Culture, Genre, and Literary Vocation

D1604445

MICHAEL DAVITT BELL

Culture, Genre, AND Literary Vocation

SELECTED ESSAYS ON
AMERICAN LITERATURE

THE UNIVERSITY OF CHICAGO PRESS
Chicago and London

MICHAEL DAVITT BELL was, at the time of his death in 1997, the J. Leland Miller Professor of American History, Literature, and Eloquence at Williams College. He is the author of *Hawthorne and the Historical Romance of New England; The Development of American Romance: The Sacrifice of Relation;* and *The Problem of American Realism: Studies in the Cultural History of a Literary Idea.*

The University of Chicago Press, Chicago 60637
The University of Chicago Press, Ltd., London
© 2001 by The University of Chicago
All rights reserved. Published 2001

Printed in the United States of America

00 09 08 07 06 05 04 03 02 01   1 2 3 4 5

ISBN: 0-226-04179-4 (cloth)
ISBN: 0-226-04180-8 (paper)

Library of Congress Cataloging-in-Publication Data

Bell, Michael Davitt
    Culture, genre, and literary vocation : selected essays on American literature / Michael Davitt Bell
        p.   cm.
    Includes bibliographical references and index.
        ISBN 0-226-04179-4 (alk. paper) — ISBN 0-226-04180-8 (pbk. : alk. paper)
        1. American fiction—History and criticism.   2. Hawthorne, Nathaniel, 1804–1864—Criticism and interpretation.   3. Wright, Richard, 1908–1960. Native Son.   4. Romanticism—United States.   5. Fiction—Authorship.
    6. Authors and publishers—United States—History—19th century.
    7. Realism in literature.   8. Naturalism in literature.   9. Culture in literature.
    I. Title.

PS371 .B395 2000
813.009—dc21

                                                                    00-029922

This book is gratefully dedicated to all my teachers and all my students,
particularly to those among them who have mastered the fine art
of playing both roles at the same time, and especially
to George Fayen,
whose course on "Problems in Fiction" during my senior year at Yale
inspired me to go to graduate school and taught me to understand
and love the specific, detailed, and elaborate ways by which
novels make their appeals to us, and
to Perry Miller
whose Harvard graduate course on "Romanticism in America"
taught me to combine that understanding and love
with a passion for the history of
American culture.

Contents

Preface

It is probably inevitable when gathering essays that represent various stages of one's career that one should adopt the retrospective view. At such times one naturally feels compelled to take stock, to try to fit what may have been random fits and reactions, well- and ill-considered impulses, into some sort of coherent, developmental narrative. This compulsion may be all the more inevitable when one's career is drawing to a close, as is the case with mine, prematurely. For memory here is prompted not only by nostalgia but by cancer, by the fact that my doctors have told me I have six months to a year to live. So I hope you will indulge me—even as we share the knowledge that the coherence of my narrative may be little more than a happy fiction, a consolation in times of trouble—by permitting me to sketch my narrative for you here. At the very least, my story should serve to explain the contents of this book, their arrangement, and the relationships among them.

My career as a literary scholar began in 1971 with the publication of a book on Nathaniel Hawthorne, a revision of my Harvard Ph.D. dissertation entitled *Hawthorne and the Historical Romance of New England.* Persons interested in the advent of this new critical voice (and God knows there was little evidence that such persons were legion) might have supposed that I was establishing myself as a "Hawthornean," as someone who would devote his career to studying the life and works of this most famous literary son of

For bibliographical information about works mentioned, see the selected list of publications included at the end of the preface.

Salem, Massachusetts. As it happens, I did no such thing; my interests soon took me elsewhere. But neither did I leave Hawthorne utterly behind, and in some quarters I am probably still regarded (to the extent that I am regarded at all) as most essentially a Hawthorne scholar. Hawthorne, in any case, was one of the five writers upon whom I focused in my next book, *The Development of American Romance: The Sacrifice of Relation* (1980), and on three occasions during the following decade I wrote solicited pieces on Hawthorne: an essay for a Cambridge University Press volume of *New Essays on* "The Scarlet Letter" (1985), the chapter on Hawthorne in *The Columbia Literary History of the United States* (1988), and an introduction to an Oxford World Classics edition of *The House of the Seven Gables* (1991). These solicited essays constitute part 1 of this volume. They are printed out of the chronological order of their appearances for a simple reason. The *Columbia Literary History of the United States* essay succinctly summarizes the various themes and aspects of the work I've done on Hawthorne over the years, and would therefore seem to deserve the prize, however dubious, of coming first. And it seems appropriate to print the other two essays—one mostly on *The Scarlet Letter* (1850), the other on *The House of the Seven Gables* (1851)—in the order in which those novels themselves were published.

In the decade following the appearance of my Hawthorne book (that is, in the 1970s), my work came to focus on two related issues or questions—at least I hope they are related. The first was a question about the generic bases of nineteenth-century American fiction. I undertook the project of interrogating two literary-historical assertions that had become commonplaces by the 1960s: that the tradition of our fiction before the Civil War had been one of "romance" (as distinguished from the supposedly "novelistic" tradition of nineteenth-century British fiction); and that following the Civil War the characteristic mode of American fiction had shifted from "romance" to "realism" (or, at the end of the century, "naturalism"). I set out to examine the first of these assertions in *The Development of American Romance* and the second in *The Problem of American Realism: Studies in the Cultural History of a Literary Idea* (1993). It was by no means my intention simply to reiterate these commonplaces, about which I was and still am quite skeptical, especially in the case of assertions about the rise of "realism" following the Civil War. On the contrary, I set out to subject them, and the version of American literary history they entailed, to skeptical scrutiny. I was interested, first of all, in uncovering the overt and covert functions the terms "romance," "realism," and "naturalism" served for writers who used them, as well as for writers who avoided them. I was equally interested in exploring the functions these terms served for the critics who had revived them in the middle of the twentieth century, following the American triumph in World War II, to create a new literary history for this triumphal and, it was assumed in the 1950s and '60s, exceptional nation.

The second development underlying my romance and realism books was a growing interest in what I came to call the "sociology of literary vocation." My ultimate aim, the deepest ambition of my overall project, was to use sociology to try to work out the relationship between works of American literature and generalizations about "culture." Central to my approach to this problem was an insistence, informed by sociological work in which I had been immersing myself, on paying close and detailed attention to the trajectories of individual literary careers. This insistence has informed almost all the scholarship I have produced since the end of the 1970s, and it is central, in one way or another, to everything collected in this volume, perhaps the introduction most particularly. There I undertake, by describing the relationship—and the very significant differences—between my project and the project of one school of what has come to be known as "New Historicism," to explain (or to offer what British Renaissance writers called an "apologie" for) the possibly eccentric path my scholarly career has followed during the past twenty-five years.

During the 1982–83 academic year—while I was on leave in New York, working on *The Problem of American Realism*—I was asked by Sacvan Bercovitch to join in the ambitious literary-historical project upon which he was then embarking in concert with Cambridge University Press: the multi-volume *Cambridge History of American Literature.* I was to be one of four authors (along with Eric Sundquist, Barbara Packer, and Jonathan Arac) of volume 2, dealing with the period from 1820 to 1865. Each of us was to write not a chapter but a substantial monograph, something like a short book, and it was this aspect of the plan that made it both attractive in prospect and often maddening in practice. Work on this project—piled on top of my responsibilities as teacher and, soon, chair of the English department at Williams College—consistently derailed my progress on the realism book, and I sometimes seemed to have abandoned the main line of my work for a kind of digression. In a deeper sense, however, my part of this project turned out to be very much of a piece with the main concerns of my scholarly career, as my section's eventual title, "Conditions of Literary Vocation," would clearly indicate. This section's two long chapters—"Beginnings of Professionalism" (dealing with the period from 1820 to, roughly, 1845) and "Women's Fiction and the Literary Marketplace in the 1850s"—constitute part 2 of this volume. I should note that while volume 2 of the *Cambridge History* did not appear until 1995, my own section was essentially finished and submitted by the summer of 1988, allowing me to return full-time to my realism book, which I completed with the help of a Guggenheim fellowship in 1990-91.

Shortly after my Guggenheim year, however, my career took a turn that had nothing to do with any scholarly project at all. In the fall of 1992, just six months before *The Problem of American Realism* appeared, a swelling in my right thigh was diagnosed as a soft-tissue sarcoma, a rather rare (for a man now in his 50s) form of cancer. The year that followed saw not writing but treatment: chemotherapy, radiation, surgery to remove the tumor, more chemotherapy, intense depression, and then recovery. In the fall of 1993 I was able to return to teaching, and by December I was planning a new book. This one was to be a departure in subject, or rather a return to a subject I'd written on in the 1960s and in which I'd remained intensely interested: twentieth-century African-American fiction.

But the project was in fact a continuation of concerns engaged by my previous two books, particularly the one on realism, and more particularly the section of that book devoted to "The Problem of American Naturalism," a section focusing on the careers and writings of Frank Norris, Stephen Crane, and Theodore Dreiser. What I wanted to do was to explore the relationship between the debate that dominated virtually all discussions of African-American writings in the 1960s—between those who insisted that black writers had a special obligation to write "protest" fiction and those who claimed that "protest" was incompatible with "art"—and the generic tradition of literary naturalism, which seemed to me central to the idea of black "protest" fiction. I was also interested in the fact that the subsidence of the "protest" debate from its centrality to discussions of African-American fiction, by the 1980s, was accompanied by a remarkable transformation in the gendering of African-American fiction. In the 1960s, when the "protest" debate reigned supreme, all the black fiction writers were men; even Zora Neale Hurston, in these days before her revival by Alice Walker and others, was rather little known. But by the 1980s, when the focus on "protest" had given way to quite different ways of theorizing the category of "African-American writing," many of them deeply influenced by poststructuralist literary theory, it is scarcely an exaggeration to say that all the black fiction writers were women, or at least all those achieving best-seller status and winning the major literary prizes. It was my working assumption that these parallel developments were by no means coincidental, and that their connection was to be sought in assumptions about writing and gender embedded deep in the discourses of both the "protest" debate and American naturalism.

The working title of this book project was *African-American Writing, 'Protest,' and The Burden of Naturalism.* The first part was to be a contrast of the antagonistic careers of Richard Wright and Zora Neale Hurston, in the context of what I hoped would be a fresh and illuminating analysis of the ideological underpinnings of the "protest" debate. The second part was to begin by considering the complex and contradictory legacy for African-American writing of the most popular American "protest" novel of all time: Harriet Beecher Stowe's *Uncle Tom's Cabin.* It was then to move on to contrast the writings and careers of Ishmael Reed and Toni Morrison, partly because both of them have written what one might consider adaptations of Stowe's novel. In Reed's case the example is obvious: his pastiche of Stowe (and of everything else in sight), *Flight to Canada.* And it was to be my contention that Morrison would seem to have had Stowe in mind, if less overtly, in the writing of *Beloved,* a book whose principal indictment of slavery is, as it was for Stowe, its disruption of the lives of slave families, a book also set in Cincinnati, the city in which Stowe had gathered her principal firsthand experiences of both slavery and Abolition.

A recurrence of my cancer, however, nipped this project in the bud. In June of 1994, a routine CT scan revealed a metastasis of sarcoma in my lung. There was only one nodule, it was small, and it was rather easily and nonintrusively removed, but its statistical implications were clear. This was a death sentence, and the outcome was only a matter of time. The next summer a large metastasis was discovered on my left kidney, which was removed by means of a procedure neither easy nor nonintrusive. And then, over the course of the 1995–96 academic year, CT scans revealed a growing accumulation of metastases in the lungs: two in November, seven more in February, spread all through both lungs ("like a shotgun," the doctor who reported the information said). By the summer of 1996, which is when I am writing this preface, the films were definitive. The original two metastases had grown quite large, the other seven were coming up right behind them, and new lesions were everywhere. It was at this point that I was told I had the proverbial "six months" to live—which I might, with a little luck and additional chemotherapy, stretch out to a year. I chose the chemotherapy, of course, but it was now absolutely clear, if it had not been before, that I was not going to be writing that book on African-American fiction, "protest," and naturalism.

During a medical leave in the fall of 1995, however, following the surgery to remove my kidney, I had managed to write an essay outlining my basic argument about naturalism and the "protest" debate, an essay focusing on the text at the center of this debate: Richard Wright's *Native Son*. And with six months to a year of something like sabbatical ahead of me, now that my departure from teaching is necessarily permanent, I set out to write a companion piece, taking up the gender portion of the argument and focusing on Toni Morrison. It is these two companion pieces that constitute part 3 of this volume. [Michael Bell was unable to complete the Morrison essay before his death in 1997. Ed.]

Selected List of Publications

Hawthorne and the Historical Romance of New England (Princeton: Princeton University Press, 1971).

The Development of American Romance: The Sacrifice of Relation (Chicago: University of Chicago Press, 1980). Paperback edition, 1984.

"Arts of Deception: Hawthorne, 'Romance,' and *The Scarlet Letter,*" in *New Essays on* "The Scarlet Letter," Michael J. Colacurcio, ed. (Cambridge: Cambridge University Press, 1985), 29–56.

"Nathaniel Hawthorne," in *The Columbia Literary History of the United States,* Emory Elliott, ed. (New York: Columbia University Press, 1988), 413–28.

Editor, *The House of the Seven Gables,* by Nathaniel Hawthorne (Oxford: Oxford University Press [Oxford World Classics Edition], 1991).

The Problem of American Realism: Studies in the Cultural History of a Literary Idea (Chicago: University of Chicago Press, 1993). Paperback edition, 1995.

"Conditions of Literary Vocation," in *The Cambridge History of American Literature, Volume Two: Prose Writing 1820–1865,* Sacvan Bercovitch, ed. (Cambridge: Cambridge University Press, 1995), 9–123.

Introduction: "Culture," New Historicism, and the Sociology of Literary Vocation

Toward the end of a generally favorable and even flattering review of my most recent book, *The Problem of American Realism* (1993), in which she quite astutely observes that "the authors themselves . . . emerge as the primary 'texts' of Bell's inquiry," Jane F. Thrailkill announces one significant reservation. My concern with writers' full careers, she writes, including their childhoods, limits the value of my work as cultural history, implying in the cases of William Dean Howells and Frank Norris, for instance, that "realism was the random result of two troubled childhoods rather than the reflexive engagement of these writers with their particular cultural moment." "In his introduction," Thrailkill continues,

> Bell suggests that his argument about these novelists extends beyond the culture of letters to American society at large. To justify the scope of this claim, however, he might have considered a wider array of cultural practices. As recent new historicists such as Walter Benn Michaels and Amy Kaplan have pointed out, American culture at the end of the nineteenth century comprised a complex engagement with artifice, to which the naive realist project Bell isolates might be seen as an anxious response. Considered in light of the fictionality of commodities trading and stock speculation, or the romance of a mass-market culture that operates by sparking consumers' desires, realist thinking might be construed not as the crude ideologies of two insecure if powerful men, but as a social practice that manifests and seeks to manage deep-seated cultural anxieties about the dissolution of stable value.[1]

1

While I will soon be questioning some of the assumptions behind Thrail-kill's critique, my main reason for quoting her review here is that her ac-count is quite accurate in its distinction of my approach to the relation of literature and "culture" from that of the school of new historicism repre-sented by Amy Kaplan's *The Social Construction of American Realism* (1988) and especially by Walter Michaels's *The Gold Standard and the Logic of American Naturalism* (1987).[2] And what she says is true not just of *The Problem of American Realism* but equally so of its predecessor, *The Development of American Romance* (1980). All I would want to add is that the distinction Thrailkill notes is quite deliberate on my part. Not that in my two books on nineteenth-century American fiction I set out self-con-sciously to be different from this school; in fact it did not yet exist when I began work on *The Development of American Romance* in the 1970s. I mean, rather, that the path I purposely chose to follow back in the 1970s did turn out to be quite different, in important respects, from the path that Michaels, Kaplan, and other new historicists would shortly be pursuing. Let me explain.

Two contexts particularly influenced my efforts to find a way to relate American literature to American "culture," a way to work out a basis for us-ing works of literature as evidence for generalizations about "culture." The first of these was the prestige, while I was in college and graduate school in the late 1950s and 1960s, of the so-called myth and symbol school of literary American Studies. Among the most influential examples of this school were Henry Nash Smith's *Virgin Land: The American West as Symbol and Myth* (1950), whose subtitle gave the school its label, and Leo Marx's *The Machine in the Garden: Technology and the Pastoral Ideal in America* (1964).[3] At the heart of these books was the assumption, usually not subjected to much the-oretical scrutiny, that patterns of meaning informing works of American lit-erature, of "'high' culture," were expressive of similar patterns in American "culture" conceived more broadly. Thus Marx began *The Machine in the Garden* by writing that "the pastoral ideal," normally associated with a liter-ary mode, "has been used to define the meaning of America ever since the age of discovery"—so that "the dream of a retreat to an oasis of harmony and joy was removed from its traditional literary context" to be "embodied in various utopian schemes for making America the site of a new beginning for Western society" (3). And Smith, having noted on his first page that he uses the terms "myth" and "symbol" to "designate larger or smaller units of the same kind of thing, namely an intellectual construction that fuses concept and emotion into an image," goes on to assert that "the myths and symbols with which I deal have the further characteristic of being collective representations rather than the work of a single mind" (v).

The ascendency of the myth and symbol school dovetailed nicely with more general habits, in American academic criticism following World War II, of stressing the exceptional nature both of our national literature and of the nation itself, and of seeing these two kinds of exceptionalism as closely related. This sort of nationalism had long been a prominent feature of literary discourse in the United States, at least since the Revolution had led to calls for a literature as independent as the new nation, and had often produced, as well, blustering declarations of our supposed superiority. "How tame will his language sound," Walter Channing had proclaimed in 1815, during the wave of nationalism that erupted following the U.S. victory in the War of 1812, "who would describe Niagara in language fitted for the falls at London bridge, or attempt the majesty of the Mississippi in that which was made for the Thames."[4] So too, in the years after World War II, American critics (by now mostly academic) called for an exceptional American literature suited to our new status as world power and came to assert that our literature, particularly in the nineteenth century, had been exceptional. Hence, for instance, the argument mounted by Richard Chase and others that the tradition of American fiction before the Civil War had been a tradition of "romance" as contrasted with the supposedly "novelistic" tradition of nineteenth-century *British* fiction.[5]

Behind all these claims, from the post-Revolutionary period on, there had of course been a good deal of anxious and compensatory defensiveness. Hovering over nationalist discourse before the Civil War, and adding fuel to the celebration of the international success of James Fenimore Cooper's novels when this success finally seemed to prove our literary worth in the 1820s, was Sydney Smith's condescending question in the *Edinburgh Review* in 1820: "In the four quarters of the globe, who reads an American book?"[6] Similarly, the resurgence of the exceptionalist argument after World War II, tying the supposed uniqueness of American literature to distinctive qualities of the nation's "culture," no doubt owed more than a little to resentment of the second-class status of American literature, and of those who taught it, that persisted in college and university English departments well into the 1950s and '60s and beyond. But toward these factors, when I was in college and graduate school, I was largely inattentive. American exceptionalism was the reigning ideology, and its dominant expression was the work of the myth and symbol school of literary American studies.

The second context that particularly influenced my thinking about the relationship of American literature and American "culture" was the collapse of this school's prestige just as I was beginning my professional career at the end of the 1960s and in the early 1970s. The most thoroughgoing and important critique of the school was probably Bruce Kuklick's essay, "Myth and Symbol in American Studies," published in 1972 in *American Quarterly,* the journal of the American Studies Association.[7] Adopting Leo Marx's term, "humanists," for the practitioners of the school, Kuklick is particularly critical of "the humanist analysis of the relation between the great work of art"—the kind of work most often central to myth and symbol scholarship—"and the culture for which it is written." He points here to what we might call the problem of the assumed cultural *representativeness* of such works.[8] How can a novel like *Moby-Dick,* for instance, which failed to find an audience in its own time, be taken again and again as evidence for generalizations about American "culture" as a whole? At the heart of this practice in much of myth and symbol scholarship, Kuklick identifies the seeming assumptions "that the work of art 'reflects' or 'expresses' historical truths about the period in question: it is a source of knowledge about some body of extra-literary experience, and a proper understanding of this art is a shortcut around masses of historical data"—or that the work of art, *because of* its "greatness," has a special, inherent ability to provide access to the past "culture" it addresses and expresses (447).

Even more interesting is Kuklick's account of the implicit philosophical premises that would seem to underlie the myth and symbol approach to cultural analysis. Here his critique, drawing heavily on Gilbert Ryle's *The Concept of Mind* (1949), indicts humanist American Studies scholarship for its "crude Cartesian view of mind," for its distinguishing completely between ideas and images which "exist *in* the mind," and that which is "'out there' in another sphere." "Moreover," Kuklick adds, "these ideas are platonic: they exist independently of the people who think them" (437). I won't repeat here Kuklick's full critique of the premises of the myth and symbol approach, but one consequence he derives from his last point—that the approach identifies "culture" with abstract ideas that are platonic or transcendent—deserves attention. "It is clear," he writes, "that the humanists adopt a platonic approach to intellectual history. They use phrases like 'archetypal form,' which commit them to something like a platonic view." "In humanist scholarship," he adds, "this view prevents an understanding of the peculiar intentions of a given thinker" (442). This would prove to be the most telling criticism of the myth and symbol school. By 1977 even Leo

Marx was describing the weaknesses of such thinking, of which he had so recently been one of the most prominent proponents, writing of the cultural historian's approach to American literature, for instance, that it had "developed considerable skill in relating individual products of mind . . . to large mental formations—myth, ethos, ideology, world view, and the like. But, until we can apprehend these formations as they are related to a concept of social structure and its operation, they will continue to seem unmoored—a ghostly, free-floating cloud of abstractions only distantly related, like the casting of a shadow, to the actual struggles of everyday life."[9]

I describe Kuklick's critique of the myth and symbol school at such length not only because of its importance to my own scholarly development but also because I'm not sure that the new historicism of the 1980s, even while it responded to many aspects of this critique, managed—or even sought— to avoid all the problems attributed to myth and symbol thinking by Kuklick and others. I think particularly of his charge that adopting a "platonic approach to literary history"—in which the "ideas" that constitute "culture" "exist independently of the people who think them"—"prevents an understanding of the peculiar intentions of a given thinker." In the review of my realism book with which I opened this essay, for instance, Jane Thrailkill argues that "realist thinking" should not be construed "as the crude ideologies of two insecure if powerful men" but should rather be seen as a "social practice that manifests and seeks to manage deep-seated cultural anxieties about the dissolution of stable value." But exactly where, one wants to know, are these "deep-seated cultural anxieties" *seated?* Or what is the precise mechanism, in Thrailkill's account of Michaels's *The Gold Standard,* by which the logic of naturalism links the phenomenon of "fictionality" in literature with its perhaps only punning cognate in the realm of commodities trading? These questions point to two important, and very closely related, qualities of this sort of new historicism. The first is a tendency to speak of societies and parts of societies as if they were minds, with anxieties and other problems amenable, for example, to psychoanalytic description and explanation. The second is a tendency to speak of societies and parts of societies—of "cultures" and "subcultures"—as if they were essentially textual, "discourses," patterns of symbolic expression to be decoded as we would decode literary texts.

This latter is the tendency most pronounced in Michaels's *Gold Standard.* In his brilliant introduction, "The Writer's Mark," Michaels teases out a list of things "whose identity involves something more than [their] physical qualities," a list which comes to include: "the commodity"; "money, which (as opposed, say, to gold) cannot be reduced to the thing it is made of and still remain the thing it is"; "the corporation, which cannot be reduced to the men and women who are its shareholders"; and finally (and crucially) "writing." "For writing to be writing," Michaels adds in justification of adding this last term, "it can neither transcend the marks it is made of nor be reduced to those marks" (21). All of this climaxes in a well-known dismissal of the idea that a scholar might "posit a space outside the culture in order to interrogate the relations between that space (here defined as literary) and the culture." "But," Michaels explains, "the spaces I have tried to explore are all very much within the culture, and so the project of interrogation makes no sense; the only relation literature as such has to culture as such is that it is part of it" (27). The trouble is that "culture," conceived so broadly and abstractly, seems to be little more than the pattern of seeming correspondences among such things as commodities, money, corporations, and writing. They constitute a pattern, not because we can explain how they are linked (which is what we would expect of an historical account), but rather because we assume that when we find similar elements the similarities are significant of something. And this is precisely the kind of pattern we are accustomed to seek in works of art, works that have been designed and in which, therefore, patterns of correspondence don't require explanation. One might think, here, of the moment early in Thomas Pynchon's *The Crying of Lot 49* when Oedipa Maas, staring down into the suburban sprawl of San Narciso, senses a correspondence between it and a printed circuit she's once noticed while changing the battery in a transistor radio and finds in "both outward patterns a hieroglyphic sense of concealed meaning, of an intent to communicate," a sense that "words were being spoken." Later she meets John Nefastis, obsessed with another metaphor-like correspondence (between the outward forms of equations in communications and thermodynamics), whose "Nefastis Machine" is designed, as he puts it, "to make the metaphor not only verbally graceful but objectively true."[10] Both of these characters, it could be argued, are new historicists ahead of their time.

A bit later in "The Writer's Mark," Michaels writes that when he speaks of "the logic of naturalism" it is in order to "map out the reality in which a certain literature finds its place and to identify a set of interests and activities that might be said to have as their common denominator a concern with the double identities that seem, in naturalism, to be required if there are to be any identities at all" (27). The "logic" that holds all these realms together, then, is the resemblance among them, their "common denominator." This is also the "logic," of course, of *The Gold Standard*'s title essay, an essay concerned with "shifting the focus of literary history from the individual text or author to structures whose coherence, interest, and effect may be greater than that of either author or text" so that "the social involvement of these texts depends not on their direct representation of the money controversies [over the gold and silver standards] but on their indirect representation of the conditions that the money controversies themselves articulated" (175). Again, this model for culture and cultural interpretation—in which "conditions" get "articulated" and then the articulations, in turn, get traced back to the originary conditions—resembles nothing so much as a process of literary coding and decoding. The terms Michaels uses for what this decoding reveals, terms like "logic" and "structures," are at once abstractly "platonic," in Kuklick's sense, and functionally synonymous with one another, as they are also functionally synonymous with the master term, "culture." What remains unclear, however, is just what or where this "culture" is.

Let me hasten to point out that everything I'm describing here is quite deliberate on Michaels's part. He has no interest in describing "relations" (including explanatory, causal relations) among the elements he sees as constituting "culture," and he quite overtly and insistently distinguishes "culture" from the intentions and beliefs of the people who constitute it.[11] Still, one is reminded of what Leo Marx said in 1977 about the "large mental formations" typical of myth and symbol accounts of culture: that they "seem unmoored—a ghostly, free-floating cloud of abstractions." And Michaels himself now seems to be moving toward an analogous understanding of new historicism, even down to the notion of its dependence on the "ghostly." What "Americans, especially American academics, believe in," he writes in a recent essay, is "the myth of culture," of "cultural identities" such as African American and Jewish (13–14).[12] These identities have been divorced from biological, essentialist conceptions of "race," and even from items of religious belief, to be tied instead to a kind of "historical memory" (for instance, of American slavery) that cannot for any living individual be based on personal experience. So, Toni Morrison's *Beloved,* for Michaels, is the new historicist novel par excellence, as it sets out to redescribe "something we have never known as something we have forgotten and thus makes the historical past part of our own experience" (6). Michaels accordingly writes of the ghosts in Morrison's novel (and in Stephen Greenblatt's *Shakespearean Negotiations* [1988]) that they "cannot . . . . be explained as metaphoric representations of the importance to us of our history" because "the ghosts are not merely the figures for history as memory, they are the technology for history as memory—to have the history, we have to have the ghosts" (7). Which is to say, by way of paraphrasing Michaels's point, that to have "cultural identity," to have "culture" itself conceived in these terms, we have to have the same ghostliness Leo Marx came to find in "humanist" accounts of culture.[13]

My original response to the collapse of the myth and symbol school in the early 1970s, I repeat, had nothing to do with a reaction against new historicism—which I mostly highly value and which in any case hadn't yet come into existence. But issues and questions of the sort I'm outlining here *were* very much on my mind as I sought to formulate my own thoughts about the relation between mainly canonized American novels (works of "high" culture) and American "culture" more generally (if there was any such thing). And I chose a direction very different from the one that would lead others to the new historicism. Misguidedly or not I wished, in Kuklick's terms, to base whatever cultural insight I might derive from novels on detailed understandings of the "peculiar intentions" of particular thinkers and writers. Typed in capital letters on a file card over my desk hung Perry Miller's pronouncement (in his characteristically grandiose mode): "I HAVE BEEN COMPELLED TO INSIST THAT THE MIND OF MAN IS THE BASIC FACTOR IN HUMAN HISTORY."[14] But *whose* mind or minds, exactly, lay behind this (in its own platonic) abstraction—*which* people and which *groups* of people? To ask these questions was to carry intellectual history into the halls of social history, or into those of sociology itself.

My first step, though, was to recognize that, in Jane Thrailkill's nice phrase, authors themselves were to be the primary "texts" of my inquiry. I would like to take credit for this as an original recognition, but the truth is that I learned it, as did so many of my Americanist contemporaries, from the writings of William Charvat, particularly from the great unfinished essays on Longfellow and Melville collected posthumously in *The Profession of Authorship in America, 1800–1870.* Charvat's lesson was clear in the first sentence of the Melville essay: "Herman Melville's conflict with his readers, which lasted the whole ten years of his professional writing life and ended in a defeat which even in our time has not been completely reversed, began in the first paragraph of his first book" (202).[15] The reading of the opening of *Typee* that followed this assertion, accenting the narrator's sharp alternation between gestures of ingratiation and insult, showed immediately how works of literature, and full professional literary careers, could be read as indexes of an author's interaction with at least his or her understanding of his or her "culture."

I was equally concerned with another of the issues raised by Kuklick and others in their critique of the myth and symbol school: with the problem of the representativeness (or, to speak more precisely, the *lack* of representativeness) of the writers to whose canonized works the school's members routinely turned for evidence about American "culture." It wasn't just that *Moby-Dick,* for instance, had been a popular failure, while even *The Scarlet Letter,* compared to best-sellers by women novelists in the 1850s, had reached only a very limited audience. What seemed even more important was the fact that fiction writers, *as fiction writers,* were very far from being "typical Americans" (if this term meant anything at all). Indeed the decision to become a fiction writer—an unusual and generally far from remunerative career for most of the nineteenth century, and one with many other negative, even antisocial connotations—itself seemed sufficient reason to discount the notion that the fiction these people produced amounted, in Henry Nash Smith's phrase, to "collective representations rather than the work of a single mind."

What most came to distinguish my own approach to literary American Studies, I believe, is that instead of overlooking or minimizing this problem of representativeness I chose to make it central to my attempt to understand the "cultural" significance of American literature. This is the choice that led me to sociology, first of all for a Williams College American Studies course called "Literary Vocation and Social Identity in America." This course was meant to fit into a set of offerings (from which each American Studies major was required to take at least one) devoted to the experience of a social group from the seventeenth century to the present: business élites, African Americans, women. For my group I selected American writers—specifically those who had chosen to pursue careers, and hence to define themselves socially, as *imaginative* writers—and approaching writers as a group effectively bypassed the question of their representative status. *Of course* they weren't representative, but neither were the members of such groups as business élites, women, or African Americans; and this fact hardly diminished anyone's sense of *their* cultural significance.

Moreover if imaginative writers, through most of our history, had been unrepresentative—to some extent outsiders and even outcasts—then it followed naturally that I should turn to the sociology of deviance to understand their experience, and particularly to the "labeling" or "interactionist" school of the sociology of deviance founded in the 1950s by Howard S. Becker and others. The essence of Becker's approach to deviance was to see it not as a symptom of individual pathology or social dysfunction but as a socially constructed phenomenon by whose means so-called deviants, pursuing the fairly well-defined tracks of "deviant careers," interact with the social group that *labels* them "deviant." "From this point of view," Becker wrote, "deviance is *not* a quality of the act the person commits, but rather a consequence of the application by others of rules and sanctions to an 'offender.' The deviant is one to whom that label has successfully been applied"—and then, in his most famous sentence: "deviant behavior is behavior that people so label" (9).[16] "Deviance," he added, "is not a quality that lies in behavior itself, but in the interaction between the person who commits an act and those who respond to it" (14). Fiction writers, of course, were not full-fledged "deviants" in the same way that criminals and heretics are; they were rather what I came to call "marginal" deviants, able to negotiate (or attempt to negotiate) between accentuating and minimizing the antisocial implications of their vocations. But Becker's emphasis on the *interactions* between the "deviant" and the "larger society"—his sense that "culture" lay neither in the "deviants" nor in the "larger society" but in these interactions, in the structural relationships underlying them—seemed to offer precisely the sort of relation between the specific behaviors of fiction writers and the larger society's valuation of these behaviors that I was looking for. Analyzing writers' often complex negotiations between emphasizing and obscuring their "deviance" thus became a central part of my project.

At the heart of Jane Thrailkill's critique of my realism book—of my claim that my argument about the novelists on whom I focus "extends beyond the culture of letters to American society at large"—is a quite rigid bifurcation of these two realms, a bifurcation that is perhaps a bit odd in one whose allegiance is to the new historicism of Walter Michaels with its insistence that "the only relation literature as such has to culture as such as that it is part of it." Thrailkill distinguishes between what she thinks my book *does* and what she thinks it *should have done*. It *does*, she thinks, construe "realist thinking" as "the crude ideologies of two insecure but powerful men," in part by portraying Howells's and Norris's "realism" as "the random result of two troubled childhoods." What she thinks it *should have done* is to construe "realist thinking" as a result, rather, of "the reflexive engagement of these writers with their particular cultural moment," as "a social practice that manifests and seeks to manage deep-seated cultural anxieties." But my project has always rested on the belief that there is, in fact, no such distinction between "troubled childhoods" and "reflexive engagement" with culture, between "the culture of letters" and "American society at large," between the ideologies (crude or not) of individuals and the "deep-seated cultural anxieties" characteristic of a "particular cultural moment." Where *could* "anxieties" be "seated," after all, if not in individuals? And to suggest that these individuals might acquire their anxieties and their characteristic ways of managing or responding to them in childhood is hardly to dismiss the question of their "reflexive engagement . . . with their particular cultural moment." For is it not in childhood, in our childhood interactions with the societies of home and school and play, that the pattern of beliefs, values, customs, and practices that constitute "culture" are first passed on to us, even as specific individuals among us will respond to this acculturation, for a variety of specific reasons, in a variety of specific ways?

So it seems to me that to dismiss detailed examination of the trajectories of individual careers as somehow irrelevant to "culture" is to leave "culture" itself precisely nowhere. It is not that "culture" is located in the individuals themselves; it exists in, rather (and is sustained and transformed by), the structures of relation and interaction that make individual careers possible, that allow them to take their distinctive shapes. If I were to paraphrase Perry Miller, I might hazard that the acculturating interactions among these individuals, and the shifting subgroupings into which these individuals have gathered, or have been gathered by others with power over them, are the basic factor in cultural history. It can be extremely fruitful to speak as if societies or parts of societies were themselves minds, or to speak of societies or parts of societies as if they were essentially textual, patterns of symbolic expression to be decoded as we would decode a literary text. But we need to remember that these strategies, productive as they may be in application, are based on analogy, not fact. And if "culture" is nothing more than analogy, a set of elaborate puns, if it is not in some sense fact, a matter of actual social relations and interactions, one might wonder how it could be, at least for the purposes of history, anything at all.

Yet having said all this, I must also confess to a certain skepticism about the extent to which the purposes of history, strictly understood, have motivated those scholars (and here I very pointedly include myself) who have sought to "historicize" American literature as an expression or component of American "culture." With the exception of extreme (and extremely vulgar) varieties of Marxist (or psychoanalytic) criticism, we have hardly been bent on "explaining" works of literature as historical effects traceable to "cultural" causes. I suspect that we have needed "culture," rather, for the simple reason that without it our subject, "American literature," can scarcely be said to exist as a distinct field warranting academic study. "How tame will his language sound," Walter Channing proclaimed in 1815, "who would describe Niagara in language fitted for the falls at London bridge, or attempt the majesty of the Mississippi in that which was made for the Thames." Behind Channing's bluster is the pathos of his, and of our own, situation; for the "American literature" taught in the academy *is*, for the most part, written in "language fitted for the falls at London bridge," in English. So what allows us to rescue our study of "American literature" from this pathos, from this anxious sense of belatedness? What else but "American *culture*," the necessary if not always easily-supported assumption that our literature is distinctively "American" because it is related to (or is "part of") our "culture." We need that ghostly mechanism to keep our own vocational identities alive.

I   Hawthorne

1   Nathaniel Hawthorne

During the 1950s, the age of the "New Criticism" in literary scholarship, critics spoke repeatedly of the "ambiguity" of Nathaniel Hawthorne. Now, decades later, this term is likely to strike us as inadequate. *Our* Hawthorne is a figure not so much of ambiguity as of paradox and profound contradiction: a *public recluse,* openly and even sociably proclaiming his own isolation and alienation—a *mild rebel,* at once a conformist to the literary and social pieties of his day and an ironic underminer of these pieties. First published in ladies' magazines and annuals, whose editors' tastes he cultivated throughout his literary career, he was also praised by Herman Melville, in an 1850 review entitled "Hawthorne and His Mosses," for subverting these pieties by appealing to "that Calvinistic sense of Innate Depravity and Original Sin, from whose visitations, in some shape or other, no deeply thinking mind is always and wholly free." In 1851 Melville would dedicate his masterpiece, *Moby-Dick,* to Hawthorne, "In Token of My Admiration for His Genius." It was no small accomplishment, in mid-nineteenth-century America, to appeal simultaneously to the canons of "genteel" literary respectability and to Herman Melville's ultimately antisocial conception of "Genius."

The essential paradox at the heart of Hawthorne's life and writing is nowhere clearer than in his frequent public comments on his own career. Indeed the very frequency of these autobiographical excursions is itself paradoxical, since their point is usually to insist on the author's retiring nature—even on his personal and social insignificance. What is most striking in these prefaces to volumes of tales and sketches and later to novels is

Hawthorne's public insistence on his *literary* insignificance. For instance, in his preface to an 1851 edition of *Twice-told Tales,* a collection originally issued in 1837 (and expanded in 1842), Hawthorne expresses surprise that his tales "have gained what vogue they did," while noting that this "vogue" was in any case "so little and so gradual." He then goes on to enumerate the defects of his tales—to write, in effect, a hostile review of his own work. He also insists that he was never "greatly tormented by literary ambition," by a "craving desire for notoriety."

Hawthorne's self-effacing pose was by 1851 characteristic, but by 1851 it was also at the very least disingenuous. Although *The Scarlet Letter,* which had appeared in 1850, was not exactly a best-seller, it had firmly consolidated Hawthorne's literary reputation; in fact, his publisher chose to reissue *Twice-told Tales,* in 1851, in order to capitalize on its author's newfound fame. Nor should Hawthorne's disavowal of "literary ambition" and a "craving desire for notoriety" be taken at face value: few of his American contemporaries in the first half of the nineteenth century pursued a literary career with such single-minded application over such a long period of time. Behind Hawthorne's public disavowal of ambition lurks a sense of dedication bordering on obsession; and obsession and the concealment of obsession were, from first to last, Hawthorne's great literary subjects.

Hawthorne was born on the Fourth of July, 1804, in Salem, Massachusetts, into a family descended from influential seventeenth-century New England Puritans. Four years later, his sea-captain father died in Surinam, and young Nathaniel grew up in genteel poverty, often dependent for support on his more prosperous maternal relations. This support enabled him to attend Bowdoin College from 1821 to 1825, where his classmates included Henry Wadsworth Longfellow, who would become the most popular American poet of his generation, and Franklin Pierce, who would serve as President of the United States from 1853 to 1857. In an 1821 letter to his mother Hawthorne announced his literary plans with a characteristic mixture of ambition and self-deprecation: "What do you think of my becoming an Author, and relying for support upon my pen. Indeed I think the illegibility of my handwriting is very authorlike. How proud you would feel to see my works praised by the reviewers. . . . But Authors are always poor Devils, and therefore Satan may take them."

Following his graduation in 1825, Hawthorne returned to Salem to live in his mother's house and pursue his literary career. In 1828 he published, anonymously, a novel, *Fanshawe,* which he would later seek to suppress; but he devoted most of his energies to short tales and sketches. These began appearing, also anonymously, in 1830—most frequently, in the early 1830s, in Samuel G. Goodrich's *The Token*, an annual published in Boston. Although Hawthorne planned at least three book-length collections, he could persuade no publisher to take the risk of issuing them, and it was not until 1837, twelve years after he initially set out to become a writer, that his first published collection, *Twice-told Tales*, brought his name before the public. This was not an auspicious moment to seek a living through literature; 1837 was the year of a great financial panic in the United States, and the literary marketplace—with book prices depressed by the competition of cheap, pirated editions of foreign works—was in even worse shape than the general economy. Not very surprisingly, *Twice-told Tales* achieved only a modest success; 600 or 700 copies, of an edition of 1,000, were sold in two months, but then sales pretty much stopped. Still, the collection received favorable reviews—including high praise in Boston's *North American Review* from Hawthorne's former classmate, Longfellow.

In an 1837 letter thanking Longfellow for this review, Hawthorne recalled the years of his anonymous apprenticeship with something close to bewilderment:

> By some witchcraft or other—for I really cannot assign any reasonable why and wherefore—I have been carried apart from the main current of life. . . . I have secluded myself from society; and yet I never meant any such thing. . . . I have made a captive of myself and put me into a dungeon; and now I cannot find the key to let myself out—and if the door were open, I should be almost afraid to come out. . . . For the last ten years, I have not lived, but only dreamed about living.

Thus began Hawthorne's cultivation of the myth of his "solitary years" of writing in Salem. This myth has been challenged; it has been argued that Hawthorne exaggerated his seclusion and alienation, that between 1825 and 1837 he was in fact involved in a number of significant social activities and relationships. What matters, though, is that Hawthorne chose to cultivate and promulgate this myth of self-isolation.

And what is most interesting about the letter to Longfellow is the way Hawthorne dissociates himself from his own activity: if he chose literary seclusion, he nonetheless "never meant any such thing." Writing is here viewed as a form of unmotivated, even compulsive behavior, and the voice that speaks to us stands far outside of this behavior. Hawthorne's application to literature—carried on for more than a decade with no public recognition and little financial reward—suggests a powerful ambition; yet here, instead of admitting this ambition, he attributes his literary seclusion to "some witchcraft or other." This stance of what we might call self-dissociation— this radical separation of the voice that speaks to us from the subjects about which it speaks, this separation of the sociable *speaker* from the antisocial *person*—lies at the heart of the narrative strategy of much of Hawthorne's best fiction. As Hawthorne himself put it in his preface to the 1851 edition of *Twice-told Tales*, his stories "have none of the abstruseness of idea, or obscurity of expression, which mark the written communications of a solitary mind with itself. They never need translation. It is, in fact, the style of a man of society."

The publication of *Twice-told Tales* in 1837 marked, in any event, a turning point both in its author's career and in his personal life. Hawthorne continued to publish tales and sketches in annuals and magazines, even though his income from these sources remained minimal. When he became engaged to Sophia Peabody of Salem in 1839, he was obliged to seek some reliable means of financial support. Very few American writers, before the Civil War, were able to earn anything close to a living from literature, and Hawthorne was never one of this select few; he had to find other work and hope to write in his spare time. So in 1839–40—while he worked at the Boston Custom House, a patronage appointment secured through his Democratic political connections with Franklin Pierce and others—he sought to tap the potentially lucrative market for children's literature by writing three small volumes of children's history, published in 1840 and 1841 as *Grandfather's Chair, Famous Old People,* and *The Liberty Tree.* A fourth volume, *Biographical Stories for Children,* was added to the series in 1842. Hawthorne briefly joined the transcendentalist utopian community of Brook Farm (in West Roxbury, Massachusetts) in 1841. In 1842 he published an expanded version of *Twice-told Tales* that, although it sold even less well than its predecessor, elicited a highly favorable review from Edgar Allan Poe, in which Poe first formulated his well-known argument for the "unity of effect" of short fiction.

In the same year Hawthorne and Sophia Peabody were married, and they settled at the Old Manse, in Concord, Massachusetts. Here they lived for three years, and here Hawthorne wrote many of the tales collected in *Mosses from an Old Manse* (1846). This brief experiment in literary self-sufficiency ultimately proved unsuccessful; in 1846 Hawthorne was still unable to support himself by his writing, and reviewers increasingly spoke of him, even in praise, as an author unlikely to reach a broad public. But he was by now well known, at least in "cultured" circles, and generally admired; the self-proclaimed recluse of 1837 had become a husband, a father, a writer of some reputation, and a public figure with valuable Democratic political connections.

These connections led to Hawthorne's appointment in 1846 as Surveyor of Customs at Salem—an appointment made famous in 1850 by "The Custom-House," the autobiographical preface to *The Scarlet Letter.* Hawthorne and his family lived with his mother in Salem, and while there was little time for writing he was at least able to support his wife and children. Then, in 1849, things changed dramatically. In January, the Whigs having defeated the Democrats in the previous year's national elections, Hawthorne was dismissed from his customhouse position. Six months later, his mother died. At this point—with no means of earning a living, and profoundly affected by his mother's death—he returned to his writing, with new dedication. The result was *The Scarlet Letter,* completed in February 1850, and published in March. In May the Hawthornes moved to Lenox, in the Berkshire hills of western Massachusetts, where, in August, Hawthorne first met Herman Melville, who was living nearby in Pittsfield.

Hawthorne had originally planned to include *The Scarlet Letter* as a long tale in yet another story collection, to be called "Old Time Legends," but his new publisher, James T. Fields, convinced him to publish the work (together with the "Custom-House" preface) as a novel—Hawthorne's first novel (except for the suppressed *Fanshawe*) after twenty-five years of writing fiction. While sales were not spectacular, they were better than those of any of Hawthorne's earlier books—perhaps because of the novel's scandalous theme of adulterous love and because of the preface's attack on the Whigs who had dismissed him from the customhouse. In any case, spurred on by the success of the book and by Fields's constant encouragement, Hawthorne in the next few years pursued literature at an almost frantic pace. He produced two more novels (or, as he called them, "romances"): *The House of the Seven Gables* in 1851 and *The Blithedale Romance* (based very loosely on his experience at Brook Farm) in 1852. There were also works for children: in 1851 *True Stories from History and Biography* (a revised collection of the children's histories originally published in 1840–42) and two new books of mythology for young readers, *A Wonder-Book for Girls and Boys* in 1851 and *Tanglewood Tales for Girls and Boys* in 1853. Fields sought to cash in on the reputation of *The Scarlet Letter* by reissuing *Twice-told Tales* in 1851, and *The House of the Seven Gables* was followed in 1852 by a new collection (mostly of earlier, previously uncollected stories) called *The Snow-Image, and Other Twice-told Tales.* And in 1852

Hawthorne published a campaign biography of his friend Franklin Pierce, who was running for President on the Democratic ticket. Meanwhile, in November 1851, the Hawthornes had moved once again, from the Berkshires to West Newton, Massachusetts, just outside Boston.

It has been argued that Fields exhausted Hawthorne by forcing him to produce so much material so rapidly, but while it is certainly true that Hawthorne would never match this pace again, he had reasons other than exhaustion for turning away from literature after this flurry of activity. Franklin Pierce won the election of 1852, and in 1853 he rewarded his friend and campaign biographer by appointing him American consul at Liverpool, a truly valuable bit of patronage. By the time Hawthorne left this position in 1857, he had managed to *save* $30,000—which one might compare to his total lifetime *earnings* from American sales of *The Scarlet Letter* of $1,500.

Following their four years in Liverpool, the Hawthornes spent two years in Italy, living in Rome and Florence. Here, as in Liverpool, Hawthorne's writing was confined to his notebooks; he was storing up materials for future "romances." Ultimately he managed to extract only one more "romance" from this horde: *The Marble Faun,* set in Italy, appeared in 1860. Following its publication the Hawthornes returned to the United States, to the "Wayside" in Concord, where Hawthorne wrestled with his increasingly intractable materials until his death in 1864. He did get a book of social observation out of his English notebooks—*Our Old Home,* published in 1863; but except for *The Marble Faun* his fictional exertions in the late 1850s and 1860s produced only confused fragments. Portions of these unfinished manuscripts were published posthumously as *Septimius Felton; or, The Elixir of Life* (1872), *The Dolliver Romance* (1876), *Dr. Grimshawe's Secret* (1883), and "The Ancestral Footstep" (1883).

"An old man," says a character in *Dr. Grimshawe's Secret,* "grows dreamy as he waxes away. . . . But I should think it hardly worth while to call up one of my shifting dreams more than another." One suspects that this character speaks for his author. In 1837 or 1851 the disavowal of literary ambition had been for Hawthorne a paradoxical or ironic pose. By the 1860s, following the years of financial and social success in England and Italy, this pose had apparently become a reality; Hawthorne could no longer remember, it would seem, what he wrote for, why he had called up his "shifting dreams" in the first place. Having forgotten this, having finally disguised his ambition and the sources of his inspiration even from himself, he could no longer write. Following a long period of illness and depression, he died on

May 19, 1864, at the age of fifty-nine, while visiting the White Mountains of New Hampshire with his friend Pierce.

In his laudatory 1837 review of the first edition of *Twice-told Tales,* Longfellow described the book in terms characteristic of the way Hawthorne would come to be valued and understood by most of his contemporary admirers. Longfellow praised Hawthorne for his "bright, poetic style," for revealing the "poetry" of the commonplace; and, like most of Hawthorne's readers in the 1830s and 1840s, he preferred the fanciful sketches or essays—for instance, "The Vision of the Fountain," "Sunday at Home," "A Rill from the Town-Pump"—to the "tales" (what we would now call the "short stories"). Of these latter, Longfellow's favorite was "The Great Carbuncle," an allegory of the search by "a party of adventurers" for a legendary jewel in the White Mountains. He did not mention, that is to say, the works modern readers most admire and anthologize—for instance, "The Gray Champion," "The Minister's Black Veil," "The May-Pole of Merry Mount," "The Gentle Boy," "Wakefield," "The Prophetic Pictures." A review of the 1837 *Twice-told Tales* in New York's *Knickerbocker Magazine* expressed what would soon become near-consensus even more explicitly. Singling out for special praise "A Rill from the Town-Pump," a light sketch "spoken" by the pump at the corner of Essex and Washington Streets in Salem, the reviewer went on to mention "Sunday at Home," "Mr. Higginbotham's Catastrophe," "The Gentle Boy," and "Little Annie's Ramble"—while noting that "'The Minister's Black Veil,' and 'The Prophetic Pictures,' are less to our taste."

In 1850, at the close of his "Custom-House" preface to *The Scarlet Letter,* Hawthorne caustically imagined that future citizens of Salem might "sometimes think kindly of the scribbler of bygone days, when the antiquary of days to come, among the sites memorable in the town's history, shall point out the locality of THE TOWN-PUMP!" Still, Hawthorne deliberately cultivated the taste he here mocks; he was careful to leaven the more somber works we now tend to admire with the lighter sketches most of his readers apparently preferred. Indeed, among the tales already published in magazines and annuals by 1837, and therefore available for collection in *Twice-told Tales,* Hawthorne passed over some of the grimmest ones, stories now considered to be among his finest works. "Roger Malvin's Burial" (1832) and "Young Goodman Brown" (1835) were not collected until 1846, when they appeared in *Mosses from an Old Manse.* "My Kinsman, Major Molineux" (1832) was not collected until 1852, when it was included in *The Snow-Image, and Other Twice-told Tales.* Of *Twice-told Tales* Longfellow wrote in

1837, "A calm, thoughtful face seems to be looking at you from every page; with now a pleasant smile, and now a shade of sadness stealing over its features. Sometimes, though not often, it glares wildly at you, with a strange and painful expression." Hawthorne was usually careful to keep such "painful expressions" to a minimum.

A few contemporary readers, however, dissented from the general preference for the "calm, thoughtful" Hawthorne of the sketches. Poe—in his 1842 review of the expanded edition of *Twice-told Tales,* published in Philadelphia's *Graham's Magazine*—objected to the *"repose"* of the sketches and insisted on the superiority of the tales. "Of Mr. Hawthorne's Tales," he wrote, "we would say, emphatically, that they belong to the highest region of art." Eight years later—in "Hawthorne and His Mosses," published in New York's *Literary World*—Herman Melville observed that "where Hawthorne is known, he seems to be deemed a pleasant writer, with a pleasant style— . . . a man who means no meanings." But Melville vigorously rejected this view. "The world," he insisted, "is much mistaken in this Nathaniel Hawthorne," some of whose stories "are directly calculated to deceive—egregiously deceive—the superficial skimmer of pages." Melville then went on to praise "Young Goodman Brown" (which Hawthorne had kept out of both the 1837 and 1842 editions of *Twice-told Tales*) for being "deep as Dante."

"Young Goodman Brown," however uncharacteristic it may be of what Hawthorne's contemporaries admired, is in many respects typical of what most readers now value in his best fiction. For one thing, it is concerned with the great theme of many of the stories first published in magazines and annuals in the 1830s, New England's colonial past. Hawthorne turned away from this theme in the 1840s, the "Old Manse" period, but at the end of the decade he returned to Puritan history in his masterpiece, *The Scarlet Letter.* Critics used to argue (as many, in fact, still do) that Puritan history in Hawthorne is only incidental to his more "universal" moral or psychological concerns. More recently, however, a number of scholars—most notably Michael Colacurcio, in *The Province of Piety* (1984)—have shown how Hawthorne's fiction demonstrates among other things a serious and coherent interest in, and understanding of, the history of colonial New England. Their point is not so much that Hawthorne "used" or "drew on" New England's past as that in many of his best historical tales, especially if we take them together, we can perceive an underlying *interpretation* of colonial history. The general lines of this interpretation are perhaps clearest in an 1849 sketch, "Main Street" (collected in *The Snow-Image, and Other Twice-told Tales*). Of the first generation of Puritans, those who migrated from England in the 1630s and 1640s, Hawthorne here writes that "the zeal of a recovered faith burned like a lamp within their hearts." However, he continues, this generation was able to transmit only "its religious gloom, and the counterfeit of its religious ardor, to the next. . . . The sons and grandchildren of the first settlers were a race of lower and narrower souls than their progenitors had been."

A few of the historical tales collected in 1837 relate incidents—in effect heroic legends—of the nobility of the first-generation Puritans. In "The Gray Champion," a story set in Boston in 1689 (and first published in 1835), the Royal Governor's effort to subdue a restless crowd of Puritans is successfully resisted by the appearance of a mysterious figure who turns out to have been one of the judges who condemned Charles I to death during the Puritan Revolution in England. This "Gray Champion," we are told at the close, "is the type of New-England's hereditary spirit," of its tradition of resistance to "tyranny." In "Endicott and the Red Cross" (1838), based on an event that took place in Salem in 1634, John Endicott dramatizes the spirit of New England by cutting the red cross from the British banner used by the Salem militia. Here again, for Hawthorne, seventeenth-century history prefigures the spirit of liberty, of the American Revolution.

Such patriotic filiopietism, however, is not altogether typical of Hawthorne's historical tales, and even in "Endicott and the Red Cross" the main focus is elsewhere. The scene in Salem is dominated by tokens of Puritan intolerance and persecution of those whose ideas of "liberty" differ from Endicott's: a suspected Catholic (confined in the pillory), a boisterous drinker (in the stocks), a woman who has spoken against the elders of her church (forced to wear a cleft stick on her tongue). There is also a young woman (a brief preliminary version of Hester Prynne in *The Scarlet Letter*) "whose doom it was to wear the letter A on the breast of her gown" in token of having committed the sin of adultery. Hawthorne's general view even of the first generation of Puritans is at best mixed.

And many of Hawthorne's historical tales (including the ones now generally most admired) focus not on the founders but on those "sons and grandchildren of the first settlers" who, as he writes in "Main Street," "were a race of lower and narrower souls than their progenitors had been." In "The Gentle Boy" (1835), the title character, whose mother is a Quaker unwelcome in the colony, ultimately dies, a victim to the persecution of sec-

ond-generation Puritans. In "Roger Malvin's Burial" (1832), the young protagonist—one of the few survivors of a disastrous Indian battle that he fled
with his dying father-in-law (whom he abandoned while still living)—works
out his guilt many years later by killing his own son. In "My Kinsman, Major
Molineux" (1832), a Boston crowd defying the authority of the colonial gov-
ernment in the 1730s is portrayed as an unruly mob, whose cruelty provides
the backdrop for the problematic coming of age of the young protagonist,
Robin Molineux. And in *The Scarlet Letter* the patriarchal community of
the founders—of a Boston "which owed its origin and progress, . . . not to
the impulses of youth, but to the stern and tempered energies of manhood,
and the sombre sagacity of age"—is repeatedly contrasted with the "tremulous" and "melancholy" weakness of the "young minister," Arthur Dimmesdale.

　　At the beginning of "Young Goodman Brown" (1835) the title character,
a naïvely pious third-generation Puritan, leaves his new wife to visit a
witches' sabbath in the forest outside Salem village. In the forest, perhaps in
a dream, he sees the "shapes" of the civil and religious leaders of the colony,
of his father, and finally of his wife, Faith. As he calls to Faith to "resist the
Wicked One," the whole scene disappears. Brown returns to Salem village,
and lives out his days "a stern, a sad, a darkly meditative, a distrustful, if not
a desperate man," convinced that all those in whose virtue he had believed
have joined in worshiping the devil. Like the judges who condemned
"witches" to death in Salem in 1692 (including Hawthorne's famous ancestor, Judge John Hathorne), Brown accepts what was known as "specter evidence"; he blames his wife and neighbors for what he has seen their
"shapes" (or "specters") doing. The deeper irony is that he clings to his own
"virtue" by blaming them for doing what he, after all, was also doing; the one
fact he ignores is the only one he can know with certainty, that *he* chose to
visit the forest. Thus is Brown's piety revealed to be but a "counterfeit," as
Hawthorne puts it in "Main Street," of the "ardor" of the fathers.

　　If "Young Goodman Brown" is typical of Hawthorne's fiction in its concern with Puritan history, it is typical in at least one other sense as well: the
mode of "Young Goodman Brown," as of many of Hawthorne's tales and romances, is the mode of *allegory*. Objects and characters, in Hawthorne, often seem to matter less for what they *are* than for the ideas they *represent* or
illustrate. Losing his wife, Brown loses his "Faith," just as we are told at the
beginning of *The Scarlet Letter* that the town Beadle, leading the proces-
sion, "prefigured and represented in his aspect the whole dismal severity of
the Puritanic code of law"—or as we are told of the scaffold, on which Hes-

ter Prynne's shame will soon be made public, that "the very ideal of ig-
nominy was embodied and made manifest in this contrivance of wood and
iron." Many readers, including Poe, have complained about Hawthorne's
reliance on allegory, but there is something peculiar we should recognize in
these examples. While Faith, the Beadle, and the scaffold represent ideas,
they do not represent *Hawthorne's* ideas. It is young Goodman Brown, not
Hawthorne, who loses his "faith" when he thinks he sees his young wife at a
witches' sabbath, and it is the Puritans of Boston, not Hawthorne, who have
made the Beadle and the scaffold into allegorical symbols of their own strict
social code. It is Hawthorne's characters who are allegorists, who try to find
meanings in symbols or to turn others into symbols by imposing meanings
on them. Thus in *The Scarlet Letter* the story turns on the conflict between
Puritan Boston's literal effort to subsume Hester Prynne's "individuality"
under the symbol of the scarlet *A* and Hester's efforts to reconcile her "individuality" with this imposed allegorical identity.

Such a dehumanizing, allegorical tendency is not confined to Hawthorne's historical fiction; it is also the besetting sin of the characters in
many of the best tales of the "Old Manse" period. In "The Birth-mark" (first
published in 1842), it is the scientist, Aylmer, who sees in the birthmark on
the face of his wife Georgiana a shocking symbol of "earthly imperfection,"
and who kills her in his effort to remove it. In "The Artist of the Beautiful"
(1844), it is the artist, Owen Warland, who considers his mechanical butter-
fly a representation of "the intellect, the imagination, the sensibility, the
soul, of an Artist of the Beautiful," and who turns from life to the perfection
of this symbol. And in one of Hawthorne's greatest stories, "Rappaccini's
Daughter" (1844), it is Giovanni Guasconti, a young man in many respects
similar to Goodman Brown, who becomes obsessed with the poisonous
qualities of Beatrice Rappaccini, and who kills her, as Aylmer killed Georgiana, in his effort to "purify" her. Beatrice's final words might stand as a
condemnation of all of those characters in Hawthorne who substitute allegory for human sympathy. "Oh," she says to Giovanni as she dies, "was there
not, from the first, more poison in thy nature than in mine?"

Yet if Hawthorne, as narrator and moral historian, stands outside the obsessions of his characters, if his style (as he put it in 1851) is "the style of a
man of society," the obsessions of these characters are still remarkably similar to his own—or at least to the way he characteristically described his own
behavior, to what was earlier called his posture of self-dissociation. One of
the most striking and even comic features of "Young Goodman Brown" is
that Brown himself never recognizes or even thinks about *why* he is going to

the forest to meet the devil. While his whole experience may be a projection of the "poison" in his own "nature," this is precisely what he never permits himself to understand. In his 1837 letter to Longfellow, we might recall, Hawthorne expresses a similar bafflement about his previous twelve years of supposed literary seclusion: "I have secluded myself from society," he writes; "and yet I never meant any such thing." "I have been carried apart from the main current of life," he insists (two years after the first publication of "Young Goodman Brown"), "by some witchcraft or other—for I really cannot assign any reasonable why and wherefore." This is not to say, however, that Hawthorne's vision of Puritan history, or of moral history generally, is simply a projection of personal psychological conflict or neurosis. Rather, it would seem that Hawthorne's understanding of himself and of his need to conceal this understanding provided him with an acute comprehension of the experience of others.

The titles or subtitles of the four full-length fictions Hawthorne published between 1850 and 1860—*The Scarlet Letter: A Romance; The House of the Seven Gables: A Romance; The Blithedale Romance;* and *The Marble Faun; or, The Romance of Monte Beni*—identify these works as "romances" rather than "novels." In a well-known passage from the preface to *The House of the Seven Gables* Hawthorne sets out to explain this distinction:

> When a writer calls his work a Romance, it need hardly be observed that he wishes to claim a certain latitude, both as to its fashion and material, which he would not have felt himself entitled to assume, had he professed to be writing a Novel. The latter form of composition [that is, the Novel] is presumed to aim at a very minute fidelity, not merely to the possible, but to the probable and ordinary course of man's experience. The former [that is, the Romance]—while, as a work of art, it must rigidly subject itself to laws, and while it sins unpardonably, so far as it may swerve aside from the truth of the human heart—has fairly a right to present that truth under circumstances, to a great extent, of the writer's own choosing or creation.

For Hawthorne, this is to say, the romancer, unlike the novelist, is not tied to conventional reality ("the probable and ordinary course of man's experience"); he has the freedom (or "latitude") to depart from novelistic realism.

In the 1950s and 1960s, many literary scholars—most notably Richard Chase in *The American Novel and Its Tradition* (1957)—used Hawthorne's terms to distinguish generally between the supposed "romance" tradition of American fiction and the "novelistic" tradition of Great Britain. American fiction-writers, they argued, should be judged by standards different from those we apply to Jane Austen or George Eliot. In spite of the great value of their insights into the literature they discussed, these scholars were often rather vague (as they were often far from agreement) about just what qualities distinguished a "romance" from a "novel"; and Hawthorne's *Seven Gables* preface provided surprisingly little help. While Hawthorne tells us what the romance does *not* deal with ("the probable and ordinary"), he says almost nothing about what *does* constitute its distinctive subject; although he identifies the romance with the romancer's "latitude," he still does not say what this "latitude" is *for.*

Hawthorne, one should note, often uses the term "romance" pejoratively, as a way of describing the inferiority of his supposedly "insubstantial" works to the solid "reality" of the novels he always claimed to prefer. "It was a folly . . . ," he writes toward the end of "The Custom-House," "to insist on creating the semblance of a world out of airy matter, when, at every moment, the impalpable beauty of my soap-bubble was broken by the rude contact of some actual circumstance." This apology cannot help but seem a bit odd; terms like "airy," "impalpable," and "soap-bubble" hardly seem appropriate to the grim story of Hester Prynne and Arthur Dimmesdale; as has already been noted, Hawthorne's historical tales, and perhaps *The Scarlet Letter* above all, are deeply involved with "actual circumstance." Moreover, Hawthorne's most immediate importance to the history of fiction in English may be his development of analytic, psychological realism, foreshadowing (as he also influenced) the work of such later realists as George Eliot and Henry James. So his comments on "romance," for all their apparent forthrightness, may ultimately strike us as being at least a bit disingenuous.

One may get a better sense of what Hawthorne meant by "romance" by noticing some more casual comments in his prefaces. "If a man . . . cannot dream strange things, and make them look like truth," he writes in "The Custom-House," "he need never try to write romances." Of the setting of *The Blithedale Romance* he writes, in his preface, that he has chosen his memories of Brook Farm, not for the purposes of the novel, but "merely to establish a theatre, a little removed from the highway of ordinary travel, where the creatures of [the author's] brain may play their phantasmagorical antics." The "latitude" of romance, that is, is a latitude of *imagination,* of dreams. And romance allows the romancer both to release his private fantasies and to "make them look like truth"; Hawthorne's romancer, like so many of his characters, at once indulges "strange" fantasies and conceals this indulgence—as Hester Prynne, for instance, uses her scarlet letter simultaneously to express and to hide her forbidden "individuality."

One might note, too, Hawthorne's description of himself—in his preface to *The Snow-Image, and Other Twice-told Tales*—as one "who has been burrowing . . . into the depths of our common nature, for the purposes of psychological romance,—and who pursues his researches in that dusky region, as he needs must, as well by the tact of sympathy as by the light of observation." The key term here, one guesses, is "sympathy"—the opposite of the obsessively allegorical intolerance by whose means so many of Hawthorne's characters manage to disown their forbidden fantasies by projecting them onto others. The ideal romancer, the writer of "psychological romance," releases his own fantasies and dreams "strange things," but he does so in order to *understand* the fantasies of others—not as a form of "sin" or "poison" or "earthly imperfection" but as a token of "our common nature." The power of romance, unlike that of self-protective allegory, is above all the power of sympathy.

Hawthorne's insistence on the importance and mutuality of imagination and fantasy might seem to ally him with nineteenth-century "Romanticism" (a term closely connected to, and in fact derived from, "romance"), but Hawthorne's relationship to romanticism, like so much else in the case of this self-contradictory writer, is essentially paradoxical. The great Romantics—such figures as William Wordsworth in England or Henry David Thoreau in the United States—sought to turn from the artificial constraints of commercial civilization to what they saw as the superior truth of "Nature." The same movement occurs again and again in Hawthorne's fiction: young Goodman Brown journeys from Salem village to the forest; in *The Scarlet Letter* Hester Prynne and Arthur Dimmesdale meet in the forest to confess their abiding passion and plan their escape from Puritan Boston; in *The Blithedale Romance* a group of would-be idealists flees the "artificial life" of nineteenth-century Boston to begin "the life of Paradise anew" in a rural utopia. Yet Hawthorne hardly shares the Romantics' valuation of this movement from civilization to nature, or at least their confidence that such a return to nature is possible. Goodman Brown is destroyed by his wilderness experience, and the vows Hester and Arthur Dimmesdale exchange in the forest prove illusory. So do the reformist schemes of the idealists at Blithedale, whose dream of a natural society based on "familiar love" soon gives way to the nasty reality of sexual competition among the four major characters, Hollingsworth, Zenobia, Priscilla, and the narrator, Miles Coverdale.

As the Romantics valued nature and the natural, so they also valued sincerity—the direct, personal expression of *human* nature. Hawthorne's fre-

quent autobiographical excursions might link him to this Romantic valoriza-
tion of sincerity, but these prefaces are exercises more in personal concealment than in self-disclosure. As he writes of the author's "talk about his
external habits, his abode, his casual associates, and other matters entirely
upon the surface," in his preface to *The Snow-Image, and Other Twice-told
Tales:* "These things hide the man, instead of displaying him." Or there is his
comment, at the beginning of "The Custom-House," on his increasingly
characteristic "autobiographical impulse": "we may prate of the circumstances that lie around us, and even of ourself, but still keep the inmost Me
behind its Veil." And veils, as we know, occur repeatedly in Hawthorne's fiction. For instance, in "The Minister's Black Veil" (1836), Parson Hooper, another descendant of the Puritans, protests against secrecy, paradoxically, by
covering his face with a veil—a veil he refuses to have removed even on his
deathbed.

The transcendentalism of Ralph Waldo Emerson and his followers was,
among other things, an American variant of European Romanticism, and
Hawthorne, in the 1840s, had a number of associations with the transcendentalists. He joined the transcendentalist community at Brook Farm for
six months in 1841, and he lived in Concord—where Emerson, Thoreau,
Margaret Fuller, and Bronson Alcott were among his neighbors—from
1842 to 1845. Yet he regarded the thinking of these neighbors with the considerable skepticism that he recorded, for instance, in "The Old Manse"
(1846), his autobiographical preface to *Mosses from an Old Manse.* "Never
was a poor little country village," he writes of those who came to Concord to
worship Emerson, "infested with such a variety of queer, strangely dressed,
oddly-behaved mortals, most of whom took upon themselves to be important agents of the world's destiny, yet were simply bores of a very intense water." Hawthorne satirized the optimism of those who flocked to Emerson—
particularly their easy denial of the reality of sin and evil—in a number of
sketches, most notably "The Celestial Rail-road" (1843), and he gave full expression to his antitranscendental skepticism in *The Blithedale Romance.*

"Our age is retrospective," Emerson complained in *Nature* (1836). "It
builds the sepulchres of the fathers." Emerson exhorted his contemporaries
to reject this fealty to the past: "Let us demand our own works and laws and
worship." Such an exhortation is echoed in the forest scene in *The Scarlet
Letter* when Hester Prynne urges Arthur Dimmesdale to flee Boston: "Begin all anew! Hast thou exhausted possibility in the failure of this one trial?
Not so! The future is yet full of trial and success. There is happiness to be
enjoyed! There is good to be done! Exchange this false life of thine for a true

one!" Even Hester's style here, relying on brief assertions and imperatives, echoes or parodies Emerson, an effect clearly quite deliberate on Hawthorne's part. Hawthorne, fully aware of the repressive intolerance of Puritanism, is more than a little sympathetic with Hester's aspirations, as he is sympathetic with similar aspirations expressed by women characters in his later romances—by Zenobia in *The Blithedale Romance* and by Miriam in *The Marble Faun*. The passionate *women* in these romances, in significant contrast to the often tremulous and even prurient defensiveness of the *male* characters, embrace with sincerity and passion the most revolutionary ambitions of Romanticism.

Nevertheless, these ambitions, in the romances of the 1850s, are always defeated by the force of circumstances and guilt and by the abiding pressure of the past. Hester and Dimmesdale do not escape; at the close Dimmesdale ascends the scaffold to confess his sin, and years later Hester returns to Boston, "of her own free will," to resume wearing the scarlet letter she had thrown off in the forest. *The House of the Seven Gables* relates a story of the working out of a seventeenth-century curse in the nineteenth-century—illustrating "the truth," as Hawthorne puts it in his preface, ". . .that the wrong-doing of one generation lives into the successive ones." This sense of the continuing pressure of the past, of the futility or tragedy of efforts to escape its influence, sets Hawthorne apart from the forward-looking, revolutionary optimism of Emersonian Romanticism, and it lies at the heart, once again, of the last romance Hawthorne completed. In *The Marble Faun,* the artist Miriam seeks to escape a mysterious figure associated both with her own past and with the distant past of Rome. Sympathetic to her plight, an innocent Italian, Donatello, murders the pursuer. At the close, however, Donatello, increasingly wracked by guilt, has given himself up to the authorities, and Miriam, like Hester, has embraced a life of penitence. She is last seen kneeling in a Roman church, her face "invisible, behind a veil or mask."

It would be a gross distortion, however, to categorize Hawthorne simply as an anti-Romantic dissenter from the enthusiasms of his literary contemporaries. After all, Herman Melville, whose early career was fueled by precisely these enthusiasms, found in Hawthorne a fellow "Genius." Hawthorne's real scorn was not for Romanticism as such but for the bogus popular Romanticism, the easy "spirituality," which seemed to him to pervade the culture of his own nineteenth-century America, the culture portrayed with such telling irony, for instance, in *The Blithedale Romance*. If the voice that addresses us in Hawthorne's fiction, to return to the 1851 preface to *Twice-told Tales,* speaks in the sociable "style of a man of society," the subjects about which it speaks, in however "veiled" a fashion, are nevertheless the great themes of the great Romantics: alienation, solitude, nature and natural impulse, unconscious fantasy and dream. That Hawthorne sometimes viewed such things skeptically, and far more often in the light of tragedy, does not mean that he dismissed their power or their truth. "Truth," writes the narrator of "The Birth-mark," "often finds its way to the mind close-muffled in robes of sleep, and then speaks with uncompromising directness of matters in regard to which we practise an unconscious self-deception, during our waking moments." From first to last the tension between this sort of "truth" and the "self-deception" that resists such "uncompromising directness" constituted both Hawthorne's main subject and the most significant model for his art.

2   Arts of Deception: Hawthorne, "Romance," and *The Scarlet Letter*

To many readers, both distinguished literary critics and high school students forced to read *The Scarlet Letter* as a duty, Hawthorne's fiction has seemed mainly solemnly moral and allegorical: "serious," of course, and important, but for these very reasons—to state the matter bluntly—boring. This vision of Hawthorne set in early, and it was early challenged by Hawthorne's admirer, Herman Melville. "The world," Melville proclaimed in 1850, "is mistaken in this Nathaniel Hawthorne. He himself must often have smiled at its absurd misconception of him." "Where Hawthorne is known," Melville observes, "he seems to be deemed a pleasant writer, with a pleasant style—a sequestered, harmless man, from whom any deep and weighty thing would hardly be anticipated: a man who means no meanings"; but the truth, Melville insists, is that Hawthorne is "immeasurably deeper than the plummet of the mere critic." Many of his stories (Melville was reviewing a collection of tales, *Mosses from an Old Manse*) seem "directly calculated to deceive—egregiously deceive—the superficial skimmer of pages."[1]

This was a perceptive comment, and it has proved prophetic of recent developments in Hawthorne criticism. What Melville saw, or claimed, in 1850 is that the "superficial" Hawthorne (the solemn classic now enshrined in literary history and high school curricula) is in fact a sort of mask, half-covering a different Hawthorne, far more subversive and anarchic, certainly far from having the sort of genteel complacency with which Hawthorne has so often been associated. In the past twenty years or so, we have become more sensitive to this hidden quality in Hawthorne's fiction. We have now

come to value the ways in which Hawthorne's overt moralizing and allego-
rizing seem designed to deceive us, to play with our needs and fears, as "superficial skimmers of pages," in order to insinuate a vision that would seem
to have little to do with conventional morality or allegory.[2]

What has been less often recognized is that a similar quality of playfully
subversive deception is also characteristic of Hawthorne's *critical* writings:
his comments on fiction in his prefaces—notably in "The Custom-House,"
his preface to *The Scarlet Letter.* Many passages in these prefaces have been
quoted, again and again, as straightforward statements of artistic intention;
they have even been used to bolster sweeping general theories of the distinctive nature of American fiction. What we need to recognize is the extent
to which these very passages, to use Melville's words, seem "directly calculated to deceive—egregiously deceive—the superficial skimmer of pages."

I considered calling this essay "The Scarlet Herring"; taste, happily, intervened, but the title did have a serious point. *Webster's* dictionary defines
"red herring" as "a diversion intended to distract attention from the real issue."[3] This is precisely the covert function of many of Hawthorne's best-
known statements about fiction, those generalizations about its nature and
purpose that have long been taken at face value, and it is time we looked at
these statements more closely. We need to drop our "plummets"—to quote
Melville again, while recognizing that "plummets" may be a bit ponderous
for the enterprise—as deeply as possible. Only then can we understand
both the drama and the humor of Hawthorne's apparently "official" pro-
nouncements. Only then can we uncover the deepest connections between
the play of fiction in "The Custom-House," for instance, and the action of
The Scarlet Letter.

Hawthorne always insisted that he wrote "romances," rather than "novels,"
and most of the general comments on fiction in his prefaces have to do with
defining the nature of romance and the difference between the romance
and the novel. In 1850 *The Scarlet Letter* was subtitled *A Romance,* and
in the following year, in the preface to *The House of the Seven Gables,*
Hawthorne set out, apparently, to define his terms. "When a writer calls his
work a Romance," the preface begins, "it need hardly be observed that he
wishes to claim a certain latitude, both as to its fashion and material, which
he would not have felt himself entitled to assume, had he professed to be
writing a Novel." The novelist, Hawthorne explains, is confined to "a very
minute fidelity, not merely to the possible, but to the probable and ordinary
course of man's experience." The romancer, on the other hand, is free to

present "the truth of the human heart . . . under circumstances, to a great extent, of [his] own choosing or creation" (vol. II, p. 4).[4]

For Hawthorne, this is to say, a romance is more *fictional*, and therefore less *realistic* (although the term "realism" was not in use in pre–Civil War America), than a novel. Unlike the novelist, the romancer is not tied to conventional reality ("the probable and ordinary course of man's experience"); he is free to indulge the fantastic and the marvelous. For the rest of his life, apparently in these terms, Hawthorne continued to characterize himself as a romancer and his works as romances. In 1852 the key word appeared in the main title of *The Blithedale Romance,* and in 1860 *The Marble Faun* was subtitled *The Romance of Monte Beni.* Moreover, the prefaces to these two works continue to use the definition of "romance" begun in "The Custom-House" and the preface to *The House of the Seven Gables.*

Hawthorne's reputation as a fiction writer—unlike Melville's, for instance—endured into the years after the Civil War, into the era we are now accustomed to call the "age of realism." But to such post–Civil War admirers as Henry James and William Dean Howells, his insistence that he wrote romances rather than novels was a significant embarrassment. In the climate of the new realism, Hawthorne's affection for romance could only seem unfortunate and old-fashioned, a matter for apology or condescending explanation.[5] This situation persisted well into the twentieth century, and its persistence had a good deal to do with the solidification of Hawthorne's reputation as serious but somehow irrelevant or outmoded.

After World War II, however, things began to change, and quite dramatically. In 1947 Lionel Trilling, in an essay entitled "Manners, Morals, and the Novel," contended that the novel "has never really established itself in America"—where, he argued, the novel has always diverged "from its classic intention which . . . is the investigation of the problem of reality beginning in the social field." "The fact is," he wrote, "that American writers of genius have not turned their minds to society." Trilling, in this essay, was not directly concerned with Hawthorne, but he did turn to Hawthorne's prefaces to support his own general assertions. "Hawthorne was acute," he wrote, "when he insisted that he did not write novels but romances—he thus expressed his awareness of the lack of social texture in his work."[6]

Trilling's argument that America has had a distinct tradition in fiction soon became a critical commonplace; and although Trilling himself, like the post–Civil War realists, mainly deplored the effects of this tradition, the modern critics who followed his lead turned his ideas to the purposes of something like national celebration. In 1957, for instance, in *The American*

Novel and Its Tradition, Richard Chase argued that "the tradition of romance is major in the history of the American novel but minor in the history of the English novel," giving us our own distinctive answer to the novelistic "great tradition" in British fiction described by F. R. Leavis. A year earlier, Perry Miller had delivered a series of lectures entitled "The Romance and the Novel," similarly arguing that the tradition of American fiction was distinctive, and was a tradition of romance. At this same time, more traditional literary romance (for instance, in Spenser or in Shakespeare's late plays) was acquiring new prestige, largely as a result of Northrop Frye's influential *Anatomy of Criticism* (1957), and such prestige was not unwelcome to proponents of the formal or generic "Americanness" of American fiction. By 1968, in any case, Joel Porte, in *The Romance in America,* felt confident in simply assuming that ours was a distinctive tradition of romance. "It no longer seems necessary," he wrote on the first page of his study, "to argue for the importance of romance as a nineteenth-century American genre."[7]

Needless to say, this rapid shift in academic critical opinion, this sudden conversion to the belief that romance constitutes a distinct and distinguished tradition in American fiction, produced a comparable shift in critical opinion about Hawthorne's comments on fiction in his prefaces. What had made him seem old-fashioned in the later nineteenth century all at once, in the 1950s and 1960s, made him seem central. Again and again, from the 1950s to the present day (although there has been a growing current of dissent[8]), Hawthorne's prefaces have been brought forward as evidence that American fiction writers—at least before the Civil War—*knew* that they were creating a distinctive fictional tradition, a tradition at once specifically national and nevertheless tied to the august tradition of European romance.

One can hardly help speculating about why American romance, a kind of literary embarrassment up to World War II, suddenly became a matter of national pride and an arena of critical consensus. Perhaps, having emerged from the war as a world power, we had to discover a tradition of our own, and the claims of Hawthorne and some of his contemporaries that they wrote romances rather than novels were too convenient to be ignored. During these same years, it is worth noting, the study of American literature as a distinct subject first gained general acceptance in American colleges and universities.

Whatever it may have been, it seems likely that there was *some* external reason, in the 1950s and 1960s, for the growing consensus about American romance, because the actual arguments presented to support the romance hypothesis were often fraught with problems. Chase, for instance, cites the preface to *The Marble Faun* as evidence of Hawthorne's belief that "romance, rather than the novel, was the predestined form of American narrative." The problem is that this is in fact precisely the opposite of what Hawthorne actually says in his preface—his point being, rather, that it is almost *impossible* to write a romance about America, given its lack of ruins, legends, and the like. This, he explains, is why he has chosen to set *The Marble Faun* in Italy.[9] Now Richard Chase was no "superficial skimmer of pages"; he was an astute reader. That he so blatantly misread what Hawthorne says suggests that he very much wanted Hawthorne to have said something else. And although his misreading is an extreme example, it is in many respects typical of the way proponents of the American romance tradition have used Hawthorne's comments on fiction to support their own arguments.

Taken together, moreover, these critics produce no genuine consensus on what romance is or what it does. One could argue, of course, that romance may combine a number of different forms and impulses, but such an argument simply assumes, as a given, what must first be demonstrated— that there *was* a common tradition in nineteenth-century American fiction that it makes sense to describe as romance. The classic studies of American romance produce no such demonstration. Trilling, for instance, locates the distinctiveness of fictional romance in its lack of what he calls "social texture" or "social reality"; unlike novels, he argues, romances do not deal with social "manners." Chase more or less agrees with Trilling, but he locates the *central* distinction of American romance elsewhere: in its cultivation, as he puts it, of "radical forms of alienation, contradiction, and disorder"—all of which he distinguishes from the sense of reconciliation and order supposedly achieved by the most characteristic English novels. For Miller, to cite one more example, what distinguishes American romance is mainly its supposed concern with the wilderness and the irrational. "Nature with a capital N," he writes, "Nature as meaning both universal human nature and natural landscape," is what romance signified in the first half of the nineteenth century.[10]

The more one reads these critics, even as one profits immensely from their insights into the literature they are describing, the more one comes to feel that they are using the term "romance" not to describe a particular literary form (which is what the term is supposed to do), but as a convenient label for *any* qualities they find typical of American fiction, or even of American life generally. Yet this vagueness and confusion are understandable. It is not just that academic critics after World War II felt compelled to discover a uniquely American tradition in fiction. Even more important, one suspects, is the fact that for their evidence that American fiction writers *meant* to cultivate a kind of fiction different from that of England, they turned to Hawthorne's prefaces;[11] the truth is that Hawthorne's definitions of "romance" are as confusing—and in their own way apparently as insufficient— as the twentieth-century theories that have been based on them. It is thus hardly surprising that literary historians drawing upon Hawthorne's "generic" categories have found themselves in a state of confusion. The problem is not so much that they have misunderstood what Hawthorne was saying as that they have paid insufficient attention to the way he was saying it. Such attention now needs to be paid. We need to reexamine the well-known descriptions of "romance" in Hawthorne's prefaces, not just as statements but as performances.

We might take another look, for instance, at Hawthorne's most frequently quoted definition of "romance" in the first paragraph of his preface to *The House of the Seven Gables:*

> When a writer calls his work a Romance, it need hardly be observed that he wishes to claim a certain latitude, both as to its fashion and material, which he would not have felt himself entitled to assume, had he professed to be writing a Novel. The latter form of composition [i.e., the Novel] is presumed to aim at a very minute fidelity, not merely to the possible, but to the probable and ordinary course of man's experience. The former [i.e., the Romance]—while, as a work of art, it must rigidly subject itself to laws, and while it sins unpardonably, so far as it may swerve aside from the truth of the human heart—has fairly a right to present that truth under circumstances, to a great extent, of the writer's own choosing or creation. (Vol. II, p. 1)

The first thing we might note here is a kind of slippery evasiveness. What the writer wishes to claim "need hardly be observed"; what matters is what he would feel himself "entitled to assume"; the writer might have "*professed* to be writing a Novel"; that form "is *presumed* to aim at a very minute fidelity." The key terms here seem to have meaning, not in and of themselves, but only in the context of a process of negotiation or even pretense. What is the difference, one wonders, between *writing* a novel and *professing* to write a novel? Hawthorne's assumption that the novel/romance distinction is so widely accepted as hardly to require explanation is also somewhat disingenuous. As Nina Baym has pointed out, after examining reviews of fiction in

American periodicals from 1840 to 1860, this distinction was neither very important nor very clear to Hawthorne's contemporaries.[12] Moreover, if the meaning of calling one's work a romance were so clear as hardly to require explanation, one wonders why Hawthorne feels compelled to explain it.

Briefly summarized, what this opening paragraph from the *Seven Gables* preface says is, as I have already noted, that a romance is distinguished by its "latitude," by its freedom from the novel's obligation to "minute fidelity . . . to the probable and ordinary course of man's experience." This is fine as far as it goes, but it does not, in fact, go very far at all. This is a curiously negative definition: It tells us what romance does *not* do, but tells us almost nothing about what it *does*. More importantly, and closely related to this first sort of reticence, the preface says nothing at all about *why* a writer might wish to depart from ordinary, novelistic realism.

My point might be more clearly expressed in slightly different terms. Hawthorne, in the *Seven Gables* preface, clearly identifies what we might call the *authority* of the novelist. The authority behind his fictions—the "truth" of which those fictions are an expression or representation—is the kind of "fact" studied by historians or, in our own time, by psychologists and sociologists: "the probable and ordinary course of man's experience." What the preface does not identify is the authority of the *romancer.* We learn nothing about the distinctive sorts of truth on which the romancer's fictions are based (both the novel and the romance, apparently, deal with "the truth of the human heart"), and this omission is crucial. The romancer presumably writes a different kind of fiction because he is concerned with a different kind or order of truth. What Hawthorne doesn't tell us is what this truth is.

What seems most interesting about the *Seven Gables* preface, then, is what it does *not* say, and it seems likely that Hawthorne's silence here about what romance is—about the sort of truth that authorizes it—is quite deliberate. This silence allows him to conceal the nature of romance even as he seems to explain it, and if this is what Hawthorne was up to, his strategy has proved remarkably successful. Generations of critics have quoted this passage as a straightforward and complete definition of "romance" without noticing how little it actually says. Instead, they have filled in the gap with their own ideas about the distinctive truth of the romancer: the absence of social "reality" for Trilling, alienation and radical disorder for Chase, "Nature with a capital N" for Miller.

If Hawthorne wrote the *Seven Gables* preface to conceal, rather than reveal, the true authority behind romance, if he set out here "to deceive—egregiously deceive—the superficial skimmer of pages," he had good reason for doing so. According to conventional opinion in the first half of the nineteenth century, imaginative fiction, as opposed to literature based on fact, was deeply dangerous, psychologically threatening, and even socially subversive. Thomas Jefferson, for instance, wrote of fiction in 1818 that "when this poison infects the mind, it destroys its tone and revolts it against wholesome reading. Reason and fact, plain and unadorned, are rejected. . . . The result is a bloated imagination, sickly judgment, and disgust towards all the real businesses of life." Jefferson may sound a bit hysterical to modern readers (although his warning is strikingly similar to modern alarm about the dangerous effects of television on impressionable viewers), but what he says here is quite typical of early-nineteenth-century American comments on the dangers of fiction; and these attitudes endured, albeit in less virulent forms, into the middle of the century and beyond. To Hawthorne's contemporaries, what I have called the authority of romance, of imaginative fiction as opposed to factual history, was clear, and it was clearly dangerous. Romance, according to conventional opinion, derived from "sickly" imagination rather than from "wholesome" reason or judgment. To indulge in the delusions of romance was to undermine the basis of psychological and social order, to alienate oneself from "the real business of life."[13]

The term "romance," at least implicitly, was thus less a neutral generic label than a revolutionary, or at least antisocial, slogan. To identify oneself as a romancer was to reject far more than "the probable and ordinary course of man's experience"; it was to set oneself in opposition to the most basic norms of society: reason, fact, and "real" business. In 1848 Herman Melville, who would later delight in Hawthorne's deceptions, wrote a letter to his British publisher, John Murray, announcing that his third book, *Mardi,* would be quite different from its more or less factual predecessors, *Typee* and *Omoo.* "My *instinct,*" Melville declared, "is to out with the Romance, & let me say that instincts are prophetic, & better than acquired wisdom."[14] To "out with the Romance" was, for Melville, to rebel, to reject the authority of "acquired wisdom" (of reason, fact, and judgment) for the subversive authority of "instinct" and imagination. Melville's publisher understood him perfectly. A conservative purveyor of safely factual narratives, John Murray was not at all pleased by this letter, and when Melville finally finished his romance, Murray refused to publish it.

In this context, the *Seven Gables* preface is a truly remarkable performance. Hawthorne was fascinated with the antisocial and abnormal, but he never openly identified himself with them. Thus, in the preface, Hawthorne, or the persona he adopts, openly announces that his book is a romance; yet this persona manages to seem wholly ignorant, as Hawthorne himself surely was not, of the subversive implications of such an announcement. He makes it sound perfectly safe, straightforward, morally neutral; the "superficial skimmer of pages" would see no reason to be alarmed. Still, the careful reader would notice that although Hawthorne ignores the conventional sense of the subversive authority of romance, he does not specifically reject it, and he puts nothing else in its place.

Melville openly and repeatedly announced his decision to reject "acquired wisdom" for rebellious "instinct," and this is one of the reasons he lost his reading public during the 1850s. As he became more and more open, critics and readers became more and more hostile.[15] Hawthorne was far more circumspect, which is surely one of the reasons why, unlike Melville, he *was* able to keep his reading public. When Hawthorne proclaimed his own decision to "out with the Romance," he was careful, to use Melville's phrase, "to deceive—egregiously deceive—the superficial skimmer of pages." To miss this quality in the *Seven Gables* preface is to fall for the deception.

The same sort of deception is at work in Hawthorne's discussion of fiction in the "Custom-House" preface to *The Scarlet Letter*. "Romance is there defined, in another often quoted passage, as "a neutral territory, somewhere between the real world and fairyland, where the Actual and Imaginary may meet, and each imbue itself with the nature of the other" (p. 36). This sounds like a pretty safe (hence, "neutral") definition, certainly a far cry from Melville's defiant rejection of fact for fantasy. Romance, as Hawthorne here describes it, seems to *reconcile* fantasy and fact, the "Imaginary" and the "Actual." But there are serious problems lurking in even this celebrated formulation, problems we see clearly if we place the passage in the context of Hawthorne's preface as a whole.

"The Custom-House" is mainly devoted to describing Hawthorne's experience as Surveyor of Customs at Salem from 1846 to 1849. It also tells the story—which Hawthorne, of course, made up—of what he found, one day, in the attic of the Custom-House: a frayed scarlet A, made of cloth, and a manuscript summarizing the life of the woman who wore the letter, one Hester Prynne. We are told that the manuscript was the work of Hawthorne's eighteenth-century predecessor, Surveyor Pue, and we are assured (as readers had been assured of the historical truth of many a work of fiction) that the facts he gathered provide the basis for the story of *The Scarlet Letter*. For this reason, Hawthorne writes, his "Custom-House" preface has "a certain propriety, . . . as explaining how a large portion of the following pages came into my possession, and as offering proofs of the authenticity of [the] narrative therein contained." His own "true position," he adds, is merely that of "editor, or very little more," of *The Scarlet Letter* (p. 4).

Now everybody recognizes that this self-effacing claim of authenticity is a joke, since Hawthorne himself invented the manuscript he identifies as his source, but we need to recognize the full impact of this joke. As a mere editor, Hawthorne is claiming for his story the very sort of authority his culture approved, the authority of what Jefferson called "reason and fact, plain and unadorned." But by making this claim into a joke, Hawthorne is in effect dismissing "reason and fact" every bit as much as Melville, writing to John Murray, was dismissing "acquired wisdom." The difference is that while Melville chose outright defiance, Hawthorne characteristically chooses irony, but for both writers the point is much the same. Melville rejects conventional wisdom; Hawthorne (as the title of his preface suggests) rejects accepted custom. The reader of "The Custom-House" must thus ask what sort of authority Hawthorne turns to once he has turned away from the conventional authority of fact, judgment, and custom.

This question seems to be answered, more or less, in the discussion of the "neutral territory." This passage occurs rather late in the preface, as part of Hawthorne's account of sitting in his parlor late at night, after a day of custom-house routine, contemplating familiar objects transformed by moonlight. This experience becomes, for him, a metaphor for the working of the imagination upon everyday reality. The objects in the room, Hawthorne writes, "are so spiritualized by the unusual light, that they seem to lose their actual substance, and become things of intellect." The moonlight invests them "with a quality of strangeness and remoteness"; defamiliarized, they come to seem as much imaginary as real. "Thus," Hawthorne concludes, "the floor of our familiar room has become a neutral territory, somewhere between the real world and fairy-land, where the Actual and the Imaginary may meet, and each imbue itself with the nature of the other" (35–36).

As I have said, this seems to be a pretty safe account of romance, apparently *reconciling* the authority of imagination with the authority of fact, of the "Actual," apparently *combining* "the real world and fairy-land." The problem, however, is that even metaphorically, this well-known passage doesn't quite make sense—at least as an account of the special art of the romancer. The imaginative quality of this scene comes from the scene itself, from the real combination of familiar objects and ethereal moonlight, and not from Hawthorne's own creative imagination; and this would seem to be the point. Hawthorne can claim to reconcile fact and fantasy because he can claim that his facts are already fantastic. If what results seems like romance, it is thus not his fault but the fault of his materials.

This idea, that romance stems not from the writer's art but from his materials, becomes even more important in Hawthorne's later prefaces. In the preface to *The Marble Faun*, for instance, he writes that "Italy, as the site of his Romance, was chiefly valuable . . . as affording a sort of poetic or fairy precinct, where actualities would not be so terribly insisted upon, as they are, and must needs be, in America" (vol. IV, p. 3). In the preface to *The Blithedale Romance*, the same argument is used to explain the use of Brook Farm as the setting for a work of fiction. "The Author," Hawthorne writes, "has ventured to make free with his old, and affectionately remembered home, at BROOK FARM, as being, certainly, the most romantic episode of his own life—essentially a daydream, and yet a fact—and thus offering an available foothold between fiction and reality" (vol. III, p. 2). *The Marble Faun* and *The Blithedale Romance* are romances, this is to say, because the very facts of Italy and Brook Farm are already essentially romantic.

This is an appealing argument, allowing Hawthorne to advertise his works as romances without quite having to admit that he is himself a romancer. He thereby frees himself from personal responsibility for the romantic or imaginative quality of his works. Yet we should see this argument for what it is (and is not). It is clearly not a straightforward declaration of artistic intention, and it is certainly not a theoretical definition of a distinctively American mode of fiction. Rather, it functions as a rather devious strategy for concealing or evading the more subversive implications of being a romancer, the implications Melville, to his peril, proclaimed openly. The trouble with the descriptions of Italy, Brook Farm, and the moonlit parlor as definitions of romance is that they really don't *define* romance. Like the passage in the *Seven Gables* preface, they tell us nothing about what the romancer actually does, or about why he might wish to do it. In fact, they divert our attention from these matters, and arguably do so quite deliberately. We might recall *Webster's* definition of "red herring": "a diversion intended to distract attention from the real issue." This is precisely the function of the "neutral territory" passage in "The Custom-House"; it distracts our attention from the real issue. And the frequency with which this passage is quoted by modern critics as a definition of "romance" suggests that it has fulfilled its function admirably, allowing Hawthorne to engage in something like subversion without appearing to do anything of the sort.

Still, despite his fondness for deception and concealment, Hawthorne knew very well what the real issue was, and there are other passages in "The Custom-House," passages not very often discussed by modern critics, that hint at his true sense of the nature of romance, his true sense of the source of his own power as a fiction writer. For instance, at the close of his description of the moonlit parlor, we are told: "Then, at such an hour, and with this scene before him, if a man . . . cannot dream strange things, and make them look like truth, he need never try to write romances" (36). "Dream strange things, and make them look like truth": Here, for just a moment, the cat is allowed to peek out of the bag. The phrase reveals that the real source of romance is not some romantic quality in the setting but the "strange dreams" of the romancer. Even more important, the idea of reconciliation—of a "neutral territory" or an "available foothold between fiction and reality"—is revealed to be itself a fiction, a sham, a form of deception. The romancer tricks the reader into accepting his "strange dreams" by making them *look* like the sort of truth to which the reader is accustomed.

Here, for a change, we begin to get some sense of what the romancer actually does, and in this context the most interesting and revealing passages in "The Custom-House" are those describing the supposed sources for the story of *The Scarlet Letter:* the manuscript left by Surveyor Pue and the frayed letter once worn by Hester Prynne. Hawthorne begins his account of the manuscript with another joke about its supposed authority. "It should be borne carefully in mind," he reminds us, "that the main facts [of *The Scarlet Letter*] are authorized and authenticated by the document of Mr. Surveyor Pue." We are even assured that "the original papers, together with the scarlet letter itself . . . , are still in my possession, and shall be freely exhibited to whomsoever, induced by the great interest of the narrative, may desire a sight of them" (32–33). Needless to say, scholars have not yet turned up these invaluable items.

These facetious remarks are followed, however, by comments of a quite different nature. Jefferson, we recall, insisted on "reason and fact, *plain and unadorned.*" "I must not be understood as affirming," Hawthorne writes, "that, in the dressing up of the tale, and imagining the motives and modes of passion that influenced the characters who figure in it, I have invariably confined myself within the limits of the old Surveyor's half a dozen sheets of foolscap. On the contrary, I have allowed myself, as to such points, nearly or altogether as much license as if the facts had been entirely of my own invention" (33). This curiously casual progression—from "nearly" to "altogether" (presented as if they were interchangeable synonyms) to "*entirely* of my own invention"—nicely deflates the pretense of factual authenticity. It reminds us that Hawthorne is having fun with us, that his comments are often comic performances. The function of these performances, one suspects, is to mask the more subversive, even compulsive implications of a decision "to out with the Romance," but what matters first of all is simply that we recognize the irony and comedy, recognize the fact that Hawthorne, in his critical remarks, *is* performing.

In any case, whatever Hawthorne's motive may have been, there is also a serious literary significance lurking in this particular performance. In the *Seven Gables* preface, written a year after "The Custom-House," romance is distinguished by "latitude." Here the term is "license": "I have allowed myself . . . as much license as if the facts had been entirely of my own invention." Here, moreover, we are told what we are not told in the *Seven Gables* preface; we are told what this license is *for.* It allows the romancer to *imagine* "the motives and modes of passion that influenced the characters." And the special authority of romance is also, for once, identified; it is neither fact nor reason, but sympathetic "imagining."

The nature of this sympathetic imagination, and its distance from the realm of fact and custom, are revealed most clearly, in "The Custom-House," in the description of the letter of frayed scarlet cloth, supposedly bound up with Surveyor Pue's manuscript, once worn by Hester Prynne. "It strangely interested me," Hawthorne writes; and this "strangely" surely recalls his remark about the romancer's "strange dreams." "My eyes," he continues, "fastened themselves upon the old scarlet letter, and would not be turned aside. Certainly, there was some deep meaning in it, most worthy of interpretation, and which, as it were, streamed forth from the mystic symbol, subtly communicating itself to my sensibilities, but evading the analysis of my mind" (31). Here the mask of objective historian or editor is dropped completely. There is even a tone of irrational obsession or compulsion in the author's confession that his eyes "fastened themselves upon the old scarlet letter, and would not be turned aside." The source of this strange fascination has nothing to do with reason or judgment, with what Hawthorne here calls the "analysis of my mind," nor is there any talk here of *reconciling* fact and fantasy. Rather, this compulsive fascination derives wholly from irrational "sensibilities," from feeling and imagination. It is these "sensibilities," and not any general, rational sense of "the probable and ordinary course of man's experience," that give the author imaginative access to "the motives and modes of passion" of his characters.

The passages I have just referred to are unusual because they concern themselves with what most of Hawthorne's comments on fiction conceal or evade; they describe, or at least hint at, what the romancer actually does, and why he does it. Taken together, they indicate that the deepest significance of romance for Hawthorne had little to do with the meanings modern critics have given to the term: absence of social texture, lack of resolution, concern with Nature, and the like. These passages also suggest a notion of romance quite different from the idea of reconciliation set forth in the description of the neutral territory or in the prefaces to *The Blithedale Romance* and *The Marble Faun.* For Hawthorne, finally, the most basic authority of romance is neither "reason and fact, plain and unadorned," nor some romantic quality in certain kinds of settings, but the projected imagination of the author. Not surprisingly, this notion of the authority of romance sounds a good deal like the conventional assumptions about romance proclaimed by Herman Melville, denounced by most of Hawthorne's contemporaries, and disguised or concealed in Hawthorne's most often quoted comments on fiction.

Hawthorne described his fiction, in his preface to the 1851 edition of *Twice-told Tales,* as an attempt "to open an intercourse with the world" (vol. IX, p. 6). His prefaces serve the same function, and this is what critics who mine them for theoretical ideas, for some theory of romance, tend to overlook. In the last analysis, these prefaces are not essays in critical definition but, as I have been arguing, dramatic, ironic, and often comic social performances, in which the author adopts a series of masks and poses in order to obscure—and yet still hint at—the true authority behind his fiction. Hawthorne knew very well what he was doing, and one guesses he enjoyed doing it. And in his preface to an 1852 story collection *(The Snow-Image and Other Twice-told Tales),* he for once quite openly discusses those "superficial skimmers of pages" who insist on taking his prefaces literally. His remarks here reveal a certain detached contempt. They also, in passing, provide what may be his most complete and suggestive remarks about the art of the romancer.

Some readers, Hawthorne writes, have seen his penchant for autobiography, in his prefaces, as a sign of egotism. "A person," he replies,

> who has been burrowing . . . into the depth of our common nature, for the
> purposes of psychological romance,—and who pursues his researches in
> that dusky region, as he needs must, as well by the tact of sympathy as by
> the light of observation,—will smile at incurring such an imputation [i.e.,
> of egotism] in virtue of a little preliminary talk about his external habits, his
> abode, his casual associates, and other matters entirely upon the surface.
> These things hide the man, instead of displaying him. (vol. XI, p. 4)

Having dismissed the superficiality of his literalist readers, and having described "the purposes of psychological romance" with unusual directness, Hawthorne proceeds to explain how he should properly be read. "You must make quite another kind of inquest," he writes, "and look through the whole range of [the author's] fictitious characters, good and evil, in order to detect any of his essential traits" (4).

The reader, this is to say, must, like the romancer, rely on imagination, on "the tact of sympathy." If we wish to understand the author, we must understand how he has both hidden and revealed his own "essential traits" by projecting them into his characters—including, of course, the character "Nathaniel Hawthorne" who addresses us in the prefaces. The romancer dreams "strange things" and makes them "look like truth"; he manages to present unconscious fantasy in the *disguise* of socially respectable reality. This is precisely what Hawthorne does in his prefaces. It is also the "essential trait" that ties the author of "The Custom-House" most closely to his "fictitious characters" in *The Scarlet Letter.*

Toward the end of "The Custom-House," Hawthorne contrasts what he sees as the insubstantiality of his romance of Hester Prynne to the superior reality of the novel he might have written about his actual experience in present-day Salem. "I might readily," he insists, "have found a more serious task."

> It was a folly, with the materiality of this daily life pressing so intrusively upon me, to attempt to fling myself back into another age; or to insist on creating the semblance of a world out of airy matter, when, at every moment, the impalpable beauty of my soap-bubble was broken by the contact of some actual circumstance. . . . A better book than I shall ever write was there; leaf after leaf presenting itself to me, just as it was written out by the reality of the flitting hour, and vanishing just as fast as written, only because my brain wanted the insight and my hand the cunning to transcribe it. (37).

To the reader of *The Scarlet Letter,* this declaration seems at least odd, perhaps even disingenuous. Phrases like "airy matter," "impalpable," and "soap-bubble" hardly seem appropriate to the book they are meant to describe. The story of Hester Prynne scarcely exemplifies the fanciful insubstantiality for which "The Custom-House" takes pains to apologize in advance; on the contrary, it has all the air of "actual circumstance."

To be sure, there are flights of allegorical fancifulness in the book, notably in connection with little Pearl, and all the talk of the mystic "elf-child" and her natural affinity for sunshine is inevitably unpalatable to modern readers trained on realistic fiction. Still, *The Scarlet Letter* is, in the most fundamental respects, a significantly realistic work of fiction.[16] Its greatest importance to the history of fiction in English is probably its development of analytical, psychological realism, especially in its probing and elaboration of the conscious and unconscious motives and feelings of Hester Prynne and Arthur Dimmesdale. In this respect, it foreshadows (as it also influenced) the work of such later psychological realists as George Eliot and Henry James. Moreover, in its treatment of Puritan history, as Michael Colacurcio and others have persuasively demonstrated, *The Scarlet Letter* is thoroughly and realistically concerned with both the details and the meaning of the New England past.[17] The account of romance in "The Custom-House" seems, then, curiously inappropriate to the book it claims to describe.

From another point of view, however, the discussion of romance in "The Custom-House" is a particularly appropriate gateway to the world of *The Scarlet Letter.* For while *The Scarlet Letter,* as a work of prose fiction, may seem to have little in common with the sort of romance Hawthorne describes in his preface, the behavior of the characters in the book, especially that of Arthur Dimmesdale and Hester Prynne, has a great deal in common with the duplicitous deception that, as Hawthorne describes and impersonates him in "The Custom-House," characterizes the behavior of the romancer. To read *The Scarlet Letter* as some sort of *kunstlerroman,* as an allegorical exploration of the nature and sources of "psychological romance," is to risk distorting its solidly real concern with general human psychology and Puritan history. Yet, both Dimmesdale and Hester do function in the book, in effect, as artists, manipulating appearances—much like the Hawthorne of the prefaces—in order to mediate between their own subversive impulses and the orthodox expectations of the society in which they live their public lives.[18]

From the very beginning, Dimmesdale sets out to deceive—egregiously deceive—those superficial proponents of Puritan orthodoxy whose need to see him as pious is comparable to the need of Hawthorne's readers to see him, in Melville's phrase, as "a man who means no meanings." When we first see Dimmesdale, he is openly exhorting Hester to name her child's father while, secretly, of course, urging her to do just the opposite; already, at the outset, he is a master of doublespeak. And his celebrated sermons, like Hawthorne's prefaces, permit him to confess without taking responsibility for what he is confessing. His hearers, we are told, "little guessed what deadly purport lurked in [his] self-condemning words," and this deception is quite deliberate: "The minister well knew—subtle, but remorseful hypocrite that he was!—the light in which his vague confession would be viewed" (vol. I, p. 144). Dimmesdale would thus appear to succeed, as Melville thought Hawthorne succeeded, in indulging "instinct" without seeming, at least publicly, to reject "acquired wisdom."

The problem, of course, is that the person Dimmesdale succeeds in deceiving above all is himself. If he is a kind of artist, he is nonetheless unable to regard either the inward motive or the outward expression of his art as anything but falsehood; unlike the subversive romancer, he fully shares his society's equation of the source of his art—passionate, forbidden "impulse"—with sin. "As concerns the good which I may appear to do," he insists to Hester when they finally meet in the forest, "I have no faith in it. It must needs be a delusion. . . . I have laughed, in bitterness and agony of heart, at the contrast between what I seem and what I am" (191).

Dimmesdale may dream strange things and make them look like truth, but he himself cannot *believe* in their truth. He does not indulge his forbidden fantasies; he simply represses them. And even as he distinguishes between "what I seem and what I am," he becomes hopelessly confused. "No man," we are told, "for any considerable period, can wear one face to himself, and another to the multitude, without finally getting bewildered as to which may be the true" (216). Returning from the forest, Dimmesdale imagines that he has finally determined to release "the inner man," to act on his "impulses," to fling his old self down (as Hester has just thrown off her letter and her cap) "like a cast-off garment," but his understanding of this "revolution in the sphere of thought and feeling" reveals only ever-deepening perplexity. "At every step," we are told, "he was incited to do some strange, wild, wicked thing or other, and with a sense that it would be at once involuntary and intentional; in spite of himself, yet growing out of a profounder self than that which opposed the impulse" (217).

Dimmesdale might appear, in the climax of the story, to have resolved the conflict between the competing truths of inner impulse and outward expression. Following his election sermon—beneath whose rhetoric of social progress Hester hears a "low undertone" of "the complaint of a human heart, sorrow-laden, perchance guilty, telling its secret" (243)—he does join Hester and Pearl on the scaffold, to confess his sin openly at last. He does literally cast off the garment of deception, removing the ministerial band to reveal his own scarlet letter. Yet we should remember that the art of the romancer, for the Hawthorne of the prefaces, involves not the casting off of masks—he vows at the beginning of "The Custom-House," for instance, to "keep the inmost Me behind its veil" (4)—but the manipulation of appearances to *insinuate* deeper "truths." We should also recognize that Dimmesdale's resolution of his confusion at the close is only apparent. The election sermon itself is produced out of the same perplexity Dimmesdale brought back from the forest, "at once involuntary and intentional." If it gives expression to "an impulsive flow of thought and emotion," it nevertheless does so through the medium of an officially sanctioned form—a form, moreover, that Dimmesdale, who "fancied himself inspired," must still believe to be officially sanctioned. It is not that Dimmesdale (like the arch romancer of the prefaces) subverts orthodoxy by pretending to adhere to it; rather, he himself can acknowledge "impulse" and "emotion" only when they are disguised as divine "inspiration"—wondering all the while "that Heaven should see fit to transmit the grand and solemn music of its oracles through so foul an organ-pipe as he" (225). Here Hawthorne's irony is devastating. Dimmesdale cannot recognize the significant sexual pun in "organ-pipe." Even in the privacy of his own thoughts, he must continue to distinguish between his "sin" and the source of his "artistic" power.

Dimmesdale's final confession, for all of its apparent sincerity, is also fraught with irony. He casts off imposture, after all, in an elaborately staged *performance;* he turns privacy into public spectacle. What he reveals, we should also recognize, is less an inner "impulse" than an outward *sign,* a letter—the same letter that Hester has been wearing, all along, *as* a garment. Moreover, as we learn in the "Conclusion," Dimmesdale's confession is sufficiently equivocal so as to allow "certain persons, who were spectators of the whole scene" (259), to interpret it just as his earlier "confessions" were interpreted: as a general dramatization of sinfulness rather than as a personal confession of a specific sin. From beginning to end, then, it would seem that Dimmesdale's deception remains self-deception. Hawthorne, in his preface to *The Snow-Image and Other Twice-told Tales,* distinguishes between "external habits" and "essential traits." Dimmesdale is never able to determine which is which. We might thus understand him as a kind of false or failed romancer, ultimately less an artist than a text, a text that he himself can neither control nor even read.

If any character in *The Scarlet Letter* learns to control the interplay of "external" and "essential," to become the sort of romancer Hawthorne hints at in his prefaces, that character is Hester Prynne. She does not, however, learn this lesson all at once. At the outset, she is as confused as Dimmesdale, albeit in a somewhat different fashion, about the relationship between what she seems and what she is. Hester climbs the scaffold, at the beginning of the story, as a central figure in an allegorical social drama—what contemporary sociologists would call a symbolic degradation ritual—and she thinks of her performance in overtly theatrical terms. "Knowing well her part," we are told, "she ascended a flight of wooden steps, and was thus displayed to the surrounding multitude" (55–56). All other conceptions of her identity are engulfed by her allegorical, deviant social role, and she herself fully conspires, or attempts to conspire, in this eradication of her inner personality: "She turned her eyes downward at the scarlet letter, and even touched it with her finger, to assure herself that the infant and the shame were real. Yes!—these were her realities,—all else had vanished!" (59). "In this manner," the narrator later writes, once again enforcing the metaphor of theatrical artifice, "Hester Prynne came to have a part to perform in the world" (84).

Hester, according to the narrator, gives up her "individuality" in order to become "the general symbol at which the preacher and moralist might point, and in which they might vivify and embody their images of woman's frailty and sinful passion" (79). Hester is defined as their text, and she attempts to read herself at their valuation. Yet Hester's extirpation of her "individuality," of her inner life of "impulse," is hardly so complete or successful as she wishes to believe. It is to this repressed "impulse," for instance, that she gives covert expression through the art of needlework, with which she adorns her scarlet letter and her daughter, Pearl. (We should also here recall Hawthorne's comments in "The Custom-House" about "the dressing up of the tale, and imagining the motives and modes of passion that influenced the characters who figure in it.") For all of Hester's outward social conformity, we are told, her needlework "appeared to have also a deeper meaning"; "it might have been a mode of expressing, and therefore soothing, the passion of her life" (83–84). Here Hester seems very much a figure of the romancer, simultaneously expressing and concealing the content of her strange dreams.

Like Dimmesdale, however, Hester is at this point mainly concerned with concealing her dreams from herself. To the extent that her needlework expresses "the passion of her life," we are told, "she rejected it as sin" (84). Nor can she face openly, even in the privacy of her own thoughts, the idea that one of her motives for staying in Boston may be her enduring love for Arthur Dimmesdale:

> She barely looked the idea in the face, and hastened to bar it in its dungeon. What she compelled herself to believe,—what, finally, she reasoned upon, as her motive for continuing a resident of New England,—was half

> a truth, and half a self-delusion. Here, she said to herself, had been the scene of her guilt, and here should be the scene of her earthly punishment; and so, perchance, the torture of her daily shame would at length purge her soul, and work out another purity than that which she had lost; more saint-like, because the result of martyrdom. (80)

This surely sounds like the Dimmesdale who can stand no discrepancy between "what I seem" and "what I am."

Nevertheless, by the time Pearl has reached the age of seven, Hester has changed, and seems much more like the deliberately duplicitous romancer of Hawthorne's prefaces. The great summary chapter of psychological and social analysis, "Another View of Hester," describes a woman who wears one face to herself and another to society, but who remains very much aware (unlike Dimmesdale) of the different ways in which each of these faces is true. "She never battled with the public," we are told, "but submitted uncomplainingly to its worst usage" (160). She has even convinced the public that her embroidered letter—through which she has long expressed and soothed "the passion of her life"—is "the token, not of that one sin, for which she had borne so long and dreary a penance, but of her many good deeds since" (162).

Yet, behind this mask of "acquired wisdom," Hester has been nurturing her "instinct," nurturing a thoroughly subversive sense of her "individuality." "The world's law," we are told, "was no law for her mind. . . . Hester Prynne . . . assumed a freedom of speculation . . . which our forefathers, had they known of it, would have held to be a deadlier crime than that stigmatized by the scarlet letter." But they do not know of it; they are as deceived— as egregiously deceived—as were, so Melville thought, Hawthorne's "superficial" readers. "It is remarkable," writes the narrator, "that persons who speculate the most boldly often conform with the most perfect quietude to the external regulations of society" (164). Hester dreams strange things and makes them look like truth; and what matters most, she clearly (unlike Dimmesdale) understands what she is doing.

She still, however, has another lesson to learn. In the forest, she determines to cast off the arts of deception, to act openly on the truths of "impulse" and "individuality." "See!" she proclaims, throwing off the scarlet letter, "With this symbol, I undo it all, and make it as it had never been!" (202). In this moment, she drops the duplicitous mode of Hawthorne for the open defiance of Melville. In the event, of course, this open rebellion is frustrated: Hester must reassume the scarlet letter—first to placate Pearl, then to conceal from the town her plan to escape with Dimmesdale—and

Dimmesdale's confession and death undermine this plan permanently. But there is a deeper meaning in the frustration of Hester's open rebellion, her avowal of overt sincerity. Hester, in the forest, is doing what Dimmesdale does in his final confession on the scaffold: She is turning inner feeling, defined all along by its repression and concealment, into outward display, public spectacle. She thereby betrays the most essential character of this feeling, of her experience of this feeling. Her repudiation of symbolism in the name of freedom—"See! With this symbol, I undo it all!"—is itself, inevitably, a symbolic gesture. Pearl, who has all along been tied to her mother as a symbol simultaneously of inward rebellion and outward conformity, is right to refuse to recognize this new Hester.

When Hester returns to Boston in the book's "Conclusion," she has returned as well to something like the art of deception described in "Another View of Hester." She finds "a more real life," we are told, "here, in New England, than in that unknown region where Pearl had found a home. Here had been her sin; here, her sorrow; and here was yet to be her penitence" (262–63). This sounds ominously like the self-deceiving Hester, earlier, to whom only the tokens of shame were "realities," the Hester who masked her abiding passion, even from herself, in the language of "guilt," "earthly punishment," and "martyrdom"; but there are major differences. For one thing, this language now seems to apply truly to Hester's feelings; she is now apparently sincerely penitent, or at least bereft of any opportunity to gratify her love for Dimmesdale. What may be even more important is that she has now "resumed,—of her own free will, for not the sternest magistrate of that iron period would have imposed it,—resumed the symbol of which we have related so dark a tale" (263). The crucial term here is "free will": Paradoxically enough, it is by *forsaking* open rebellion, by reassuming her part in society, that Hester is at last able to realize her individuality and freedom. And this paradox lies at the heart, not only of Hester's story, but of Hawthorne's conception of the art of fiction.

Nor does outward conformity prevent Hester from proclaiming her quite revolutionary and "firm belief, that, at some brighter period, when the world should have grown ripe for it, in Heaven's own time, a new truth would be revealed, in order to establish the whole relation between man and woman on a surer ground of mutual happiness" (263). To be sure, Hester, in view of her own sinfulness, renounces all pretension to being herself the "destined prophetess" of this new order, but we should attend to the irony here. It is her outwardly humble renunciation of this role that allows her, in fact, to play it; for in what sense is a woman who announces a "firm belief" in a new order *not* a prophetess"?

Seeking a moral for his story, Hawthorne's narrator proclaims, in the "Conclusion": "Be true! Be true! Be true! Show freely to the world, if not your worst, yet some trait whereby the worst may be inferred!" (260). What matters most about this avowal of sincerity is the speed with which it is qualified, the speed with which a call for sincere openness succumbs to a recognition of the need for indirection; and in this qualification we see both the truth of Hester's story and the central assumption underlying Hawthorne's writing about romance. Melville's open avowal of instinct, as he himself rapidly discovered, led not only to alienation but to distortion. Hawthorne, like Hester, rebels rather through indirection, through ironic subversion, through showing not the worst but something whereby the worst might be inferred—or not inferred, for that matter, at least by the "superficial skimmer of pages." We can only speculate about *why* Hawthorne was impelled toward subversion, but what matters is that we recognize the subversive impulse, and the ways this impulse is managed and masked, in both his fiction and his critical writing. For as Melville was one of the first to recognize, the art of the romancer, for Hawthorne, was above all an art of deception.

3   *The House of the Seven Gables*

The House of the Seven Gables (1851) was the second of three novels Nathaniel Hawthorne published in rapid succession at the beginning of the 1850s, following *The Scarlet Letter* (1850) and preceding *The Blithedale Romance* (1852). While these novels secured Hawthorne's enduring literary reputation, his career as a professional writer had in fact begun more than two decades earlier. In 1828, three years after graduating from Bowdoin College, he had published a novel called *Fanshawe*, which reached few readers and which he soon sought to suppress. Then, in 1830, he began publishing sketches and tales in newspapers, magazines, and annuals—all anonymously. His first collection of these short pieces, *Twice-told Tales*, did not appear until 1837. Hawthorne earned little money from the magazines or from the collection (which sold only 600 or 700 copies), but *Twice-told Tales* at least named him as its author, and the book elicited some positive reviews, including valuable praise from Hawthorne's Bowdoin classmate, Henry Wadsworth Longfellow, in Boston's prestigious *North American Review*.[1]

Over the next thirteen years Hawthorne continued to publish in magazines. He produced three books of popular history, designed for children (and clearly, as well, for making money) in 1840 and 1841. And there were two more story collections: an expanded edition of *Twice-told Tales* in 1842 and *Mosses from an Old Manse* in 1846. The latter was published in New York as part of Wiley and Putnam's new "Library of American Books," edited by Evert Duyckinck—a short-lived but important series that also included Edgar Allan Poe's *Tales* (1845) and *The Raven and Other Poems* (1845) and Herman Melville's *Typee* (1846). But Hawthorne's writings in the 1830s and 1840s never came close to supporting him, and he had to earn his principal living by other means: an abortive career as a magazine editor in 1836; a Democratic political appointment in the Boston Custom House in 1839–40; a brief stint at the Brook Farm Utopian Community, outside Boston, in 1841; and another political appointment as surveyor at the Salem Custom House, from 1846 until he was removed by the new Whig administration in Washington in 1849. By 1849 Hawthorne had been married for seven years, to Sophia Peabody, and they had two children (a third child would be born in 1851). Even with the Custom House job, support was still a problem—in 1849 Nathaniel, Sophia, and the children were living with Hawthorne's mother and sisters—and work at the Custom House left little or no time for writing. Hawthorne was at this point a professional writer only in a rather attenuated sense.

   The Scarlet Letter—to which Hawthorne turned in the summer of 1849, following his removal from the Custom House in June and the death of his mother in July—ended up significantly transforming his literary status. This transformation was in large measure the accomplishment of his new publisher, Boston's James T. Fields.[2] Hawthorne conceived and wrote *The Scarlet Letter* as a long "tale," to be the centerpiece of yet another collection, but Fields talked him into publishing it as a novel, with the autobiographical sketch, "The Custom-House," as introduction. Fields also promoted the book skillfully and successfully, arranging for advertising and, less openly, for favorable reviews. *The Scarlet Letter* was by no means a "best-seller"; while it sold 6,000 copies in its first year, one should note that Harriet Beecher Stowe's *Uncle Tom's Cabin,* two years later, sold 300,000 copies in *its* first year. But the commercial and critical impact of *The Scarlet Letter* was unprecedented in Hawthorne's experience, and Fields did everything in his power to capitalize on his author's new fame. Early in 1851 he brought out a new edition of *Twice-told Tales,* with a new preface by the author; in the same year (in addition to publishing *The House of the Seven Gables*) he reissued the children's histories of 1840–41 as *True Stories from History and Biography,* and Hawthorne wrote (and Fields published) a new book of mythology for young readers, *A Wonder-Book for Girls and Boys.* In 1852 Fields would publish (in addition to *The Blithedale Romance*) a "new" Hawthorne collection (containing mostly old, previously uncollected work) called *The Snow-Image, and Other Twice-told Tales.* A continuation of *A*

Wonder-Book, called *Tanglewood Tales for Girls and Boys,* would follow in 1853, and in 1854, when he finally secured the copyright from Wiley and Putnam, Fields brought out a new edition of *Mosses from an Old Manse.*

This information about the marketing of Hawthorne in the early 1850s is relevant to *The House of the Seven Gables* for at least two reasons. Most obviously, the success of *The Scarlet Letter* provided an incentive for producing a new work—and for producing it as rapidly as possible. Hawthorne began *The House of the Seven Gables* in August 1850, only five months after publishing *The Scarlet Letter,* and he predicted to Fields that the new novel would be done by November. For his own part, Fields was applying plenty of pressure; already in October of 1850 he was advertising the new book. Hawthorne's November prediction proved over-optimistic, but not by much; he completed *The House of the Seven Gables* in January 1851, less than a year after finishing *The Scarlet Letter,* and the new novel was published in April. The sudden change in Hawthorne's professional status has another, deeper relevance to *The House of the Seven Gables.* The "Nathaniel Hawthorne" who set to work on the new novel in the summer of 1850 was quite different from the "Nathaniel Hawthorne" who had written *The Scarlet Letter,* and he knew it. He had moved from Salem to the Berkshires, in western Massachusetts, where he planned to support himself and his family by writing. He clearly intended his new book to register or ratify the recent transformation of his literary identity. And on many levels, both superficial and fundamental, this transformation informs the action and meaning, the very fabric, of *The House of the Seven Gables.*

In January 1851, as he was finishing *The House of the Seven Gables,* Hawthorne took time off to write a brief preface for Fields' new edition of *Twice-told Tales.* He used the occasion to reflect on his past status as, in his words, "the obscurest man of letters in America" and to deprecate the writings Fields was reissuing. These early tales and sketches, he wrote, "have the pale tint of flowers that blossomed in too retired a shade." "The book, if you would see anything in it, requires to be read in the clear, brown, twilight atmosphere in which it was written; if opened in the sunshine, it is apt to look exceedingly like a volume of blank pages."[3] The imagery here is important and characteristic; sunshine is associated with everyday reality, while pallor and shade are associated with tameness and unreality.

Hawthorne often lamented the seclusion of the so-called solitary years between his graduation from Bowdoin in 1825 and the publication of the first edition of *Twice-told Tales* in 1837, years when he lived alone in Salem in a room in his mother's house, writing. In the 1851 preface he is striving to distance himself from this early association of literature with isolation, and even, perhaps, to revise his earlier literary motives. His early tales, he writes, "are not the talk of a secluded man with his own mind and heart, . . . but his attempts, and very imperfectly successful ones, to open an intercourse with the world." Thus Hawthorne claims the only merit he can now find in these early tales is that they "have opened the way to most agreeable associations, and to the formation of imperishable friendships" (CE, ix, 6–7). In *The Scarlet Letter* and in such stories as "The Artist of the Beautiful" (1844), Hawthorne had clearly linked creativity and imaginative power with isolation, but here he insists that his motives have been social from the first and that the movement of his career has been from insubstantiality to reality, from seclusion to social intercourse. A similar movement underlies *The House of the Seven Gables*—where it is also figured, at times even obsessively, as a transformation of shade into sunshine.

The same figure dominates Hawthorne's comments on the differences he saw, or intended, between *The House of the Seven Gables* and its predecessor. He complained to Fields that while writing *The Scarlet Letter* "I found it impossible to relieve the shadows of the story with so much light as I would gladly have thrown in"; to his friend Horatio Bridge he wrote that the narrative "lacks sunshine," that it is "positively a h–ll-fired story, into which I found it almost impossible to throw any cheering light" (CE, xvi, 307, 311–12). In the midst of writing *The House of the Seven Gables*, Hawthorne wrote to Fields that the story "darkens damnably towards the close, but I shall try hard to pour some setting sunshine over it"; he later commented to Evert Duyckinck that "in writing it, I suppose I was illuminated by my purpose to bring it to a prosperous close; while the gloom of the past threw its shadow along the reader's pathway" (CE, xvi, 376, 421). The literalness with which Hawthorne took this "purpose" is indicated by the prevalence of sunshine and "natural" blooming towards the end of *The House of the Seven Gables* (in the chapters entitled "Alice's Posies" and "The Flower of Eden") and by the significance to the book's sunny conclusion of Phoebe Pyncheon. "Phoebe" was one of Hawthorne's nicknames for his wife, and Sophia Hawthorne reacted to the final chapters of *The House of the Seven Gables* exactly as her husband would have wished. "Mr. Hawthorne read me the close, last evening," she wrote in January, 1851. "There is unspeakable grace and beauty in the conclusion, throwing back upon the sterner tragedy of the commencement an ethereal light, and a dear home-loveliness and satisfaction"—with "the flowers of Paradise scattered over all the dark places."[4] (By contrast, Hawthorne reported that when he read his wife the conclusion of *The Scarlet Letter,* "It broke her heart and sent her to bed with a grievous headache" [CE, xvi, 311].)

Hawthorne's professed goal in *The House of the Seven Gables* was, most essentially, to certify his own normalcy by transforming or simply disowning whatever might have seemed abnormal in his literary past. In a letter to Duyckinck, thanking him for a favorable review, he wrote: "It appears to me that you like the book better than the Scarlet Letter; and I certainly think it a more natural and healthy product of my mind, and felt less reluctance in publishing it." He wrote to Bridge, in a similar vein: "I think it a work more characteristic of my mind, and more proper and natural for me to write, than the Scarlet Letter" (CE, xvi, 421, 461). Herman Melville—Hawthorne's neighbor in the Berkshires, who in the summer of 1851 was completing his own "h–ll-fired" romance of the whale fisheries—praised what he saw as the secret defiance of *The House of the Seven Gables:* "There is the grand truth about Nathaniel Hawthorne," he wrote in a letter to Hawthorne. "He says NO! in thunder; but the Devil himself cannot make him say *yes.* For all men who say *yes,* lie."[5] Reviewers, however, mostly stressed the book's healthy, "natural" propriety. "The impression which it leaves on the reader's mind," said an anonymous writer in *The Christian Examiner,* "is . . . much pleasanter than that produced by its predecessor," and the *Southern Quarterly Review,* for similar reasons, thought *The House of the Seven Gables* "a more truthful book" than *The Scarlet Letter.* Amory Dwight Mayo, a Unitarian minister surveying Hawthorne's career in the *Universalist Quarterly,* described a "tendency to disease" in Hawthorne's nature, "a sort of unnaturalness in his world," a tendency that "reached its climax in the 'Scarlet Letter.'" But in *The House of the Seven Gables,* Mayo proclaimed, "we see the author struggling out of its grasp, with a vigor which we believe ensures a final recovery."[6]

We might also describe the self-transformation Hawthorne hoped to demonstrate in *The House of the Seven Gables* in terms of a shift in genre, a shift in the kind of fiction he wished to write, or to be seen as writing. In the famous first paragraph of his preface, Hawthorne insists that he has chosen to write a "Romance"—permitting "a certain latitude," especially with respect to incorporating "the Marvellous"—rather than a "Novel"—requiring "a very minute fidelity, not merely to the possible, but to the probable and ordinary course of man's experience" (1).[7] The distinction Hawthorne makes here and in other prefaces, similar to the contrast between unreal "twilight" and healthy "sunshine" in the 1851 preface to *Twice-told Tales,* has produced a good deal of critical controversy over just what he meant by "romance," and has even led some critics to argue that the major tradition of nineteenth-century American fiction was a tradition of "romance" as contrasted with the supposedly "novelistic" tradition of British fiction.[8] Yet Hawthorne's preface, in context, is a bit misleading: he well knew that in *The House of the Seven Gables* he was in important respects moving away from the romantic into something like novelistic realism. "Many passages of this book," he wrote to Fields in November, 1850, "ought to be finished with the minuteness of a Dutch picture, in order to give them their proper effect" (CE, xvi, 371).

Hawthorne clearly associated this realistic "minuteness" (foreshadowing the "minute fidelity" he would cite, in his preface, as characterizing the "Novel") with what made the book "a more natural and healthy product of my mind," "more proper and natural for me to write," and once again his most sympathetic critics got the point. Henry T. Tuckerman—in a review in the *Southern Literary Messenger,* for which Hawthorne expressed deep gratitude—praised the book's "local authenticity"; in its details, he wrote, "we have the truth, simplicity and exact imitation of the Flemish painters," and its sketches of background are "so life-like in the minutiæ . . . that they are daguerreotyped in the reader's mind." Amory Dwight Mayo, who saw in *The House of the Seven Gables* signs of "recovery" from the "disease" and "unnaturalness" of *The Scarlet Letter,* wrote of the later book that, "as a whole, it is nearer actual life, and more comprehensively true to human nature, than any former work of its author."[9]

Whatever its meanings for twentieth-century critics, "romance" had some clear and fairly uncomplicated associations for Hawthorne's contemporaries. It was linked, above all, with the tradition of *Gothic* romance—the mode popularized in England in the 1790s by Ann Radcliffe, which relies on apparently haunted mansions, secret chambers, bleeding statues, and other seeming supernatural horrors, all of which are explained rationally at the close. From the very beginning of his career, Hawthorne had drawn on the tradition of Gothic romance, and there are plenty of Gothic props and conventions in *The House of the Seven Gables,* from the house itself to the mysterious painting to "Maule's Curse" on the male descendants of Colonel Pyncheon. At the close all of this gets explained away in good Radcliffean fashion: Maule's curse, for instance, turns out to be only a hereditary (if strangely selective) propensity towards apoplexy. But the undermining of Gothic sensationalism in *The House of the Seven Gables* goes far beyond the conventions of Radcliffean rational explanation: throughout the novel the Gothic is persistently subjected to sarcastic mockery. For instance, as Phoebe prepares an Indian cake, the narrator speculates that "perchance . . . the ghosts of departed cook-maids looked wonderingly on" (99)—or when Phoebe imagines that Jaffrey Pyncheon is a ghostly reincarnation of his ancestor, the Colonel, the narrator wonders if "on his arrival from the other world, he had merely found it necessary to spend a quarter-of-an-hour at a barber's," and had then visited "a ready-made clothing establishment" (120). Nor does Phoebe, confronted with the mysteries of the decaying Pyncheon mansion, have much in common with the quivering heroines of Ann Radcliffe; she is never frightened, we are repeatedly told that she is not "morbid," and on her first night in her cobwebby and desolate bedchamber (always a moment of titillating terror in Gothic romances) she simply uses her "gift of practical arrangement" to give the room "a look of comfort and habitableness" (71). And there is something deeper than mockery of the Gothic at work in the novel's ending. The scene of Judge Pyncheon's death becomes the setting for, and in a sense the guarantee of, the love of Phoebe and Holgrave. The haunted house is not simply, as we might put it, de-Gothicized; as the sunshine returns, and as Alice's posies bloom on the roof, in the angle between the two front gables, it is also domesticated. One recalls Sophia Hawthorne's blissful comment on the "dear home-loveliness and satisfaction" of the ending. At the book's close, the haunted house of Gothic romance gets transformed into the feminized "home" of realistic, domestic fiction.

With all of its apparent accommodations to accepted notions of the "natural" and "healthy," *The House of the Seven Gables* might have been expected to be more popular than *The Scarlet Letter.* In the long run, such expectations were not borne out; in its first thirteen years the later book sold 11,550 copies, as compared to 13,500 for its predecessor,[10] and it is *The Scarlet Letter* that has come to be regarded as Hawthorne's masterpiece. The ultimate success of *The Scarlet Letter* may in fact be connected to what contemporary readers saw as its unhealthy morbidness; even Amory Dwight Mayo, who thought the later novel "more comprehensively true to human nature, than any former work of its author," stated flatly, and without any apparent recognition of paradox, that "the 'House of the Seven Gables' is inferior to the 'Scarlet Letter' in artistic proportion, compactness and sustained power."[11] Still, *The House of the Seven Gables* continues to be read and admired almost a century and a half after its publication, and it actually had slightly better sales than its predecessor in its first year (6,710 copies as compared to 6,000).[12] Such sales were at least sufficient to sustain Hawthorne at his new creative pace. "As long as people will buy," he wrote to his friend Bridge, "I shall keep at work; and I find that my facility of labor increases with the demand for it" (CE, xvi, 462). One also suspects that financial considerations, while they clearly mattered to Hawthorne, may have been somewhat less important to him than the psychological or vocational transformation he wished to accomplish or affirm with *The House of the Seven Gables,* the transformation of the isolated artist into the man who had supposedly always sought, through his writing, "to open an intercourse with the world." In this sense Mayo may have been right about Hawthorne's ambition for *The House of the Seven Gables:* it would be "better" than *The Scarlet Letter* precisely because it would be less "artistic."

Hawthorne's desire to leave his old literary identity behind gets thematized in his novel in a more general repudiation of the past, of the weight of history. Nothing more clearly distinguishes *The House of the Seven Gables* from *The Scarlet Letter* than its interest in what the preface calls "the realities of the moment" (3)—its concern for the enumeration of up-to-the-minute facts and details of mid-nineteenth-century American culture. The explanatory notes to this edition gloss, for instance, numerous references to what were still, in 1851, recent technological innovations: galvanic batteries, daguerreotypes (the precursors of modern photographs), railroads, the telegraph, transatlantic Cunard steamships. There are references to mid-century American politics, for instance to the newly formed Free Soil party, and Hawthorne's attack on Jaffrey Pyncheon is clearly aimed, more generally, at the Whig Party that had removed him from his position at the Salem Custom House in 1849.[13] Perhaps the largest number of contemporary references, many of them associated with Holgrave, cluster around mid-century reform movements and fads: temperance lectures, Utopian communes, hypnotism or mesmerism, spiritualism, public séances, and other forms of popular pseudo-science.

The House of the Seven Gables engages its contemporary "moment" in other, more fundamental ways. The book seeks to assess the moral or spiritual significance of rapid innovations in technology and social and political culture, hoping to find here more instances of healthy transformation. Also, the book's interest in up-to-date, novelistic social realism seems to signal a corresponding interest in social or political criticism. Hawthorne describes the book's supposed moral, in the preface, as "the folly of tumbling down an avalanche of ill-gotten gold, or real estate, on the heads of an unfortunate posterity, whereby to maim and crush them, until the accumulated mass shall be scattered abroad in its original atoms" (2). One thinks of what Hawthorne's friend and former Concord neighbor, Henry Thoreau, would say in *Walden* (1854) about the misfortune of those who "have inherited farms, houses, barns, cattle, and farming tools": "How many a poor immortal soul have I met well nigh crushed and smothered under its load, creeping down the road of life, pushing before it a barn seventy-five feet by forty, its Augean stables never cleansed, and one hundred acres of land, tillage, mowing, pasture, and wood-lot!"[14] Thoreau's alternative to this burden was of course the radical simplicity of his own experimental Utopia, his socialist community of one at Walden Pond. The alternative imagined by *The House of the Seven Gables* is considerably more difficult to locate, and this difficultly brings us at once to the famous problem of the novel's ending—of the *way* it transforms darkness and isolation into sociable sunshine in order to achieve the closing "home-loveliness and satisfaction" that so gratified Sophia Hawthorne.

Hawthorne's hopes for the transformative moral-political power of contemporary innovations seem most fully embodied in the character of Holgrave. He is introduced as a radical reformer, an incarnation of change, a man of the "moment" with a particular hostility towards the past as embodied in old houses. He believes that "in this age, more than ever before, the moss-grown and rotten Past is to be torn down, and lifeless institutions to be thrust out of the way, and their dead corpses buried, and everything to begin anew" (179). In the end, with Judge Pyncheon a dead corpse, Holgrave's ideas might seem to be vindicated: Holgrave's marriage to Phoebe certifies the triumph of light over darkness, of the present over the "moss-grown and rotten Past." But when Holgrave, Phoebe, Clifford, and Hepzibah move out of the House of the Seven Gables, it is only to move into another of Judge Pyncheon's properties, his country house. Since Holgrave is a descendant of Matthew Maule, we might justify this accession to property as a matter of political justice, of the heir of dispossession coming at last into his own. What has been more troubling to many readers of *The House of the Seven Gables* is the astonishing rapidity with which Holgrave's new status swings him from political radicalism to conservatism; he even wishes the judge had built his country house out of stone rather than wood, so that it might last longer. This abrupt transformation seems to ignore Hawthorne's earlier sense of the genuine burden of property; at the same time, it seems to undermine retroactively the seriousness of Holgrave's politics.

The rapid shift in Holgrave's political principles certainly presents problems for the reader; even Phoebe exclaims, in amazement: "how wonderfully your ideas are changed!" (315). Yet to concentrate on this aspect of Holgrave's thinking may be to exaggerate the novel's interest in political ideas. We should at least recognize that Hawthorne's sense of the burden of property is very different from Thoreau's. What matters to Thoreau as false economy, as excess accumulation, matters to Hawthorne above all as *inheritance;* property is a burden, for Hawthorne, not because it is grotesquely disproportionate to actual need but because it is transmitted from the past—because ownership, founded on an act of forced appropriation, is inevitably associated with guilt. Hence the preface's other formulation of the book's supposed moral: "the wrong-doing of one generation lives into the successive ones, and, divesting itself of every temporary advantage, becomes a pure and uncontrollable mischief" (2). Or as Clifford puts it during the brief exhilaration of his escape with Hepzibah: "What we call real estate—the solid ground to build a house on—is the broad foundation on which nearly all the guilt of this world rests" (263). So the basis of Hawthorne's social criticism has less to do with economy, in Thoreau's sense, than with psychology, and what is therefore needed to bring his novel to a prosperous conclusion is not a Holgravian political revolution, a general redistribution of wealth, but some sort of expiation or absolution—more in the therapeutic sense, perhaps, than in the religious.

To some extent the conclusion does provide something like absolution; at least it labors mightily to dispose of all traces of guilt. Clifford, long imprisoned for the supposed murder of his uncle, is revealed to be innocent, and his uncle turns out not even to have been murdered. The rift between the Pyncheons and Maules, originating in the crime of dispossessing and executing Matthew Maule, is repaired when Holgrave, having revealed his Maule ancestry, marries Phoebe.[15] Most notably, the novel's sense of inherited evil is displaced on to the house, and especially on to Judge Pyncheon—and then exorcised. The death of the Judge, so the ending wants to assure us, signals the end of Matthew Maule's curse on the Pyncheons.

Nevertheless, problems remain. Clifford may be innocent of his uncle's murder, but his delight in the Judge's death, resembling the narrator's protracted exultation over the corpse in Ch. XVIII, suggests that he has at least wished to be rid of his cousin; and his praise of progress in Ch. XVII, as he and Hepzibah escape on the railroad, keeps threatening to turn into a confession of a crime he has not technically committed. If the Judge's death promises liberation, it also quite literally recapitulates the very past from which it seems to offer escape, the death of Colonel Pyncheon—just as, for example, Hepzibah's persistent knocking on the door of the silent parlor repeats the knocking on the same door on the day of the Colonel's death. Also, as guilt is displaced in order to be exorcized, it paradoxically gets only more generally diffused; even Holgrave, after Phoebe's return, confesses that "the presence of yonder dead man . . . made the universe, so far as my perception could reach, a scene of guilt, and of retribution more dreadful than the guilt" (306). The conclusion finally offers more mystification than absolution of guilt, and for a fairly simple reason. Whether in religious or therapeutic contexts, guilt usually needs to be acknowledged before it can be overcome, and here it is simply denied or escaped, as everyone climbs into a carriage to head for the country.

Readers have long debated the coherence of the ending of Hawthorne's novel, and they will surely continue to do so. There should be less debate about what is at stake in this ending. What it means for the surviving characters to leave the House of the Seven Gables finally turns out to be much the same as what it meant for Hawthorne to write *The House of the Seven Gables,* or at least what he wanted the writing of the book to mean. To leave the house is to move from darkness into sunshine, from morbid isolation into healthy sociability and normalcy, from the past into the present, from the world of the romance into the world of the novel. What remains unclear is the extent to which Hawthorne, however much he wished to do so, was able to believe in these transformations. When Phoebe returns to the house—her "healthful presence" confronting "the crowd of pale, hideous, and sinful phantoms" that occupy it—the narrator praises her "gift of making things look real, rather than fantastic, within her sphere" (297). Proclaiming Clifford's innocence and identifying with the influence of Phoebe's "sphere," the ending of *The House of the Seven Gables* endeavors to dismiss *all* guilt as fantasy, as romance. But Hawthorne had long known that to identify guilt with fantasy was hardly to render it powerless. In an 1837 sketch, "Fancy's Show Box," he had meditated on the guilt arising from deeds contemplated but never perpetrated. "Man must not disclaim his brotherhood, even with the guilties," the sketch concludes, "since, though his hand be clean, his heart has surely been polluted by the flitting phantoms of iniquity" (CE, ix, 226). This understanding of the link between guilt and fantasy lies at the heart of much of Hawthorne's writing from the 1830s down to *The Scarlet Letter.* It is above all this understanding that the ending of *The House of the Seven Gables*—endorsing sunshine, healthy normalcy, novelistic realism, in a word, Phoebe—seeks to leave behind.

II Conditions of Literary Vocation

4   Beginnings of Professionalism

In *American Renaissance: Art and Expression in the Age of Emerson and Whitman,* his seminal 1941 study of classic American writing, F. O. Matthiessen located the "renaissance" of his title in the 1850s, when Emerson, Whitman, Thoreau, Hawthorne, and Melville were all publishing major works. One might locate an earlier American renaissance (or "naissance") at the beginning of the 1820s, when three writers who would come to dominate American literature during the next two or three decades published their first important works. Washington Irving's *The Sketch Book of Geoffrey Crayon, Gent.* was issued in installments, by C. S. Van Winkle of New York City, beginning in June 1819 and running through September 1820. In September 1821, Hilliard and Metcalf, of Cambridge, Massachusetts, issued the first volume of *Poems* by William Cullen Bryant. Three months later, in New York City, Charles Wiley issued James Fenimore Cooper's *The Spy.* The earth did not, perhaps, shake at the time, but from the perspective of literary history the appearance of these three books within a little less than three years seems momentous. The careers of these writers would testify to a major change in the meaning of both literature and literary vocation in America—a change that affected almost all of their literary contemporaries.

Irving (1783–1859) was not exactly a new writer in 1819; he had been a celebrated fixture of the New York literary scene a decade earlier and was still known, for instance, as the author of *Diedrich Knickerbocker's History of New York* (1809). But he had been living in England and had been largely silent since 1815. Moreover, none of his earlier writings had achieved anything like the success of *The Sketch Book*, which was widely praised and widely purchased on both sides of the Atlantic. In England, where an edition appeared early in 1820, it was promoted by no less a lion than Sir Walter Scott, already a kind of mythological being to Americans; and Lord Byron, from Italy, declared that "Crayon is very good." *The Sketch Book* went through printing after printing in both England and America, suggesting what had previously seemed an impossibility: that international literary success could be attained by an American writer. Young Henry Longfellow, a student at Bowdoin College where he discovered Irving, was only one of many Americans enraptured by this new native celebrity. "Every reader," he would recall when Irving died in 1859, "has his first book . . . which in early youth first fascinates his imagination. . . . To me, this first book was *The Sketch Book* of Washington Irving."

The Spy was Cooper's (1789–1851) second fictional effort; its predecessor—a clumsy imitation of Jane Austen called *Precaution* (1820)—had fared poorly. The new book featured an American setting (Westchester during the American Revolution) and even a cameo appearance by George Washington, and like *The Sketch Book* it proved popular and profitable on both sides of the Atlantic. Here, it seemed, was the "American Scott," doing for American history and scenery what the author of *Waverley* had done for Scotland, and he was America's own. The success of *The Spy* set an attractive target for future striving, both for Cooper and for other would-be native authors. *The Spy* was followed by a torrent of American historical romances, often modeled on Scott but encouraged by Cooper's example to deal with native themes and settings. Cooper's own third novel, *the Pioneers,* is now valued because it introduced the character Natty Bumppo and thus inaugurated the series of five novels known as the Leatherstocking Tales. For the purposes of literary history, however, what may be more immediately important is the fact that when *The Pioneers* appeared on February 1, 1823, 3,500 copies were bought up in New York by noon. Cooper, like Irving, was a "star." During the 1820s the author of *The Spy* would earn from his writings an average of $6,500 a year, and in a single year, 1829, Irving's income from his writings would exceed $23,000. In America such professional literary success was wholly unprecedented.

Bryant's 1821 *Poems* produced no such immediate sensation. Before Longfellow in America, new poetry by native authors did not sell the way prose could sell, and publication in the Boston area, for reasons that we will turn to shortly, was also a liability. Although Bryant (1794–1878) would come to stand with Irving and Cooper as one of the foremost American writers of his generation, it would be more than a decade before he achieved such public stature, and this fame would come from the publishing centers of New York and Philadelphia, not from Boston. Of a first printing of 750 copies (compared, for instance, to 2,000 for the first number of Irving's *Sketch Book*) only 270 copies of Bryant's 1821 *Poems* had been sold by 1823. Still, the *Poems* brought their author a measure of *critical* recognition. Bryant had been encouraged by Bostonians R. H. Dana and E. T. Channing, and his *Poems* were reviewed favorably by Boston's *North American Review,* which Channing edited, and, through Dana's good offices, by the New York *American.* Even *Blackwood's Magazine* would declare from Scotland, in 1822, that "Bryant is no mean poet; . . . we should not be surprised at his assuming, one day or another, a high rank among English poets."

The Sketch Book, Bryant's *Poems,* and *The Spy* launched three enduring professional literary careers, and the simple fact of their endurance should not be overlooked. There had been an outpouring of national literature a generation earlier, spurred by the successful completion of the War of Independence—in the work, for instance, of Philip Freneau, Hugh Henry Brackenridge, the Connecticut Wits, and Charles Brockden Brown. But if this earlier outpouring was a renaissance, it was a notably abortive one; none of these men, whatever fame he achieved, succeeded as a professional author, or even devoted himself primarily to literature. Brown is now probably the best-known writer of this generation, but he in fact abandoned literature after a very brief trial. So Irving, Cooper, and Bryant accomplished what these predecessors had found beyond their reach. And this accomplishment owed at least as much to circumstances as to aesthetic considerations.

The most important of these circumstances was a transformation, or series of transformations, in the means of producing and distributing literature in America, a transformation that began to take place in the second and third decades of the nineteenth century. Irving, Cooper, and Bryant participated in, or at least responded to, the institutionalization and rationalization of nonutilitarian writing as a market commodity. Irving and Cooper, if not Bryant, were the first Americans to find something like commercial success as literary professionals. These writers did not produce these changes; rather, their careers were symptomatic of emerging innovations in the financing, manufacture, and marketing of books and periodicals. The story of the transformation of American literature in the 1820s and 1830s is among other things a story of changes in literary production and distribution—of changes in royalty arrangements, pricing, publishing, transportation, and the like. It is also a story of changes in the social status and meaning of literary vocation—of the identity, "writer"—from the ideal of the gentleman-amateur (never in America much of a reality) to the actuality of the literary professional. None of these changes was complete by the end of the 1820s, or even by the end of the 1850s; what happened during the heyday of Irving, Cooper, and Bryant was part of a longer and larger process. Still, it is important that we understand how this process affected the work and the careers of these writers and of their American contemporaries.

Book Publishing

At the beginning of the nineteenth century, the condition of American book publishing was decidedly primitive and disorganized; there simply were no literary publishers, in the modern sense of the term, in the United States. By the 1850s things had changed dramatically; our present system of publication—of capitalizing, manufacturing, advertising, and distributing literary property, and of rationalizing the different rights of author and publisher in this property—was not yet fully in place, but its outlines were clearly visible. This radical transformation of the American book-publishing industry in the first half of the nineteenth century has been ably described by a number of scholars—most perceptively by the late William Charvat, in *Literary Publishing in America, 1790–1850* (1959) and other works. The story will only be sketched in here.

The passage of the first American copyright law, in 1790, had made literature property and had therefore made authorship as a *profession* a possibility for American writers. Possibility did not immediately, of course, become actuality, for a number of reasons. First of all, no *international* copyright law would be negotiated until 1891, and the absence of such a law produced significant difficulties for native writers. Unless they could work out special arrangements abroad—as many in fact did, with varying degrees of success—American authors received no income from sales of their works in England. Moreover, they had to compete, in the United States, with cheap reprints of popular British works. Volumes of American poetry, fiction, or history, if their authors were to receive any significant income from them, were invariably more expensive than works by British writers who received no American royalties. Yet the effect of this situation was by no means wholly or even mainly negative. The wide circulation of inexpensive British books was a major factor in creating a taste and a market for literature in pre–Civil War America. Cheap editions of Scott and Byron and, later, of Dickens and Thackeray helped produce a reading public and a literary appetite to which American writers could seek to appeal. What may be more important, it was to a large extent the business of printing, advertising, and distributing British books that brought native publishing from infancy to the beginnings of maturity, and there had to be a mature and relatively stable publishing industry before a true "American literature" could come into existence.

American book production at the beginning of the century was largely dispersed or decentralized, except in the Philadelphia area. Elsewhere, local printers, who also functioned as booksellers, produced copies sufficient to meet the demands of the local audience, and authors often simply published where they lived. But as the century progressed, the manufacture and distribution of books concentrated increasingly in urban literary centers and in such major firms as Philadelphia's House of Carey, New York's House of Harper, and, later, New York's Wiley and Putnam and Boston's Ticknor and Fields—firms that often maintained offices in other centers as well. Between 1800 and 1810 nearly 50 percent of fiction by native authors was published outside New York, Philadelphia, and Boston. By the 1840s this figure had declined to 8 percent.

The major American literary centers were invariably seaport cities with access to important inland rivers, enabling publishers in these centers to distribute books at minimum expense to the interior market. Early in the period, New York, Philadelphia, and Baltimore were literary centers in this sense, and they came to dominate American publishing, with Philadelphia ultimately beating out Baltimore for control of the Susquehanna and the South. The eventual ascendancy of New York was guaranteed less by its indigenous literary culture than by the opening of the Erie Canal in the 1820s. Boston, with no important river, remained a provincial publishing center until the late 1830s and 1840s, when railroads began to supplement river shipping as a way of getting books to the crucial inland market. This partly accounts for the commercial failure of Bryant's 1821 *Poems,* printed in the Boston area, as contrasted with the successes of Irving's *Sketch Book* and Cooper's *The Spy,* both issued in New York.

Ambitious authors rapidly learned that success depended on access to the interior market. Bryant, in the 1830s, turned to New York, where the House of Harper brought out ten editions of his poems between 1836 and 1846, giving him the national circulation his first volume had failed to achieve, even though that volume had contained such future anthology pieces as "To a Waterfowl," "The Inscription for the Entrance to a Wood," "The Yellow Violet," and "Thanatopsis." Nor did authors identified with established literary centers necessarily publish in those centers. New Yorkers Irving and Cooper, in the 1820s, signed contracts with Philadelphia's House of Carey, which was able to offer excellent terms and a shrewd understanding of promotion and distribution; and both of them stayed with Carey well into the 1840s.

Access to the interior market was itself no guarantee of success; there were still basic problems in the business of publishing to be worked out. In the 1820s, for instance, most so-called publishers were both printers and booksellers, wholesalers and retailers, and inevitably there was conflict between these two functions. A firm's tendency as retailer to monopolize sales of its own titles restricted wholesale distribution of those titles; a popular book would often be available at only one store even in a large city. Early-nineteenth-century American publishers also operated with very little capital; indeed, books by native writers were frequently published at the expense of the author rather than the publisher, as was the case with both *The Sketch Book* and *The Spy*. This last arrangement, which was also common at the time in Britain, did not necessarily work to the author's disadvantage, at least if a book was successful. Since Irving and Cooper acted in effect as their own publishers, paying Van Winkle and Wiley royalties for distributing *The Sketch Book* and *The Spy,* they were able to keep a very high share of the profits on their books. But most native writers failed to achieve such sales, and even Irving and Cooper would soon choose to lease the rights to their works for set terms and fixed sums to regular publishers. The often ridiculously low capitalization of American publishing firms also produced extraordinary instability in the industry; failures were frequent, and were abetted, in the early 1840s, by cutthroat competition in cheap foreign reprints.

Yet order began to emerge from this chaos. Firms such as Carey in Philadelphia and Harper in New York soon acquired a sufficient financial base to take over the full functions of the literary publisher, including capitalization, and the most virulent forms of competition were brought under control by the mid-1840s. Moreover, the dominant publishers saw and remedied the problem of engaging in both wholesale and retail distribution. Harper, founded in 1817, restricted itself from the beginning to printing and publishing, and Carey abandoned retail bookselling in 1830. Business, in any case, expanded dramatically, spurred on not only by improvements in capitalization and distribution but by such technological innovations in book manufacturing as the introduction of cloth bindings and the cylinder press. The value of books manufactured and sold in the United States rose from $2.5 million in 1820 to $5.5 million in 1840, and then to $12.5 million in 1850.

By the 1840s, authors could begin to count on a market stability largely absent in 1820. Yet they paid a price for this stability. As publishers took over the capitalization of native works, they came to exert far more control over native writers. Publishers had good reason for trying to predict what would and would not sell (the ability to make such predictions was after all what made successful publishers successful), and they were necessarily inclined to pressure their authors to conform to their perception of the public taste. Whereas established authors might try to resist such pressure, newcomers had little choice but to accede, and even established authors ignored market considerations at their peril. A lasting result of the cutthroat competition of the early 1840s was a dramatic decline in the price of American books and hence a corresponding reduction in authors' returns from these books. At the same time, the percentage of even a popular author's effective royalty declined considerably, as publishers took over from authors the financial risk of publication. Thus by the 1840s successful professional authors like Irving and Cooper had to generate far more sales just to produce earnings equal to those they had received in the 1820s. William Charvat has calculated the specific effect of these changes on Cooper. In 1826 Cooper earned $5,000 from the sale of 5,750 copies of *The Last of the Mohicans* at $2.00 each. In 1842 *The Wing-and-Wing* sold 12,500 copies (more than twice as many as *The Last of the Mohicans* in 1826), but at only fifty cents each and at a significantly lower effective royalty percentage (20 percent versus 43 percent). Thus Cooper's earnings from *The Wing-and-Wing* were only $1,187.50, less than a quarter of his 1826 earnings from *Mohicans*.

Even disregarding pressure from publishers, then, writers had reasons of their own for catering literary production to the public taste. They also had reasons for producing as much writing as possible as fast as possible. Quantity, for an established writer, was far more important to sustaining earnings than was quality. Developments in book publishing from the 1820s to the 1840s made available to the native author a new and truly national audience and a relatively stable means of reaching this audience, but they did so, inevitably, by turning the literary work into a commodity. To say that the basis of literature was shifted from culture to commerce is perhaps to oversimplify; the meaning and authority of "high culture" in America had always been ambiguous. But by the early 1840s, market considerations had clearly become an inescapable component of the new American literary profession. For those who chose to engage in this profession, the expansion and

consolidation of literary publishing presented a mixed and sometimes baf-
fling blessing.

Washington Irving

In an 1813 essay on the American poet Robert Treat Paine, in whose disastrous career he saw a vivid example of the dangers of literary vocation in
America, Washington Irving described the general situation of the imaginative writer in the United States in notably bleak terms. "Unfitted for business," he wrote, "in a nation where every one is busy; devoted to literature,
where literary leisure is confounded with idleness; the man of letters is almost an insulated being, with few to understand, less to value, and scarcely
any to encourage his pursuits." The financial difficulties of the professional
American writer at the beginning of the nineteenth century have already
been suggested, but Irving's emphasis is on a deeper sort of difficulty, ultimately social and psychological. To be a professional writer was to be a kind
of deviant—to be, in effect, un-American.

Literature itself had enormous prestige; it was taught in colleges, and its
cultivation was a mark of social status. Fiction was for the most part an exception to this generalization, although Scott's *Waverley* novels would soon
help make even fiction respectable. Still, the indulgence of imagination was
anathema to orthodox opinion, and the popularity of fiction, particularly of
sensational gothic novels and tales of seduction, cut it off from the official
esteem accorded to "higher" forms of literature, especially to poetry and
history. Yet the prestige of even these higher forms did not extend to those
who produced them for a living. The writer was caught in a double bind. On
the one hand, to devote oneself exclusively to literature rather than "business" was perceived as mere "idleness." Thus Hawthorne (1804–64), in his
1850 "Custom-House" preface to *The Scarlet Letter,* would imagine the
hostile reaction of his Puritan ancestors to their descendant's literary vocation: "What is he? . . . A mere writer of story-books! What kind of a business
in life . . . may that be? Why, the degenerate fellow might as well have been
a fiddler!" On the other hand, to the extent that one pursued literature *as* a
"business," one was betraying its true "gentlemanly" nature. Small wonder
that Irving saw the American writer, in 1813, as an "insulated being."

The example of Irving's own career would suggest how the financial difficulties facing the American writer might be overcome and would help
neutralize the American perception of the professional writer's social insu-
lation. In 1835, Baltimore novelist John Pendleton Kennedy would thank
the author of *The Sketch Book* for having "convinced the wise ones at home

that a man may sometimes write a volume without losing his character." This effect was quite deliberate on Irving's part. Throughout his career he sustained his professional standing by carefully considering the shifting tastes of his audience; and, what may be more important, he carefully managed his image as a writer in order to mitigate public hostility or indifference to the man of letters. Irving ultimately managed the extraordinary feat of engaging in literature as a business enterprise (thus disarming public suspicion and perhaps his own guilt about "idleness") while at the same time maintaining the public pose of amateur (thus avoiding the appearance of debasing culture with commerce). He perceived that if literature was becoming a commodity, it was also inevitably a form of public relations, and he became a master of public relations.

Irving was born in 1783, six years before his namesake's inauguration as first president of the United States. His father was a New York merchant, and a number of the sons entered the family business, but Washington was trained for the law. Although he passed the bar exam in 1806, he never practiced very actively, gravitating instead toward the provincial literary world of New York, modeled—in its own perception anyway—on the literary society of eighteenth-century London. Literature for these young men, all of whom were engaged in business or professional activities, was primarily a social affair, a diversion, a provincial imitation or invention of British gentility. It might promise a release from the boredom of commercial responsibilities and access, in a bourgeois democracy, to something like aristocratic style, but it could hardly offer a living.

Yet Irving engaged in the activities of this world with unusual energy, perhaps out of frustration with his destined social role or out of guilt concerning his apparent inaptitude for this social role. In 1802 he began publishing his satirical *Letters of Jonathan Oldstyle, Gent.*, in the *New York Morning Chronicle*, which his brother Peter edited. In 1807, together with brother William and brother-in-law James Kirke Paulding, he began publishing *Salmagundi; or the Whim-Whams and Opinions of Launcelot Langstaff, & Others*—another collection of essays, mainly satirical. Then in 1809 the death of his young fiancée, Matilda Hoffman, daughter of the judge who had offered him a legal partnership, drove him from even his desultory pursuit of the law. Instead he turned furiously to a literary project conceived the previous year: the burlesque *Diedrich Knickerbocker's History of New York*, an immediate success when it was published in 1809. His brothers, in order to give him more time for writing, made him an inactive partner in the family business.

Irving was by no means, yet, a successful professional author, or even a professional author at all. *Knickerbocker's History* was surprisingly successful (Irving made $3,000 on it), but it had no immediate successor except for a revised edition in 1812. In that year Irving became editor of a Philadelphia literary journal, the *Analectic Magazine,* which printed mostly extracts of British literature, but it folded in 1814. By this point Irving, now thirty-one, had come pretty much to the end of his rope; he had renounced business, more or less, but he was not really an author, whatever that might have meant in America at the time. So in 1815, at loose ends and with no plans, he sailed for England, where his brother Peter was running the Liverpool office of the family business.

At first, England was a disaster; Peter was ill, and Washington had to take over the Liverpool office, which was in trouble and which finally went bankrupt in 1818. Yet this disaster contained both an important lesson—that the "business" so touted by bourgeois orthodoxy was far from dependable—and an equally important imperative—that Irving, having seen the fragility of family support, would have to support himself. He had also, in 1817, met Sir Walter Scott, whose professional success was far more heartening than the literary dilettantism of New York, and who offered generous encouragement and advice. Irving set to work, first on a never-finished novel and then on the essays and tales that would become *The Sketch Book.*

He sent the first number of *The Sketch Book* to New York, to his brother Ebenezer, early in 1819. "My talents," he wrote in an accompanying letter, "are merely literary . . . If I ever get any solid credit with the public, it must be in the quiet and assiduous operations of my pen, under the mere guidance of fancy and feeling." The judgments in this statements are typical: although Irving did not publicly contest, and indeed openly shared, the conventional devaluation of literature (hence his "mere" and "merely"), he still held up literature as a *form* of "business," a means toward "solid credit." He would ingratiate himself with his audience, this is to say, by openly advertising his agreement with accepted opinions, even accepted opinions of his own vocation.

The Sketch Book was well calculated to turn mere idleness into profit. The alleged author, Geoffrey Crayon, was a professed idler, hardly one to challenge orthodoxy. Irving had used pseudonymous personae before (Jonathan Oldstyle, Launcelot Langstaff, Diedrich Knickerbocker), and he would use them repeatedly for the rest of his career. He thus protected himself (although everyone knew who actually wrote his sketches and satires) from overt personal identification with literature. Moreover, the "Gent," following "Geoffrey Crayon" in the title—like that following "Jonathan Oldstyle" seventeen years earlier—assured the reader that this work of literature, actually written by the son of a New York merchant, was the production of a gentleman-amateur. And gone now was the often acerbic or scatological satire of the earlier writings, replaced by a more gentle humor and a general suffusion of sentiment. There were sentimental tourist-sketches on such subjects as "Westminster Abbey" and "Rural Funerals," and there were the instant-classic short stories, attributed by Crayon to Diedrich Knickerbocker: "Rip Van Winkle" (which appeared in the first number) and "The Legend of Sleepy Hollow."

Irving has often been regarded as a mere imitator, a recycler of outworn British modes and styles, a charge already being lodged against him by contemporary detractors at the height of his greatest celebrity. It is certainly true that his works promote nostalgia, whether about old Britain or about old Dutch New York; such nostalgia was Irving's stock-in-trade. And he certainly drew on British models; he soon came to be known as the "American Goldsmith." All of this was no doubt deliberate. There was no reason to imagine that the American reading public wanted what they were not accustomed to, and what they were accustomed to was British writing. Still, Irving was also an important innovator, or at least profoundly influential. The pose of the idle lover of Europe and the picturesque, made famous by Geoffrey Crayon, established an important school of American writing, including much of the work of Nathaniel Parker Willis and of the early Longfellow. Irving might also lay claim to having invented the American short story; he was the only other American writer praised by Poe in the latter's laudatory 1842 review of Hawthorne's *Twice-told Tales*. The two Knickerbocker stories in *The Sketch Book*, "Rip Van Winkle" and "The Legend of Sleepy Hollow," turning the contrast between Dutch tradition and Yankee progress into a kind of elegiac allegory, might be cited as the source of the American tradition of local-color fiction, which moved through Hawthorne's "Custom-House" and *House of the Seven Gables* (1851) into the outpouring of women's local-color writing in the 1880s and 1890s and, ultimately, in the twentieth century, into the fiction of Sherwood Anderson and William Faulkner. Moreover, without Irving's sentimental popularization of the British "Christmas" (another *Sketch Book* essay), Charles Dickens would hardly have had a tradition to draw on in *A Christmas Carol;* and Dickens, for all his social seriousness one of the great sentimentalists of the nineteenth century, was indebted to Irving in many other ways as well.

In any case, *The Sketch Book* was a resounding transatlantic success, a sensation. John Murray, who had first declined the work, published five British editions between 1820 and 1823. In the United States, Van Winkle produced the same number of editions between 1819 and 1826. In the next sixteen years there were nine more American reprints, and since he was living in England, Irving was able to reap returns from both American and British sales. He had indeed found "solid credit with the public," and he rapidly sought additional returns. *Bracebridge Hall,* also attributed to Geoffrey Crayon, appeared in 1822. Although it did not achieve the huge popularity of *the Sketch Book,* of which it was an obvious imitation, it came close, and Murray paid 1,200 guineas for the right to publish it in England.

In 1824 Irving issued his last effort to work the vein of *The Sketch Book—Tales of a Traveller, by Geoffrey Crayon, Gent.*—but here there were important differences. The influence of German gothic fiction, to which Scott had introduced Irving, was far more overt, and unlike *The Sketch Book* and *Bracebridge Hall, Tales of a Traveller* consisted entirely of short stories—works of fiction, generally considered the lowest of current literary modes. Irving apparently knew that he was taking a risk; many of the *Tales* deal quite self-consciously with the fictionality of fiction, and a quarter of the book, "Buckthorne and His Friends," takes the insubstantiality of the literary life as its subject. Irving's nervousness about fiction is also indicated by the fact that even Crayon, the alleged author of the *Tales,* himself attributes the stories to other invented tellers—a "nervous gentleman," Diedrich Knickerbocker once again, and others—thus placing the book's fiction at minimally two pseudonymous removes from the identity of Washington Irving.

Irving was right to be worried. Although Murray paid him 1,500 guineas for *Tales of a Traveller,* reviews on both sides of the Atlantic ranged from unfavorable to overtly hostile. To a considerable extent this reaction was justified; Irving was trying, a second time, to repeat an earlier success, and much of the writing in *Tales* is perfunctory. Yet some of the stories, in their humorous and sophisticated self-consciousness, are extraordinary, for instance, "The Adventure of the German Student"; and it was "The Story of the Young Italian," from *Tales,* that Poe would single out for praise in 1842. Still, Irving had his eye on "credit with the public," and he took immediate instruction from the failure of the *Tales.* Never again would he devote an entire volume to fiction, let alone self-conscious fiction. The legacy of this phase of his career was in the future work of Poe, Hawthorne, and others. Irving himself turned to history.

Early in 1826 he went to Madrid, at the invitation of the American ambassador, Edward Everett. This visit, which lasted until 1829, was extremely fruitful. *The History of the Life and Voyages of Christopher Columbus,* a history published in four volumes in 1828, earned Irving more than $25,000. *A Chronicle of the Conquest of Granada* (attributed to a new pseudonymous persona, Fray Antonio Agapida) began appearing in August of the same year. Then, in 1829, Irving completed a sequel to *Columbus—The Voyages and Discoveries of the Companions of Columbus,* published in 1831—and he began work on what came to be known as his "Spanish Sketch Book," *The Alhambra,* which was published in 1832 by Carey in Philadelphia and in London by Richard Bentley, who would thenceforth replace John Murray as Irving's British publisher.

Irving had hardly become a genuine historian. *The Alhambra* was a work of sentimental tourism, the *Conquest of Granada* mixed historical fact with fancy, and the *Columbus* volumes, although they were more conventionally historical, drew all their facts from a Spanish source that had appeared in 1825; indeed, the Columbus project had begun, at Everett's suggestion, as a translation of this source. Nevertheless, the *pose* of historian was of great importance to Irving in the management of his image following the debacle of *Tales of a Traveller.* Thus, he wrote to a friend, before the appearance of *Columbus,* with a mixture of apprehension and calculation: "If the work succeeds, it will be of immense service to me; if it fails it will be, most probably, what many have anticipated, who suppose, from my having dealt so much in fiction, it must be impossible for me to tell the truth with plausibility." *Columbus,* of course, did succeed, exploiting what Irving elsewhere called the "credence and dignity of history" in order to restore the author's "credit" with his public. An appointment as secretary of the American legation in London in 1829, secured through the patronage of Democrat Martin Van Buren, indicated the extent to which Irving had managed to neutralize the deviant implications of literary vocation and turn himself into a respectable and responsible public figure. A medal from the British Royal Society of Literature and an honorary degree from Oxford further secured his stature.

When Irving finally returned to America in 1832, he was a full-scale celebrity. That most of his writing had been concerned with Europe might have raised questions about his patriotism, but he set out, again quite deliberately, to make himself into a thoroughly "American" author. Indeed, even his return home, after an absence of seventeen years, was in part a move to cement the loyalty of his American readers. His first American-based work, *A Tour of the Prairies,* appeared in 1835; the tourist was still a tourist, but he had shifted his ground from England and Spain to that most "American" of American settings, the West. The year 1835 also saw the appearance of *The Crayon Miscellany,* another collection in the mode of *The Sketch Book;* Irving was playing all his cards. He then set to work on *Astoria; or Anecdotes of an Enterprise Beyond the Rocky Mountains* (1836), a work promoting John Jacob Astor and in fact commissioned by Astor. In Melville's "Bartleby the Scrivener" (1853), the narrator's obsequious deference to the good opinion of Astor may be an allusion to this arrangement. Melville's dig is in a sense unfair; Irving's "American" works have a genuine interest and an important place in the emerging literature of the West. Still, there can be no doubt of the calculation, even what we would now call the image management, in Irving's choice of subject.

The rest of Irving's career need not be described here in detail. In 1832 he had moved into Sunnyside, his home in Tarrytown, New York, and here he lived on as an American institution until his death in 1859—except for the years from 1842 to 1846 when, having shifted his loyalties from the Democrats to the Whigs, he served as U.S. minister to the court of Spain. This American, who had originally turned from business and politics to literature, had by now, on the basis of his literary reputation, firmly entrenched himself *in* the worlds of business and politics. Although he still published fairly steadily, most of his "new" writings were culled from earlier manuscripts, and most of his literary earnings came from the republication of old books. Literature, for Irving, had become a wholly commercial enterprise. His literary income had fallen dramatically when book prices collapsed in the early 1840s, which is one of the reasons he disengaged himself from dependence on literature as a profession. Nevertheless, the income from republication could be impressive. Between 1848 and 1850 George Palmer Putnam, in New York, brought out a uniform edition of all of Irving's works to date. In an era of low book prices such recirculation of earlier titles was a shrewd way of maximizing earnings, far preferable to producing new works at the pace necessary, by the 1840s, to sustain an income comparable to the scale of the 1820s. And Putnam's "Author's Revised Edition" managed to sell almost 150,000 copies by 1853, netting Irving $22,000.

In the years immediately preceding his death, Irving produced his last work, the five-volume *The Life of George Washington,* (1855–59), another of what he called his "regular historical works." He was still a celebrity when he died, and his example had clearly inspired many other Americans to regard literature as a possible profession. From the perspective of literary history this may have been the most important legacy of his career. Yet there was an irony in this achievement all the same, in the use Irving made of his literary eminence; for what his professional success finally permitted him to do, during the last twenty years of his life, was to become in fact the kind of literary gentleman-amateur he had sought to pose as from the beginning. He had managed to become the image he created, and he would hardly be the last American writer to do so.

James Fenimore Cooper

Washington Irving and James Fenimore Cooper rose to literary eminence almost simultaneously, both were New Yorkers, and both signed long-term publishing contracts in the 1820s with Philadelphia's House of Carey. There, however, the similarity ended, or so Cooper, at least, would come to insist. At first he joined in the general praise for Irving, but his attitude soon hardened into a public scorn that embarrassed even his friends and that Irving, both publicly and privately, refused to reciprocate. Cooper's hostility to Irving owed at least something to professional rivalry and something, as well, to a clash of personalities and politics. Cooper, a loyal if often acerbic Democrat, was outraged by what he saw as Irving's opportunism—exemplified by his desertion of Democrat Martin Van Buren for the Whigs in 1840 (earning him the post of minister to Spain in 1842) and by his cozy relationship with wealthy Whig businessmen. "Columbus and John Jacob Astor!" Cooper fumed when he heard of the commission for *Astoria*. "I dare say Irving will make the latter the greatest man." Yet Cooper's public criticisms of Irving also grew out of sincere convictions about the proper role of the man of letters in the United States. Irving's "faults," he wrote in 1842, "were all meannesses, and I confess I can sooner pardon crimes, if they are manly ones." Irving, in Cooper's view, was "effeminately" deferential not only to his readers and to American plutocrats but to the standards of British literary taste. "This country," Cooper wrote, "must outgrow its adulation of foreigners, Englishmen in particular"; and Irving was not, he insisted, "a true American in feeling." Cooper sought, as a literary professional, to be both "manly" and "American"—terms often nearly synonymous for him, and synonymously vague.

In 1848, hearing the unfounded rumor that Irving had received a generous bequest in Astor's will, Cooper reacted with immediate credence and characteristic disgust: "What an instinct that man has for gold!" Yet Cooper's own instinct for gold, in spite of his public stance of "manly" independence from commerce, was hardly less intense than that of his rival. Cooper too succeeded as a writer, at least in the 1820s, by appealing to the public taste;

the main difference is that he did not wish to appear to do so. Moreover, Cooper worked as a professional writer far more consistently than Irving, who was also a businessman, a politician, and a diplomat. Cooper was for his entire career mainly a professional author, and the only American author before 1850 to support himself wholly by earnings from his writings. His aloofness was in large part compensatory fantasy; he wished to see or present himself not simply as a professional supplier of market commodities (although on occasion he was willing to cultivate this pose) but as a national prophet, an instructor and castigator of the very public and marketplace he depended on for his income. The story of his career is a story of the conflict between these different visions of American literary vocation, a conflict further exacerbated by the need, in an era of falling book prices, for ever-expanding sales. Thus Cooper's unpleasant public denunciations of Irving (who was only one of many targets for such abuse among contemporary literary figures) may ultimately have expressed, and conveniently displaced, his sense of how his *own* "manliness" was simultaneously manifested and threatened by his status as literary professional.

Cooper, like Irving, pursued his involvement in literary commerce as a self-proclaimed "gentleman"—to the extent, after the first flush of celebrity in the 1820s, of willfully imperiling his popularity and antagonizing his market, often simply for *being* a market. Yet whereas Irving accentuated the "gentle," Cooper sought to accentuate the "man," and his equation of national loyalty and democratic principle with aggressive masculinity, making even hostility on the part of his reading public a badge of demonstrated integrity, set a pattern for later male American writers. For instance, Herman Melville (who in 1851 would describe Cooper's works as being "among the earliest I remember, as in my boyhood producing a vivid, and awakening power upon my mind") would proclaim literary nationalism in 1850 in the tones of his admired predecessor: "No American writer should write like an Englishman, or a Frenchman; let him write like a man, for then he will be sure to write like an American." Nevertheless, the question remained: what did it mean, exactly, to "write like a man" at a time when "writing" and "manhood" were considered to be fundamentally antithetical?

James Cooper (he himself would add the "Fenimore," his mother's maiden name, in 1826) was born in New Jersey in 1789. A year later he moved with his family to Cooperstown, on Lake Otsego in upstate New York, where his father, William, had bought a large parcel of land as a speculation in 1786. The speculation proved immensely successful; settlers bought tracts eagerly, and the future novelist's father presided over his community as the sort of gentleman the son would later idealize in his fiction. William Cooper was no landed aristocrat however; Cooperstown, for all its aura of a fiefdom, was still a commercial venture. The ambiguity of the son's status was foreshadowed in the ambiguous status of his father.

James was educated at the local academy, then sent to Albany. He entered Yale in 1803 but was dismissed for some sort of misconduct in 1805. He went to sea as a common sailor in 1806 and then enlisted in the U.S. Navy in 1808, serving for three and a half years on Lake Ontario, an experience that would help make him a future master of American sea fiction. Late in 1809, Judge William Cooper, an active Federalist, was physically assaulted by an opponent following a political meeting and died of his injuries. James inherited $50,000 and a share, with his brothers, of his father's estate. In 1811 he married Susan Augusta DeLancey, daughter of a prominent Westchester family, and ended up settling as a gentleman-farmer in Westchester. The violence of his father's death was hardly consonant with the life of genteel stability this death made possible, and the tension between aristocratic control and disruptive violence would animate much of Cooper's later fiction.

Cooper's family-based prosperity proved as fragile and short-lived as Washington Irving's. Between 1813 and 1819 all five of his brothers died, and James was confronted with their debts as well as with his own. By the early 1820s his father's estate was gone and Otsego Hall, the family mansion in Cooperstown, was sold. The gentleman-farmer had to look about him for a means to make a living, and it was at this point that he became an author, impelled first of all, like Irving, by financial considerations. Moreover, Cooper, unlike Irving, was a husband and father; his situation was truly desperate.

Cooper's literary career began with characteristic truculence. Reading a British domestic novel to his wife he proclaimed, so the story goes: "I could write you a better book than that myself." His wife challenged him to do so, and the result was *Precaution*, published in 1820. *The Spy*, whose commercial success has already been described, followed in 1821. Cooper had not, at least in his own mind, sacrificed the status of gentleman (whatever that title meant in the new America) for that of professional author; rather, his writing would *sustain* his status as gentleman. Yet *The Spy* itself suggests deep-seated anxieties about this status. The title character, Harvey Birch, is an American revolutionary patriot, disguised as a peddler, working for George Washington. But Birch's true identity, for reasons that are far from clear, can never be revealed. His manly patriotism remains a secret for the

rest of his life, and it hardly seems farfetched to see in the plight of this figure Cooper's sense of his own situation as a patriot engaging, to his embarrassment, in commerce. Nevertheless, since *The Spy* proclaims what its title
character can never himself reveal about the blamelessness of his own motives, the book perhaps also serves as a vindication of its author and his new
vocation, defining authorship itself as a form not finally of commerce but of
secret, manly heroism.

Similar anxieties lie beneath the surface of Cooper's next novel, *The Pioneers* (1823), and here they are located closer to home. The book's "Templeton," on the shores of Lake Otsego, is a thinly disguised version of
Cooperstown, and the community's presiding founder, Judge Marmaduke
Temple, is a thinly disguised, idealized version of Cooper's father, Judge
William Cooper. Judge Temple stands for restraint and principle against the
commercial greed and excess of the new settlers of Templeton, but the
book's plot calls the legitimacy of his position into serious question. The War
of Independence enabled him to buy out the share in Templeton of his original partner, Edward Effingham, who had fought on the Loyalist side, which
would seem to implicate both Judge Temple and the American Revolution
in the very greed and commercialism Temple denounces in others. And
now, in 1793, Effingham and his son have returned to expose the judge's behavior. It turns out, though, that Temple has preserved the Effinghams'
share in a secret trust, just as Harvey Birch, the peddler in *The Spy,* turned
out to be a secret patriot. Judge Temple's claim to his property and status is
thus transformed from a matter of corrupt business into a species of principled altruism, and when young Oliver Effingham marries the judge's daughter (Elizabeth), the book's potential conflict, linked to both commerce and
revolutionary violence, is simply dissipated.

Another character in *The Pioneers,* however, presents a more profound
challenge to the judge's authority and legitimacy. Natty Bumppo (later
Cooper's famous "Leatherstocking"), a crusty old hunter loyal to the Effinghams, protests not simply against the judge's specific title to the land but
against the whole idea of commercial civilization. All ownership, to Natty, is
a form of unjust appropriation and excess. He therefore rejects the judge's
distinction between his own principled conception of property and the
greed of the self-interested settlers. Natty cannot remain in the community
affirmed by the book's happy resolution but departs for the West, "the foremost of that band of pioneers who are opening the way for the march of the
nation across the continent." As the irony of this final sentence indicates,
even Natty's radical individualism is implicated in the spread of the civiliza-

tion he seeks to flee: "the march of the nation across the continent." Yet he also suggests that Cooper was far from content with the reconciliation of gentlemanliness and commerce imaged in Judge Temple. Natty too is a projection of his author, who would revive him twice in the next four years, in *The Last of the Mohicans* (1826) and *The Prairie* (1827). Originally intended as a minor character, Leatherstocking would soon become Cooper's paradigmatic hero.

If Cooper was troubled, his doubts did not immediately upset his public reputation. The 1820s were for him a period of extraordinary success. In 1822 he moved his family to New York City, to be closer to his publisher, Charles Wiley. In 1823, along with *The Pioneers,* he published two stories, allegedly by "Jane Morgan," under the title *Tales for Fifteen. The Pilot*— Cooper's first sea novel, involving John Paul Jones and inspired by Cooper's contempt for Scott's supposed demonstration of nautical expertise in *The Pirate*—followed in 1823. Cooper then turned to a vast projected series, Legends of the Thirteen Republics, each volume to deal with the Revolution in a different colony, beginning with *Lionel Lincoln,* set in Boston and published in 1825. This was the only part of the series he ever wrote. In spite of heavy advance advertising, sales were not impressive; of a first printing of 6,000 copies, Wiley had sold only 4,500 by January 1826, and in that month Wiley himself, long in financial difficulty and poor health, died. So Cooper abandoned the Legends of the Thirteen Republics, turned to Philadelphia's Henry Carey, and returned to Natty Bumppo.

He had learned a lesson from *The Pioneers,* which in spite of an early triumph and high critical praise had ended up selling only moderately well, apparently because Cooper here neglected, as he had admitted to John Murray in 1822, "the present taste . . . for action and strong excitement." In *The Last of the Mohicans,* published in 1826, Cooper gave his readers what they apparently wanted, and confirmed his reputation in the United States and abroad as America's "national novelist." Natty Bumppo is here much younger, and his Indian friend Chingachgook (the drunken "Indian John" of *The Pioneers*) is now a vigorous warrior, accompanied by his warrior son, Uncas. These three—coming to the aid of two half sisters, Alice and Cora Munro, quite improbably wandering in the New York wilderness at the time of the French and Indian War—engage in an unrelenting sequence of "action and excitement." It is *A Midsummer Night's Dream* with weapons, and Cooper's readers loved it.

The Last of the Mohicans, for all its excesses and improbabilities, is in fact a masterpiece of mythic invention. What matters first of all, however, is that we recognize the calculation behind it, and behind most of Cooper's professional literary activity in the early 1820s. He would soon be denouncing Irving's "gold"-oriented obsequiousness, but the future patriot had first presented himself in *Precaution,* after all, as a British writer, assuming there was no market for native subjects. Cooper's turn to the American materials in his second novel was a commercial gamble, one whose American success determined the course of his immediate future career. *The Pilot's* open taunt to Scott mainly served to associate its author with the most popular British writer in America, while asserting, in the best tradition of what would later come to be known as public relations, the superiority of the advertised product. Assuming from the successes of *The Spy* and *The Pilot* the commercial value of the American Revolution, he began Legends of the Thirteen Republics, only to abandon it when *Lionel Lincoln* did not sell as well as he had apparently hoped. And in *Tales for Fifteen,* although he would later claim he did so only to aid his troubled publisher, "manly" Cooper was even happy to adopt the pseudonymous pose of sentimental woman author. The best of Cooper's writings from 1820 to 1826 reveal both a power beyond commercial speculation and a "gentlemanly" discomfort with dependence on commerce, a discomfort that would become his major political theme. Still, Cooper's conduct of his career in this period was thoroughly opportunistic, and not without reason. He had a family to support.

Following the publication of *The Last of the Mohicans,* Cooper moved himself and his family to Europe. In France he completed *The Prairie*— once again reviving a now older Natty Bumppo, who dies at the end of the book—and he published it first in England, in 1827, thus giving him (through a pattern already established by Irving) a greater assurance of income from British sales of the book. In America, however, sales were not impressive. *The Prairie* would sell steadily over time, but by the beginning of 1828, his American publisher, Carey and Lee, had not yet completely sold their first edition of 5,000 copies. Three more adventure stories followed, American books written in Europe: *The Red Rover* (1827), another sea tale, which sold 6,500 copies in America; *The Wept of Wish-ton-Wish* (1829), set in seventeenth-century New England at the time of King Phillip's War; and *The Water-Witch* (1829), a nautical romance set in New York Bay in the early eighteenth century. Cooper was working proven material, the wilderness and the sea, and he was maintaining his output, since 1823, of a book a year, for each of which Carey paid him $5,000. To this sum he added his more modest British earnings (Richard Bentley, to whom he had turned when relations with John Murray proved difficult, paid £250 for *The Prairie* and £400 for *The Red Rover*). He was also keeping journals of his European experiences and observations as material for travel books to be written when he returned to America. But one book produced early in this period was a departure from the pattern. *Notions of the Americans: Picked up by a Travelling Bachelor* (1828), supposedly written by a British visitor to the United States, was begun as an account of the Marquis de Lafayette's 1824–25 tour of the United States and was written at the request of the great French supporter of the American Revolution. Although the opinions expressed were almost wholly favorable to the democratic culture of the United States, the book did not do well; Carey, who thought it ill-advised, produced a first edition of only 2,500 copies. But Cooper had crossed a crucial bridge; he had become a spokesman, a role he would soon adopt in his own voice and with increasing vehemence.

In the early 1830s he embarked on a new venture, a trilogy of historical novels with European settings, concerned with serious political issues: *The Bravo* (1831), dealing with the corruption of democracy in Venice; *The Heidenmauer* (1832), casting a rather cold eye on the commercial underpinnings of the German Reformation; and *The Headsman* (1833), set in early-eighteenth-century Switzerland. This move was not immediately a disaster; Bentley paid £1,300, his highest payment ever to Cooper, for the right to publish *The Bravo* in England. Cooper's income from a particular book, however, had nothing to do with that book's sales; his publishers paid him a fixed fee in advance for the right to publish a book for a specific period of time, usually on the basis of only a description of the book's contents. His fee thus depended on the popularity of *earlier* works, and a commercial failure affected his earnings only as it inclined publishers to offer lower fees for subsequent productions, which is precisely what they became increasingly inclined to offer. They were proud to publish Cooper, but they wanted him to stick to his proven modes.

And there were ominous undercurrents in Cooper's European novels. The great patriotic but still expatriate novelist was apparently forsaking his native land as a subject. Even worse, to the extent that these books might be construed as being indirectly about America, neither *The Bravo*'s depiction of democracy nor *the Heidenmauer*'s portrayal of a revered revolution was flattering. Both books raise doubts about the legitimacy of democratic revolution similar to those implicit in the plot of *The Pioneers,* but here these doubts are not dissipated. Moreover, Cooper had embroiled himself, again out of friendship for Lafayette, in a French political controversy, which ended up pitting him against those Americans at home who were coalescing as a Whig party in opposition to Andrew Jackson's attack on the Bank of the United States. In 1832 an extraordinarily hostile review of *The Bravo* appeared in the Whig *New York American*. An enemy, for Cooper, was an enemy for life, and although he would have disliked the Whigs in any case, this review guaranteed the intensity of his future hostility toward American Whiggery.

Oddly or perversely enough, it was at this point, in November of 1833, that Cooper chose to return to America, purchasing and refurbishing Otsego Hall, his father's mansion, and settling in Cooperstown. The event was a far cry from Washington Irving's triumphant and calculated return a year earlier. First Cooper picked a quarrel with his fellow Americans. In *A Letter to His Countrymen* (1834) he attacked his treatment by the American press, castigated American political thinking, and announced his decision to retire from authorship. Then, this announcement notwithstanding, he immediately produced *The Monikins* (1835), its title sardonically echoing the "Mohicans" of his most celebrated success. This book, a nasty satire in which Britain and the United States are portrayed as two nations of monkeys, hardly advanced his public reputation. Between 1836 and 1838 Cooper also published five volumes of travel writings and observations. The pace of publication was as furious as ever, even more so; in need of income, he had little choice. But he was failing to match his earlier earnings, and he even seemed to be defying his public to buy his books.

The hostility of his relations with American Whiggery was matched by his antagonism to his more immediate neighbors in Cooperstown. These neighbors had become accustomed to picnics on Three Mile Point, a Cooper family property on Lake Otsego, but in 1837 the returned proprietor of Otsego Hall asserted his own title to the land. The story got into the papers, and Cooper filed the first of many lawsuits, for libel, against the account in the Whig *Otsego Republican*. This and similar libel suits would occupy him for much of the rest of his life. Unlike Natty Bumppo, Cooper was more than willing to air his grievances before the bar. He also aired them in an extraordinary flurry of publications in 1838. *The American Democrat,* a rather Tocquevillian discussion of the cultural implications of democracy, was a genuine contribution to American political discourse, and small wonder: Cooper's predicament gave him a special sensitivity to one of the greatest issues of his time. How, he asked, was one to reconcile the ideals of personal legitimacy and distinction (ideals associated with the status of "gentleman") with the actualities of a commercial democracy? The Whigs were working their own compromise, but for this compromise, which he perhaps rightly regarded as mere commercial wealth masquerading in the sheep's clothing of democratic pretense, Cooper felt only contempt. And in any case the Whigs were turning against him and would soon be denouncing him as an "aristocrat"—a bitter irony, since Cooper was far more immediately dependent on commerce than such Whigs as, for instance, Boston's Lowells and Lawrences or Irving's patron Astor. In his own dilemma Cooper saw an image of his nation's, a time-honored American habit since the days of the Puritans. We can call his reaction principle or we can call it pique; it hardly matters. What does matter is that, for Cooper, the only imaginable way of asserting his integrity became, increasingly, to openly insult the tastes, values, and personalities of his public. He would not write an *Astoria*—not even if asked, and he hadn't been.

The American Democrat was followed in the same year by a pair of semiautobiographical novels; *Homeward Bound* and *Home as Found*. The first describes the voyage home from Europe of the Effingham family (descendants of Oliver and Elizabeth of *The Pioneers*). The second describes their experiences in New York City and their resettlement in Templeton, including a replay of the Three Mile Point controversy (which also appeared in *The Chronicles of Cooperstown,* another publication of 1838). Cooper gives the Effinghams' pushy American antagonists—notably the democratic demagogue, Aristabulus Bragg—a genuine vitality, but this was hardly his intention, and the effect was lost on his enemies. The Whig journals, especially James Watson Webb's *Morning Carrier and New York Enquirer* and William Leete Stone's *New York Commercial Advertiser,* leapt on the "Effingham Novels" with glee, and Cooper responded with more libel suits, simply supplying his antagonists with more material. In 1838 the erstwhile "American Scott" also chose to publish, in New York's *Knickerbocker Magazine,* a review of John Lockhart's *Life of Sir Walter Scott,* which took pains to attack the revered novelist's principles and character in terms similar to those in which Cooper was by now attacking Irving (with whom he more than once linked Scott). But insult and invective did not sell; they did not solve the problem of what a self-respecting professional author could write in order to support himself.

It is easy to describe Cooper's transformation in the 1830s as a movement from commerce to principle, from an ignoble to a noble understanding of democracy. This was basically his own view (although he would hardly have admitted to anything ignoble in his early success), and it is the way literary history has often chosen to regard this change. But the same literary history has always preferred the works he produced in the 1820s—notably *The Spy, The Pioneers, The Last of the Mohicans,* and *The Prairie*—to the more "principled" works of the 1830s. It is equally easy, on the other hand, to dismiss Cooper's professionally self-destructive behavior in the 1830s as a kind of personal aberration, which it surely was in part, but this is also far too easy. For one thing, Cooper's hostility to the growing ascendancy of the Whigs, who would win the national presidential election in 1840, was not simply an expression of personal resentment; it grew, as well, out of a serious belief in the potential of America's still-new political experiment, a potential Cooper felt the Whigs were betraying. In any case, Cooper's literary celebrity makes his behavior almost a litmus test of the conditions of literary vocation at the very time these conditions were first being established. Cooper, to his credit, was fully aware of what we might call his national-experimental status; if he was lashing about, even in unattractive ways, he had reasons for lashing about. He was admittedly nasty to Irving and others, but he was interested in asking questions Irving and others had chosen not to ask, even if he himself had no answers to these questions. This hardly makes him better as a person, or a better writer, but it does give him a special interest for the late twentieth-century literary historian interested in the very questions Cooper was agitating. What sort of literature *could* an American write—without, on the one hand, becoming simply commercial and without, on the other hand, simply losing his or her audience? This is the issue Cooper confronted in the 1840s. He did not resolve it, any more than any of his successors have; and the early 1840s, an era of collapsing book prices, may have been one of the worst times to try. Nevertheless, after the possibly self-inflicted fiasco of 1838, Cooper set out to restore his American literary reputation (he still had a family and a family mansion to support), and the results of his striving are at the very least instructive.

His first attempt to refashion his image involved the abandonment of both fiction and, so he hoped, controversy. Just as Irving had turned from fiction to history after the failure of *Tales of a Traveller* in 1824, so Cooper now turned from the Effinghams to *The History of the Navy of the United States of America,* published in 1839. He regarded this work as more important than his fiction and more likely to be lasting. Sales, however, were poor; in the next few years Bentley would cite his losses on *The History of the Navy* as grounds for arguing down Cooper's British fees for subsequent productions. In America the financial picture was better, but hardly what Cooper had hoped, and *The History of the Navy*'s impartial handling of the battle of Lake Erie embroiled its author in yet another controversy—this time between the family of Commodore Oliver Perry (all Whigs) and partisans of Jesse D. Elliott, a Jacksonian Democrat whom Perry had accused, some time after the famous battle, of neglect of duty. Cooper ignored these charges for plausibly good historical reasons, but in the era of "Tippecanoe and Tyler, Too," the Whigs could hardly resist another chance to abuse a prominent supporter of the Democrats—a supporter this party of wealth could accuse, as it had accused "King Andrew" Jackson, of "aristocratic" pretension.

It was at this point that Cooper once again revived Natty Bumppo, first in a work he described to Bentley in 1839 as "a nautico-lake-savage romance." The term is wonderful, foreshadowing the bravura with which modern advertising proclaims a combination of new, secret ingredients; in a single book Cooper would play all the cards that had proved so winning in the 1820s: nautical adventure (on Lake Ontario), the wilderness, and a Natty Bumppo now one or two years older than at the time of *The Last of the Mohicans*. *The Pathfinder* was published in 1840, and Natty was revived once more for *The Deerslayer* (1841), containing, as Cooper wrote to Bentley, "the *early* life of Leatherstocking—a period that is only wanting to fill up his career." The polemicist of the 1830s had apparently learned his lesson: he was returning to what his readers and publishers wanted. Indeed, in these last two Leatherstocking novels there are no Effinghams or even Temples; Natty is no longer an attendant or guide but a hero in his own right, failing at love (in *The Pathfinder*) or resisting it (in *The Deerslayer*). Yet the absence of genteel protagonists in these books is also ominous. For instance, in *The Deerslayer*, set on Lake Otsego well before the establishment of Cooperstown or Templeton, white civilization is represented only by Tom Hutter, a former pirate motivated entirely by naked greed, a grim parody of the Judge Temple of *The Pioneers*. Beneath the adventure tale of Natty's "First Warpath" lurks a somber and apocalyptic picture of the rise and fall of American civilization.

Still, one could simply read these books for the adventure. Bentley, for example, expressed his pleasure at Cooper's return in *The Pathfinder* to "the ground where you earned for yourself such great reputation" and paid him £500 for the right to publish it (less £200 to help cover his own losses on *The History of the Navy*). In the United States, meanwhile, Lea and Blanchard (the current incarnation of the House of Carey) offered $3,600 for the right to publish 5,000 copies of *Pathfinder* and 2,000 more copies of *The History of the Navy*. Considering the state of the economy in general, and of the American publishing business in particular, these were impressive figures, and Cooper fully appreciated them. "Lea has sold near 4000 of Pathfinder," he wrote to his wife in May of 1840. "It has great success, in the worst of times—Indeed, it is the only thing that does well." Critical reaction, after a decade of embattlement and still at the height of the libel suits, was equally gratifying. *The Pathfinder* was praised in Europe by no less a figure than Balzac, and it was also widely praised at home, its public supporters including Washington Irving. Even a negative notice by Park Benjamin, another of Cooper's Whig enemies, was able to find "one merit" in the work: "The book does *not* contain the mass of political, philosophical and philological ravings which have spoiled so many of the author's preceding works."

Nor were these Leatherstocking novels Cooper's only attempts to recover his reputation and his earning power. Between *The Pathfinder* and *The Deerslayer* he also published, in 1840, *Mercedes of Castille,* a tale drawing on the voyages of Columbus, which, to its author's surprise, did not sell. In 1842 he published two romances of naval warfare: *The Two Admirals* and *The Wing-and-Wing.* In 1843 appeared *Wyandotté,* set in the American wilderness during the Revolution; *Ned Meyers, or A Life Before the Mast,* Cooper's rendition, as "editor" of the life of a sailor he had known at sea and recently rediscovered; and *The Autobiography of a Pocket-Handkerchief,* dealing with a French noblewoman reduced to menial labor after the July Revolution of 1830. This last book perhaps expressed Cooper's sense of his own situation, because he was now averaging two books a year and still failing to match his earnings from one book a year in the 1820s. And the pace continued. In 1844 Cooper published the two-part *Afloat and Ashore* and *Adventures of Miles Wallingford.* In 1845 and 1846 he produced a trilogy, the Littlepage Manuscripts (*Satanstoe, The Chainbearer,* and *The Redskins*), supporting the position of the Hudson Valley landowners in the current "Rent Wars."

Cooper had recovered from the debacle of the 1830s. Irving, facing the collapse of the economy in 1837 and of book prices in the early 1840s, had moved increasingly into other endeavors. In the parlance of modern business, he had "diversified." Cooper stuck with literature, but it was hardly clear that his renewed success in the 1840s was worth the price, or that it really *was* "success." In an 1846 letter to James Kirke Paulding, who had inquired about his publishing arrangements, Cooper summarized his situation in remarkably grim terms:

> My pecuniary benefits, in this country amount to nothin worth naming. . . . The cheap literature has destroyed the value of nearly all literary property, and after five and twenty years of hard work, I find myself

comparatively a poor man. Had I employed the same time in trade, or in traveling as an agent for a manufacturer of pins, I do not doubt I should have been better off, and my children independent. The fact is, this country is not sufficiently advanced for any thing intellectual, and the man who expects to rise by any such agency makes a capital mistake, unless he sells himself, soul and body, to a faction.

"If I were fifteen years younger," Cooper concludes, after noting that he expects to earn only $500 each from his three most recent books,

I would certainly go abroad, and never return. . . . You and I have committed the same error; have been American—whereas our cue was to be European, which would have given us success at home. The time was, when these things pained me, but every interest seems so much upside down, here, that another feeling has taken the place of even regret.

If Cooper saw his career as a kind of national experiment, it was to this, by 1846, that he thought the experiment had come.

By "cheap literature" Cooper probably did not mean sensational fiction aimed at a large, lower-class audience, although one of the first sensational American best-sellers, George Lippard's *Quaker City,* had appeared in 1844, just a year before the letter to Paulding. Rather, one guesses, Cooper was referring to the general collapse of book prices as a result of the competition of the early 1840s. *This* "cheap literature" consisted mainly of pirated European works, but Cooper's letter refers not to foreign competition, but to the pressure on *American* writers to "be European," and one suspects that, once again, he has Irving in mind. The irony, of course, is that Cooper's envy is here inflating Irving's "success at home," for in the 1840s Irving was no more able than Cooper to rely comfortably on the value of his "literary property."

Cooper continued writing for a living until his death in 1851, one day short of his sixty-second birthday. *The Crater* appeared in 1847, *Jack Tier* and *The Oak Openings* in 1848, *The Sea Lions* in 1849, *The Ways of the Hour* in 1850. Not all was the bleakness proclaimed in the letter to Paulding. With *The Sea Lions,* in 1849, Cooper moved to a new American publisher, New York's George Palmer Putnam, who began issuing a uniform edition of his works (as he was also doing with Irving's). And in a review of *The Sea Lions,* a member of the new literary generation, Herman Melville, praised Cooper as "our national novelist." Yet for British rights to *The Ways of the Hour,* Richard Bentley was willing to offer, and Cooper was compelled to accepted, only £100. Cooper's mood was increasingly revealed by the endorsement of aristocratic withdrawal in such works as the Littlepage Manuscripts, or by the apocalyptic energies of works like *Wyandotté* or *The Crater*. In the former, a settlement darkly modeled on the Templeton of *The Pioneers* is attacked by Indians at the time of the Revolution and its founder is killed. In the latter the founder is luckily absent when his Pacific island community, overrun with commercial excess, is destroyed in a volcanic eruption.

Cooper was indeed a "national novelist." Far more so than any of his American contemporaries, indeed virtually uniquely among these contemporaries, he had succeeded for over three decades in the new profession of literature. In his effort to reconcile "manliness" with the commercial requirements of his profession, however, he had in his own judgment failed. Cooper's ideal of manly integrity, expressed again and again in dramas (or melodramas) of beset manhood, was at least in part a response to the fragility of his own fortunes, a compensatory myth. This myth, embodied most purely in the nostalgic evocation of Natty Bumppo and of Indian life in the wilderness, is one of considerable power; it has become an enduring component of the ideology of "America." Still, it is important to recognize that even Cooper's great tragic theme of the destruction of Indian culture by the march of white commercial civilization is closely tied to his own personal and professional situation as he understood it. The major fear of his Native Americans, after all, is that someone—the whites, another tribe— may have "made women" out of them, and Natty Bumppo maintains his integrity, above all, by avoiding women.

Cooper, who distinguished Irving's supposed "meannesses" from manly (and therefore morally superior) "crimes," helped establish the equation of "America" with "masculinity," and the concomitant equation of commercial popularity with "feminization," that have lain at the heart of much nineteenth- and twentieth-century thinking about American literature. For instance, in Fanny Fern's *Ruth Hall* (1855), the heroine's effeminate brother is editor of a journal called the "Irving Magazine." The truth is that Cooper hardly knew what he wanted, which is why his ideas of manhood and America, so nearly synonymous in his thinking, are also so vague, so reactively negative. What matters, however, is that the equation of the American with the masculine (and with resistance to the feminine) has appealed to so many of Cooper's male American successors, successors faced with the same commercial predicament. As Irving helped create a taste and market for native tales and sketches, so Cooper suggested the possibilities of the novel, and both writers would have many American imitators. But their most important legacy, beyond demonstrating the possibility of professional literary success for Americans, lay in their promotion of contrasting and even antagonistic images of American literary vocation, of the writer's relationship to the public, and ultimately of the meaning of America and American identity. In effect, Cooper and Irving established, by their examples, contrasting schools or traditions of American literature. Twentieth-century literary historians have generally seen Cooper, rather than Irving, as the seminal American fiction writer, and not without reason. The myth or ideology of American identity and literary vocation to which he gave currency can be traced in the stances and careers of such later Americans as Melville, Mark Twain, and even Ernest Hemingway, and these male writers occupy central positions in the twentieth-century literary "canon." We should not, however, ignore Irving's legacy. Poe and Hawthorne, for instance, turned most consistently to the tale rather than the novel, and it was Irving, far more than Cooper, whose influence lay behind the most deliberately popular body of pre–Civil War American literature, especially the magazine writing that would signal in the 1840s and 1850s the real beginnings of mass literature.

Novels and Novelists in the 1820s

In 1820, according to Lyle H. Wright's *American Fiction, 1774–1850* (1948), five volumes of new prose fiction by native authors were published in the United States, only a marginal increase over the average of three and a half per year for the previous decade. The figure began to rise dramatically after 1820: to eighteen in 1825, to twenty-six in 1830, and to fifty-four in 1835. Severe economic conditions, both in the nation at large and in the publishing business, momentarily slowed the pace of expansion and even reduced the rate of production: to an average annual figure, from 1836 through 1842, of thirty-nine new titles. Then, with the national economy recovering and with the most virulent forms of competition in book publishing largely under control, production once again took off. In 1843, seventy-seven new titles entered the ranks of American fiction; in 1844, one hundred and two; in 1845, one hundred and fifty-eight. In quantitative terms at least, the period from 1820 through 1845 clearly marked the first major "renaissance" in American fiction.

More than a few of these new books were collections of tales and sketches, including the first and second series of Nathaniel Hawthorne's *Twice-told Tales* (1837 and 1842) and Edgar Allan Poe's *Tales of the Grotesque and Arabesque* (1840). But most were novels, which almost always, then as now, sold far better than story collections. Although Irving's influence would spawn such blatant imitations as Henry Wadsworth Longfellow's *Outre-Mer* (1833) and Henry T. Tuckerman's *Italian Sketch Book* (1835), and although Irving's mode would receive wide currency in magazines, in the 1820s Cooper rather than Irving provided the model most imitated, and the immediate impact of Cooper's success as an incentive to emulation is revealed quite starkly by the figures. Between 1821 (when *The Spy* gained national and international acclaim) and 1822, the rate of publication of new native fiction rose impressively from five volumes a year to fifteen. Seldom does literary history find such precise quantitative evidence of at least crude influence—of new writers and publishers, in this case, trying to cash in on *The Spy's* success.

Many of the new American novels published in the 1820s were, like *The Spy* and *The Pioneers*, works of historical fiction. What had worked for Scott and Cooper, these authors and their publishers apparently believed, might work for them. But only infrequently did such beliefs prove to be justified. For example, James McHenry (1785–1845), an Irish-born Philadelphian who produced six historical novels between 1823 and 1831, is now completely forgotten, and even during his lifetime he was better known for an 1822 verse collection, *The Pleasures of Friendship* (which had gone through seven editions by 1836), than for any of his hastily written historical fictions.

Several of the writers who turned to fiction in the 1820s did so only briefly and ultimately achieved professional success through other literary endeavors. Lydia Maria Child (1802–80) published three historical novels in the 1820s and 1830s: *Hobomok* (1824) deals with seventeenth-century Massachusetts; *The Rebels* (1825) with, as its subtitle puts it, "Boston before the Revolution"; *Philothea* (1836) with ancient Greece. These books sold well enough (new editions of *Philothea*, for instance, were issued in 1839, 1845, and 1849), but Child's most important efforts were not in fiction. In 1830 she published a manual of domestic advice, *The Frugal Housewife*, helping to establish one of the major genres of American women's literature. *The Mother's Book* followed in 1831, and from 1826 to 1834 Child edited a well-known children's magazine, Boston's *Juvenile Miscellany*. Her *Letters from New York* (1843, 1845), a collection of newspaper pieces written for the *Boston Courier*, went through eleven editions by 1850. And with her husband, David Lee Child, a founder of the New England Anti-Slavery Society, she was an active abolitionist, editing the *National Anti-Slavery Standard* from 1841 to 1849. Child was very much a successful literary professional, but fiction constituted a small and even incidental part of her professional activity. In this respect her career resembled that of Sarah Josepha Hale (1788–1879), who first made her mark with *Northwood* (1827), a New England local-color novel, and with a collection, *Sketches of American Character* (1829), but who thereafter devoted her energies mainly to magazines, especially as the influential editor of *Godey's Lady's Book* from 1837 to 1877.

The reputation of Timothy Flint (1780–1840) was also not mainly based on his works of fiction. His first historical romance, *Francis Berrian, or the Mexican Patriot,* (1826), was followed by other novels—*The Life and Adventures of Arthur Clenning* (1826), *George Mason, the Young Backswoodsman* (1829), *The Shoshonee Valley* (1830)—but he was better known as a magazine writer and editor, and his nonfictional works on the geography and history of the American West had a much wider circulation than did his novels. Born in Massachusetts and serving there as a minister from 1802 to 1814, Flint then traveled westward for the Missionary Society of Connecticut. His record of these travels, *Recollections of the Last Ten Years, Passed in Occasional Residences and Journeyings in the Valley of the Mississippi,* was published in 1826 and launched his literary career. From 1827 to 1830 he edited the *Western Monthly Review* in Cincinnati, where he also published such more-or-less factual volumes as *A Condensed Geography and History of the Western States* (1828, expanded in 1832 as *The History and Geography of the Mississippi Valley*) and *Indian Wars of the West* (1833). In 1834 Flint served briefly as editor of New York's new *Knickerbocker Magazine.* In 1833, meanwhile, he had published his *Biographical Memoir of Daniel Boone, the First Settler of Kentucky,* which went on, through fourteen editions, to become perhaps the most widely read account of the western frontier in the first half of the nineteenth century.

Not all of the new American fiction writers in the 1820s were new to literature. James Kirke Paulding (1778–1860) had been part of New York's literary culture since the beginning of the century. He was closely associated with Washington Irving: his sister had married Irving's brother William; he had collaborated with William and Washington on *Salmagundi* in 1807; and his *Diverting History of John Bull and Brother Jonathan*, a comic history published in 1812, was clearly inspired by the success of Washington's *Diedrich Knickerbocker's History of New York.* Paulding was apparently following his perception of the tastes of the American reading public, and two years after the success of Cooper's *The Spy*, he turned to historical fiction with *Koningsmarke* (1823), set in seventeenth-century Delaware. Two more historical novels followed in the early 1830s: *The Dutchman's Fireside*

(1831), dealing with Dutch New York before the Revolution; and *Westward Ho!* (1832), set on the Kentucky frontier. By the standards of the time these books were quite successful; *The Dutchman's Fireside,* for example, went through six editions in the 1830s and 1840s.

In 1819–20 Paulding had published, without the collaboration of the Irving brothers, a *Second Series* of *Salmagundi,* which included an essay on "National Literature." "By freeing himself from a habit of servile imitation," he proclaimed, the native writer "may and will in time destroy the ascendancy of foreign taste and opinions and elevate his own in the place of them." Although such literary nationalism, seventeen years before Emerson's "American Scholar," was already thoroughly conventional, Paulding was far from clear about what, exactly, would give the new "national literature" its "air and character of originality." For the most part his essay is an attack on the gothic marvels associated with the romances of Sir Walter Scott; it is a plea for what Paulding calls "Rational Fictions," based on "nature." Yet in spite of his attack on imitation, Paulding proposes a British novel, Fielding's *Tom Jones,* as the highest example of the sort of fiction most appropriate to America, and Fielding's influence is markedly evident in *Koningsmarke* and *The Dutchman's Fireside.*

Paulding played the role of American man of letters for three decades with energy, dedication, and considerable success, producing not only historical novels but short stories, verse, satire, literary criticism, essays, biographies, and plays (his *The Lion of the West,* a farce first produced in 1831, was long a popular favorite). He was also a successful man of affairs, serving as secretary of the navy under Martin Van Buren from 1838 to 1841. After this hiatus in his literary career he returned to historical fiction in the later 1840s with *The Old Continental* (1846), set in New York during the Revolution, and *The Puritan and His Daughter* (1849), which takes place in seventeenth-century New England and Virginia. Yet Paulding's very literary versatility—his cultivation of so many different modes, his following the leads first of Irving and then of Cooper, even while modeling himself on Fielding—is symptomatic of a general uncertainty in the 1820s and 1830s about just what sort of literature the American man of letters would or should produce.

The same uncertainty is clear in the more flamboyant career and writings of John Neal (1793–1876). Raised in poverty in Portland, Maine, Neal left school at the age of twelve and spent the next dozen years working in a series of mercantile establishments. Ending up in Baltimore in 1817, he began studying law and turned to literature in the hope that it might support him while he prepared for the bar. He was much enamored of Byron and wrote a hundred-and-fifty-page appreciation of the British poet for Baltimore's *Portico* magazine in four days, but he earned little money or reputation from his own literary works: a melodramatic novel, *Keep Cool* (1817); a long poem, *The Battle of Niagara* (1818); and a Byronic verse tragedy, *Otho* (1819). Undaunted, he produced four novels in 1822–23, following the success of Cooper's *Spy: Logan,* an overwrought historical romance involving an Englishman masquerading as a vengeful Indian chief; *Errata; or, the Works of Will. Adams,* a kind of melodramatized autobiography; *Randolph,* a novel risky both in its sexual concerns and in its often caustic sketches of Neal's contemporaries; and *Seventy-Six,* a historical novel of the American Revolution. In 1845 Nathaniel Hawthorne, who had been a student at Bowdoin when these books appeared, recalled "that wild fellow, John Neal, who almost turned my boyish brain with his romances," but these hastily written books hardly fulfilled their author's ambition of surpassing the reputations and commercial successes of Irving and Cooper.

Although Neal was an ardent nationalist, accusing both Irving and Cooper of being wanting on this score, it was oddly enough in England that he managed, briefly, to achieve notoriety as a representative American writer. Settling in London early in 1824, he began to place essays in Edinburgh's *Blackwood's Magazine,* most notably a series on "American Writers." Here, anonymously, he praised Brockden Brown and Paulding and criticized Irving's *Sketch Book* (in spite of its dashes of "bold poetry") for its "squeamish, puling, lady-like sentimentality"; Cooper was by no means the only American to equate Irving's popular appeal with effeminacy. Yet Neal was no kinder to the author of *The Spy,* whom he dismissed in a mere half column as "a man of sober talent—nothing more." Neal then went on to devote seventeen columns to his own work. These essays infuriated many of Neal's American contemporaries, but once the identity of their author became known, they did make him famous.

In his mixture of Byronic defiance and blatant self-promotion Neal anticipated, in different ways, Poe, Melville, and Whitman. The open preoccupation of his novels with sexual transgression and oedipal guilt makes him at least an interesting curiosity to the modern reader. And his fiction anticipates the sensational novels, aimed at a mass audience, that began appearing regularly in the 1840s. But Neal's contemporary vogue was very brief. William Blackwood brought out Neal's fifth novel, *Brother Jonathan,* in 1825, after requiring the excision of material he considered indecent, and when fewer than five hundred copies sold, out of a printing of two thousand,

Blackwood's ardor for his American genius cooled almost instantly. Neal returned to America in 1827 and settled in provincial Portland, where he lived for the rest of his life. He continued publishing for a time, mostly works planned or written in England: *Rachel Dyer: A North American Story* (1828), *Authorship: A Tale* (1830), and *The Down-Easters* (1833). He produced new short stories for American periodicals and promoted such younger writers as Edgar Poe, but the fame, or infamy, of the 1820s gave way to growing obscurity. After recalling "that wild fellow, John Neal," in 1845, Hawthorne went on to surmise that "he surely has long been dead, else he never could keep himself so quiet." By the 1860s Neal was writing Western dime novels, on order and according to formula, simply for needed money. He died in 1876, after failing to interest Boston's J. R. Osgood in reissuing *Seventy-Six* to commemorate the centennial of American liberty.

Catharine Maria Sedgwick (1789–1867), although now almost as little known as Neal, was widely admired in the nineteenth century, and she was one of the most influential American fiction writers of her generation. Never marrying, she divided her time between Stockbridge, in western Massachusetts, and New York City. Her first literary effort, *A New England Tale* (1822), began as a tract criticizing the intolerance of New England's inherited Calvinism (Sedgwick herself converted to Unitarianism), but during composition it evolved into a genuine novel, chronicling the triumph over adversity of its orphan heroine, Jane Elton. *Redwood*, which followed in 1824, is the story of another exemplary young woman, Ellen Bruce. Then Sedgwick turned to historical fiction in 1827 with *Hope Leslie*, set in seventeenth-century Massachusetts. With these novels and their exemplary heroines Sedgwick established the basic formula that would lie behind such best-sellers of the 1850s as Susan Warner's *The Wide, Wide World* (1850) and Maria Cummins's *The Lamplighter* (1854), although Sedgwick's heroines are considerably more self-reliant than those of Warner and Cummins.

Although Sedgwick was a woman of independent means, with no need to support herself by her writings, and although she herself persistently deprecated her own literary abilities and ambitions, her books sold well. *Redwood* was translated into German, Swedish, Italian, and French; *Hope Leslie*, which was compared favorably to the work of Cooper and made its author the most celebrated American woman writer before Harriet Beecher Stowe, earned her $1,100 from the sale of an edition of two thousand copies; and in 1830 *Clarence*, a contemporary story with another strong heroine, earned her $1,200. Sedgwick was equally successful, and considerably more productive, in the 1830s. *The Linwoods*, a historical romance of the Revolution, appeared in 1835, but Sedgwick was turning increasingly to didactic fiction aimed at children or working-class readers. *Home* (1835) went through twenty editions by 1846; *The Poor Rich Man and the Rich Poor Man* (1836) went through sixteen; *Live and Let Live* (1837) went through twelve. From New York's House of Harper, which published *The Linwoods, The Poor Rich Man,* and *Live and Let Live,* Sedgwick earned more than $6,000 between 1835 and 1841. Her last novel, *Married or Single?* appeared in 1857.

It is more than a little difficult to generalize about the nature of American fiction or the status of the American fiction writer in the 1820s, and this difficulty of generalization is itself important. To writers as diverse as Lydia Child, Timothy Flint, James Paulding, John Neal, and Catharine Sedgwick, Cooper's success apparently suggested the possibility of fiction writing as an American profession, but it suggested little else. Child and Flint soon abandoned fiction, and although Paulding and Neal were considerably more dedicated, their very dedication reveals, in different ways, a good deal of uncertainty about what, as American novelists, they were supposed to be doing. Sedgwick's career came closest, in the 1820s and early 1830s, to the professional consistency of Cooper's, but by the mid-1830s she, too, was beginning to turn away from fiction. And unlike Cooper, even Sedgwick, after the collapse of the literary marketplace at the end of the 1830s, did not attempt to revive the experience of the 1820s.

A laudatory review of Sedgwick's *Hope Leslie* published in Boston's *North American Review* in 1828 concludes by noting that "our authoress . . ., if the truth must be told, appears to entertain a decided partiality for her own sex." Exemplary, self-reliant heroines do dominate Sedgwick's fiction—Jane Elton in *A New England Tale,* Ellen Bruce in *Redwood,* Hope Leslie in the novel that bears her name—and yet Elizabeth Temple, for instance, in Cooper's *The Pioneers* is no less self-reliant and no less willing to combat social injustice than these young women. Cooper, who had begun his career with an inept imitation of Jane Austen, was aware (or assumed) that women constituted the bulk of his potential audience. It was only in the late 1820s and early 1830s—as Cooper increasingly shifted his interest to Natty Bumppo and other isolated male figures, while such women as Child and Sedgwick gravitated more and more toward children's fiction and advice manuals—that a pronounced differentiation of "masculine" and "feminine" American fiction began to emerge as perhaps the major fault line in the American literary landscape.

There were clearly many reasons for this increasing division of the literary marketplace. It coincided with the growing influence in the larger culture of the so-called Cult of Domesticity, the doctrine of woman's separate "sphere," to which we will turn presently. There may also be reasons more directly implicated in the professional careers of these writers. Cooper became more aggressively "masculine" and more contemptuous of the "feminine" in response to anxieties about the commodification of his work, the commercialization of his authorial identity. Male writers—at least writers like Cooper who felt their masculinity imperiled—associated commercial success with feminization long before women novelists had much actual market success. A writer like Sedgwick, on the other hand, apparently felt no alienation from her public; if her readers wanted didactic fiction and works for children, she was content to supply this demand. But this differentiation of men's and women's fictional traditions, never absolute in any case, took place later. In 1827 Sedgwick still found it perfectly natural to follow Cooper's example and write a work of wilderness historical romance, complete with Indian massacre and melodrama; and readers gratified by *The Last of the Mohicans* were happy to turn to *Hope Leslie*. This is hardly to say that the 1828 reviewer was incorrect about Sedgwick's "partiality to her own sex," but only that in the 1820s such partiality did not yet necessarily bear the nearly generic significance it would acquire by the 1850s.

Drama and Literary Vocation

In drama as in book publishing, the years from the 1820s through the 1840s witnessed extraordinary expansion. By the middle of the century there were more than fifty professional theatrical companies in the United States. Charleston, important for its theatrical productions in the eighteenth century, was on the decline, and activity centered in three northern coastal cities: Philadelphia, Boston (where the Massachusetts laws against theatrical exhibitions had been repealed as recently as 1792), and especially New York (already, by 1820, the dominant influence in American theater). But although these cities boasted the greatest number of theaters and new productions, they had no monopoly on American drama. Permanent and traveling companies appeared throughout the nation and across the frontier, and in the late 1840s two theaters even opened in California. The main attractions in American theaters were most often visiting British actors, but America was beginning to produce its own stars: for instance, Mary Ann Duff, Anna Cora Mowatt, Charlotte Cushman, and, above all, Edwin Forrest. Also, although most of the plays produced on the American stage were classics (especially plays by Shakespeare) or contemporary foreign works (for instance, melodramas by such popular playwrights as Edward Bulwer Lytton and August von Kotzebue), quite a few, including a number of major hits, were written by American playwrights.

Nevertheless, these developments in the American theater are at best incidental to the history of American literature and American literary vocation in the first half of the nineteenth century. Philip Hone, a wealthy businessman and devoted playgoer who would become a prominent New York Whig in the 1830s, expressed his hope in 1825, on the occasion of the laying of the cornerstone of New York's Bowery Theatre, that "at no distant period the latent talents of some native Bard may here be warmed into existence, who shall emulate the growing fame, acquired in other walks, by Irving and Cooper." But this hope, even though popular works by both Irving and Cooper were adapted for the stage, was disappointed. In part the problem was simply a matter of quality; none of the American plays produced before 1850, however great their interest as documents of popular culture, has survived as literature. The United States was hardly unique in its failure to produce an enduring dramatic literature at this time; it is equally true of England and Europe that the first half of the nineteenth century, from the perspective of the history of dramatic literature, is something of a black hole. There was a more basic reason for the failure of Hone's hopes, however. The careers of Irving and Cooper indicated that literature could be pursued in America as a profession. The years before the Civil War produced many important developments in *theater* as a profession, but they produced no comparable professionalizing of *playwriting*.

Professional American theaters were staffed by resident companies, whose members filled most of the parts in a remarkable (and taxing) variety of performances. Leading parts, however, were often filled by touring celebrities. On the positive side, this system meant that playgoers almost anywhere in the United States could eventually see the great actors of their day, that local actors could learn from these professionals, and that, since both star and company were most likely to have standard works in common, there was a built-in incentive for performing classic plays by Shakespeare and others. Other consequences were less salutary. The star system, together with the almost daily alternation of plays (at a time when even the largest urban populations could hardly support long runs), kept rehearsals to a minimum, at least rehearsals with the visiting star; and actors frequently forgot lines or even failed to appear for whole scenes. Unable to develop subtlety of dramatic interpretation, which was in any case not in much popular demand, American theaters tended to promote emotional and scenic spectacle, a development abetted by the shift from candles to gas lighting. The reliance on visiting stars encouraged the mounting (and commissioning) of plays dominated by single characters—often rather bombastic characters. Also, since a popular star could claim up to half a performance's total proceeds, *before* expenses, the star system further undermined the already precarious incomes of theater managers and especially of performers. Actors for the most part received only subsistence wages, supplemented, from time to time, by "benefit" performances, in which friends or supporters of a particular performer would buy tickets and the performer would receive all or some of the proceeds, *after* expenses.

A performer's abiding hope, or at least a young performer's abiding hope, was that this precarious situation might be only an apprenticeship, and a few American actors actually did rise to stardom. The most spectacular success in the years before 1850 was Edwin Forrest (1806–72). Born in Philadelphia, Forrest made his debut at Philadelphia's Walnut Street Theatre in 1820. He then embarked on his apprenticeship, first with a traveling company based in Pittsburgh and then with a resident company in New Orleans. In 1825 he landed a job in Albany, for $7.50 a week, and there he had the good luck to work with, and to learn from, the great British star Edmund Kean, playing Iago, for instance, to Kean's Othello. Then, in 1826, Forrest himself played Othello at New York City's Park Theatre and his reputation was made. New York's new Bowery Theatre signed him on for $800 a year, and the next year he was earning $200 *a night*. Forrest's success was no more typical than were the successes of Irving and Cooper, but he demonstrated that a professional American actor could not only succeed but make a fortune. No American playwright came even close to such a demonstration.

Forrest's acting style was "heroic," more physical than subtle, and his admirers were loyal and passionate, none more admiring or passionate than Forrest himself. He was fiercely nationalistic—a quality that expressed itself above all in public abuse of his British stage rivals, especially the British tragedian William Charles Macready. In May of 1849, during a Macready performance of *Macbeth* at New York's Astor Place Theatre, Forrest partisans in the house kept the play from proceeding. A public petition signed by leading New York citizens and literary figures (including Washington Irving and Herman Melville) apologized to Macready, and a repeat performance was arranged. That night the rowdies, forbidden entrance to the theater, rallied outside, some 10,000 to 15,000 strong, throwing stones through the windows, and it ultimately took three volleys from the rifles of the militia to disperse the mob.

The Astor Place Riot indicated both the passion that American audiences could feel for the theater and an apparently political dimension to Forrest's popularity. Whereas Macready's most ardent sponsors were Whig "gentlemen," Forrest's appeal in New York was especially to the so-called Bowery Boys, Democrats all. The day of the riot a poster challenged American "Workingmen" to come to the "English aristocratic opera house" and "Stand up to your lawful rights"; the same divisions would manifest themselves in the New York draft riots of 1863. On a deeper level, however, the incident suggests not so much the political seriousness of American theater as the potential of American politics for a dangerous theatricality. The Astor Place Riot—aroused not by any coherent political agenda but by the rivalry of dramatic stars, and resembling less the storming of the Bastille than the Rolling Stones' 1969 fiasco at Altamont—left twenty-two dead and thirty wounded.

Forrest's nationalism did have a more positive outlet. In 1828 he began his practice of offering prizes for works by American playwrights, and he was ultimately reported to have awarded a total of something like $20,000 to the winners of his many contests. Such munificence was hardly enough, however, to make playwriting a viable profession in the United States, and even those who produced hit plays were unable to support themselves, for a number of reasons. In the absence of an international copyright law, American theater managers could produce foreign works for free; what incentive did they have for paying more than token compensation to native authors? Even worse, there was no domestic copyright law protecting the performance (as distinguished from the publication) of plays. And there was no system of royalties governing the compensation of playwrights. Managers or star actors paid a flat fee for dramatic vehicles, which then became their property. Thus, a play running for decades was not necessarily worth any more to its author than a play that closed after its first performance. Some examples should clarify a situation that kept even hits from enriching (or, for that matter, from supporting) their authors.

The first American hit play of the 1820s was *The Forest Rose,* written by Samuel Woodworth (1785–1842) and first produced in New York in 1825. This "Pastoral Opera," as its subtitle described it, resembled what we would now call musical comedy, and its virtuous American farmers, its Yankee Jonathan, its villainous fop, its mixture of humor and melodrama, all led to enduring popularity over the next forty years. Both in the United States and in London it was performed more regularly than any other American play before 1850. Woodworth wrote many other plays and engaged in a variety of literary activities (for instance, he wrote the song "The Old Oaken Bucket"), but he received little compensation from the success of *The Forest Rose.* He abandoned literature in 1836 and died in poverty six years later.

The first of Forrest's prize competitions, in 1828, offered $500 plus half the proceeds from a benefit for a "tragedy, in five acts, of which the hero, or principal, shall be an aboriginal of this country." The winning play was *Meta-mora, or The Last of the Wampanoags,* by John Augustus Stone (1800–34), a professional actor. *Metamora* was loosely based on the seventeenth-century conflict known as King Philip's War but added such clichés of melodrama as a lascivious villain and the revelation of an orphan's true parentage. The play was first performed in New York in 1829 and was an instant sensation. It launched the American craze for Indian plays that would finally be lampooned by John Brougham in 1847 in *Metamora; or, The Last of the Pollywogs,* and it provided a dependable source of income for Edwin Forrest from 1829 to the end of his career. In 1853, for instance, it ran for six consecutive performances in Boston, an impressive run for the time, and brought in almost $4,000. But Stone, the author, earned nothing from *Metamora* beyond the original $500 and half the proceeds from the benefit. He wrote other plays but never again achieved a success on the order of *Metamora*'s; he committed suicide in 1834 in Philadelphia. In that same year, an audience for *Metamora* in Albany was so large the musicians in the orchestra had to give up their seats and retire to the wings to make room for more paying customers.

The American who came closest to establishing a viable career as a professional playwright before 1850 was Robert Montgomery Bird (1806–54). Trained to be a doctor, Bird soon abandoned medicine for literature, and in the early 1830s he won four of Forrest's prize competitions. *Pelopidas, or the Fall of the Polemarchs,* Bird's first winning entry, was never produced, but in the fall of 1831 Forrest did perform *The Gladiator* (Bird's version of the revolt of Spartacus) in New York, Philadelphia, and Boston. This play, like *Metamora,* became a staple of Forrest's repertory; between 1831 and 1854 he played the role of Spartacus at least a thousand times—an average, over twenty-three years, of almost forty-four performances per year. Bird followed *The Gladiator* with *Oralloosa, Son of the Incas* (1832) and *The Broker of Bogota* (1834), and although neither matched the success of *The Gladiator,* both received critical praise and continued to be performed by Forrest for some time. By the mid-1930s, Bird was clearly America's foremost dramatist, and his professional relationship with Forrest had warmed into friendship. Their friendship soon soured, however, not surprisingly over money. Forrest had paid Bird $1,000 each for *The Gladiator, Oralloosa,* and *The Broker of Bogota.* When the author, noting that Forrest was getting rich performing his plays, demanded a small share of the profits, Forrest refused, as he would later refuse Bird's son permission to publish his father's collected dramatic works. Bird asked for $6,000 in 1837; after Bird's death his widow estimated that Forrest must have made something like $100,000 performing *The Gladiator.* But Bird had no valid legal claim on any portion of these earnings; no wonder he abandoned drama, in the 1830s, for fiction. "What a fool I was to think of writing plays!" he wrote in his journal. "To be sure, they are much wanted. But these novels are much easier sorts of things and immortalize one's pocket much sooner."

The devaluation of playwriting in pre–Civil War America was not simply a fluke of the marketplace, or a consequence of inadequate copyright laws; it in fact represented public taste quite accurately. Anna Cora Mowatt (1819–70) was best known as an actress, but she also wrote a number of successful plays, most notably *Fashion,* a satire on American nouveaux riches first produced in 1845. Of this play Mowatt later wrote that "a *dramatic,* not a literary, success was what I desired to achieve." From our own perspective *Fashion* is a better play than much of its competition—including the inflated Forrest vehicles *Metamora* and *The Gladiator*—but Mowatt's distinction of the "dramatic" from the "literary" tells us a good deal about a theater with which, as both performer and playwright, she was intimately familiar. What succeeded were broad humor, melodrama, and spectacle. A play with Forrest was a good draw, but even better was a play with Forrest and real horses on the stage. Almost no one wanted literary subtlety, which would in any case have had to overcome both inept acting and, typically, a good deal of audible activity on the part of the audience.

A night at the theater in pre–1850 America did not simply involve seeing a single play performed; there were also curtain-raisers, songs and other entertainments during intermissions, and afterpieces (often farces). Thomas D. Rice introduced his famous blackface impersonation of "Jim Crow" as an afterpiece at New York's Bowery Theatre in 1830; by the 1840s the Virginia Minstrels and Christy's Minstrels had developed the full-fledged "minstrel show." Vaudeville and burlesque had similar origins. Such creations were hardly literature, but literature was not what most Americans went to the theater for—even, one gathers, when they went to see

Shakespeare. The night of Macready's first performance at the Astor Place Theatre, in 1849, the rowdies in the crowd began hissing the local actor playing Duncan. They thought he was Macbeth.

Spectacle and crude entertainment ruled drama even when plays were allegedly moral in purpose; and didactic purpose, by disarming religious prejudice against theater, could help attract new customers. The first great success in this vein was *The Drunkard, or the Fallen Saved,* written by W. H. Smith (1808–72) and first performed in Boston in 1844. *The Drunkard* tells the story of the descent into alcoholism and the subsequent and astonishingly sudden recovery of one Edward Middleton. It ends with a wonderful tableau in which the cast, assembled in a "rural cottage," sings verse after verse of "Home, Sweet Home." The popularity of this confection was phenomenal; in New York, it played simultaneously at four different theaters for a time, and an 1850 production at P. T. Barnum's American Museum became the first play in the United States to run for one hundred consecutive performances. Although *The Drunkard* owed a good deal of its popularity to its temperance message (it was advertised as a "moral drama" or "moral lecture"), it inevitably converted this message into popular entertainment. On occasion the famous "delirium scene," in which Middleton, writhing on the floor, fights off imaginary snakes, was even performed on its own. This popular play did enrich its author, but only because W. H. Smith, a British actor who had emigrated to the United States in 1827, was manager of the Boston Museum, where *The Drunkard* had its first great success.

The same combination of didactic intention and popular spectacle lay behind the most extraordinary and long-lasting of all nineteenth-century theatrical phenomena: the many adaptations of Harriet Beecher Stowe's *Uncle Tom's Cabin* that swept the United States from 1852 until well into the twentieth century. The first version to succeed was commissioned by G. C. Howard, manager of the Troy, New York, Museum, who wanted to feature his four-year-old daughter, Cordelia (one is really not making this up), as Little Eva. Howard, who played Augustine St. Clare, and his wife, who played Topsy, had met while performing together in the original Boston production of *The Drunkard.* Their version of *Uncle Tom's Cabin* was written by George L. Aiken, Howard's cousin, who played the part of George Harris and who received forty dollars and a gold watch for his adaptation. This Troy production was apparently seen by 25,000 people (the total population of Troy was 30,000) before moving on to New York City, and the Howard family continued performing the play until 1887, when G. C.

Howard died and when Cordelia, famous as Little Eva since the age of four, celebrated her thirty-fifth birthday.

Aiken's version of *Uncle Tom's Cabin,* which Stowe saw performed in Boston, is fairly faithful to the novel; indeed, much of the dialogue is simply lifted from the book. But Aiken included such bits of stage spectacle as Eliza crossing the Ohio on a moving block of ice, and subsequent dramatizations exploited spectacle on a much grander scale. Soon Eliza was crossing the ice pursued by real dogs, and Uncle Tom, at the close, was ascending skyward in a golden carriage, one that actually moved upstage (if the machinery was working), while the gates of heaven opened to reveal St. Clare and Eva, surrounded by angels, smiling down from golden clouds. Also, more and more elements from minstrel shows were entering into the performances and into the characterization of Tom, making the phrase "Uncle Tom" synonymous, as it had never been for Stowe, with obsequious black servility to whites. By the end of the century "Tom Shows" were available on a regular basis almost everywhere in the United States, but Stowe had never earned a penny from stage versions of her novel. Nor was her abolitionist message of much importance in the post-Reconstruction era, when "Jim Crow," first given currency by the stage, had become the label for the South's new set of repressive segregation laws. Message, as usual, had given way to crude entertainment.

Once again, none of this had much to do with literature, and no one claimed otherwise. After 1850, the efforts of such people as the actor-manager-playwright Dion Boucicault (1820–90) began to professionalize playwriting, but it would be a good deal longer before a play written by an American achieved anything close to literary distinction. The main importance of American drama for pre–Civil War American literature probably derives from its development and popularization of a number of stock characters, mainly comic stereotypes. There was the stage Yankee, who had first appeared as "Jonathan" in Royall Tyler's *The Contrast* in 1787. There was the Western boaster: for instance, Nimrod Wildfire in Paulding's *The Lion of the West* (1831). There were stage Irishmen and stage Germans and an urban variant of the rural yokel, named "Mose the Fireboy," who made his first appearance on the New York stage in 1848. There was the ubiquitous, racist stereotype of the shuffling, comic "darky," beginning with "Jim Crow" and minstrelsy but by no means confined to these formats.

It is harder to trace the influence of more "serious" pre–Civil War plays on American literature, since these plays are themselves so utterly derivative. But we might recall that a number of chapters in *Moby-Dick* are written in dramatic form and that the extraordinary impact of Shakespeare on Melville in the years immediately preceding *Moby-Dick* was undoubtedly at least partly mediated by performances of Shakespeare on the American stage, and by performances of such pseudo-Shakespearian "tragedies" as *Metamora* and *The Gladiator.* This is not to say that Melville's Ahab has very much in common with Stone's Metamora or Bird's Spartacus, beyond a love for ranting; unlike them he is a victim less of cruel external circumstance (white perfidy, Roman power) than of his own overweening conceptions of self and freedom. The deeper affinity is between Ahab and an actor like Edwin Forrest, between Ahab's monomania and the self-absorbed, "democratic" paranoia of the star who—as Metamora or Spartacus, as Macbeth or Lear—held American audiences in the palm of his hand. This is not to argue that Ahab was consciously based on Forrest but only that if the kind of magnetic power Forrest exercised over his audiences made its way anywhere into what we now regard as American literature, it was surely in Melville's portrayal of the charismatic captain of the *Pequod.*

Magazines

American magazine publishing, like book publishing and theatrical production, expanded dramatically from the 1820s to the 1840s. At the beginning of this period the situation was much as it had been for the previous quarter century. In 1794 a new Postal Act had admitted magazines to the mails at a reduced rate ("when the mode of conveyance and the size of the mails will permit of it"), a privilege until then granted only to newspapers. The immediate result—as Frank Luther Mott describes it in his *History of American Magazines, 1741–1850* (1930), still the fullest account of this subject—was a flurry of new periodicals; seven were launched in 1795, and there were usually more than ten new entries a year thereafter. The number of magazines in the United States rose from five in 1794 to almost one hundred by 1825.

The success of these ventures, however, was at best tenuous. The typical American magazine before 1825 failed in less than two years (often in considerably less than two years), and the reasons for this ephemerality are quite clear. Circulation was local, usually confined to the city in which a magazine was published, and it was extremely limited. Joseph Dennie's *Port Folio,* a weekly published in Philadelphia, was the most successful American periodical before the 1820s; in 1811 it became the first American magazine to survive for a decade. Yet it had only 2,000 subscribers in 1801 (each of them charged $5.00 a year), and at the time even a circulation of 2,000 was extraordinary. Closer to the norm were the sales of Boston's *Monthly Anthology* (440 subscribers in 1805) and of its successor, the *North American Review* (between 500 and 600 subscribers in 1820). There were no literary magazines aimed at mass or lower-class audiences. Moreover, subscribers were chronically delinquent in their payments. Thus neither editors nor authors could expect much remuneration for their efforts. The income of editors was usually tied to prospects of commercial success, which were seldom if ever realized, and it was not until 1819 that an American magazine (New Haven's *Christian Spectator*) proposed to pay contributors (at the rate of $1.00 per printed page).

Nevertheless, new literary magazines *were* launched in increasing numbers between 1795 and 1825, often to provide an outlet for local pride or talent—as in the case, for instance, of Baltimore's short-lived *Portico* magazine (1816–18), in which John Neal got his start. There was also the oft-expressed desire to counter British aspersions, especially following the War of 1812, on the intellectual capacity of the new American nation (even as magazines proclaiming their nationalism relied heavily on reprinted selections from British and European journals). As time passed, magazines began to target specific audiences: religious groups, farmers, physicians, children, women (although the great age of "ladies' magazines" was still in the future). The contents of American literary periodicals also changed. Political controversy, often vicious and scurrilous, gave way gradually to belles lettres, as fiction, poetry, and literary reviews began to overtake the periodical essay as the dominant forms of magazine writing. Although literary periodicals were notoriously short-lived, they were continuously replaced, often with more or less the same personnel, and not all of them failed. Boston's *North American Review*—founded in 1815 in imitation of the great British quarterlies and drawing on the resources of Harvard and of a local elite seriously devoted to culture—became a truly national journal in the 1820s and remained influential, even with a limited circulation, throughout the nineteenth century.

The intellectual and cultural ambitions of the *North American Review* would become increasingly anomalous as America entered its first great age of popular magazines in the late 1820s. Far more characteristic of future trends was the *New York Mirror,* a weekly founded in 1823 by George Pope Morris and Samuel Woodworth (the latter of whom would achieve fame, but not fortune, as author of the popular stage musical *The Forest Rose*). Woodworth soon dropped out of the business, leaving Morris to run the *Mirror,* in various incarnations, for twenty-one years, assisted in his editorial efforts by such writers as Theodore Sedgwick Fay and especially Nathaniel Parker Willis. The *Mirror* avoided overt discussion of politics, idolized Sir Walter Scott, cultivated gentle humor and sentiment in the manner of Washington Irving, and announced in its first number its ambition to appeal "to the LADIES, in particular." In fact from 1823 to 1831 it was subtitled, in part, the *Ladies' Literary Gazette,* and it featured both works by women writers and articles on such "feminine" topics as fashion and female education. Also, as early as 1824 Morris was using prize competitions to attract contributors, an innovation soon widely imitated. Boston's *North American Review,* holding to the intellectual seriousness of the early 1800s, survived, and its example helped spawn such later quarterlies as Philadelphia's *American Quarterly Review* (1827–37) and the *New York Review* (1837–42). But the *Mirror,* launched in New York in the 1820s with the intention of expanding circulation by *entertaining* its readers, was the truer harbinger of things to come.

Between 1825 and 1850, according to Mott's estimate, the number of magazines published in the United States rose from less than one hundred to something like six hundred; and although failure remained the norm, a growing number of these ventures achieved enduring commercial success and circulations unheard of earlier. Subscriber delinquency was still notorious; when, for example, Timothy Flint's *Western Monthly Review* (founded in 1827) failed in 1830, it was owed about some $3,000 in back payments. Nor were other problems immediately solved. A new regulation of 1825 fixed postal rates for magazines at one and a half to two and a half cents per sheet—well above the rate for newspapers (one to one and a half per *issue*). As a result, editors sought alternative means of shipping their products or sought to present these products as newspapers in order to reduce postal costs. On the positive side, inland transportation was improving rapidly—in 1825, for instance, the Erie Canal was completed—and, what may be most important, an increasing number of native writers were available to produce magazine material. The contents of a typical magazine at the beginning of the century were written mainly by the editor or his friends or reprinted from British journals. By the 1830s a growing group of known and unknown Americans was eager to appear in print, and in the 1840s some magazines began to stimulate productivity by offering liberal compensation, at least to writers with bankable public reputations. Readers were further enticed with woodcut and copperplate illustrations. The practice of using advertising for income, fundamental to modern magazine publishing, was still in its infancy.

Some of the most important literary "magazinists" (as they came to be called) got their starts in Boston. In 1829 Nathaniel Parker Willis founded the *American Monthly Magazine,* which launched the magazine career of Park Benjamin. Two years later Joseph T. Buckingham (editor of a Whig newspaper, the *Boston Courier*) founded the *New-England Magazine,* whose contents (compensated at the handsome rate, for 1831, of $1.00 a page) included works by Henry Wadsworth Longfellow, Oliver Wendell Holmes, John Greenleaf Whittier, and Nathaniel Hawthorne (who placed fifteen stories in this journal). Neither of these periodicals lasted long however. Boston literary society was not amused by Willis's flippant irreverence (or by the dandified personal style he affected), and in 1831, having failed to achieve the success he sought, Willis sold his subscription list to George Pope Morris, moved to New York to serve as assistant editor of Morris's *Mirror,* and went on to become one of the most popular writers of the age. The *New-England Magazine* survived only until 1835, and Park Benjamin, after a stint as its editor in 1835, followed Willis and the action to New York, joining the *American Monthly Magazine* (which soon absorbed the *New-England Magazine*).

Later Boston literary magazines were for the most part equally short-lived. The Transcendentalists' *Dial,* founded in 1840 and edited first by Margaret Fuller and then by Ralph Waldo Emerson, collapsed in 1844, and its circulation never exceeded three hundred. James Russell Lowell's *Pioneer,* founded in 1843 and including contributions of high quality (Hawthorne's "The Birthmark," for example), failed after only three issues. Boston's oldest equivalent to an enduring popular magazine was a giftbook, or "keepsake," called *The Token,* an annual collection of tales, verse, and illustrations aimed quite overtly at women readers, founded in 1827 and edited by Samuel Goodrich. There were many such annuals in America, forerunners of the popular "ladies' magazines." Perhaps the principal interest of *The Token* now is that it published many tales by Nathaniel Hawthorne (always anonymously) in the early 1830s. It was not until 1857, with the founding of the *Atlantic Monthly,* that Boston acquired an important and enduring popular literary magazine; until then, ambitious New England magazinists had to seek their success elsewhere.

Two of the most successful literary magazines of the 1840s were published in Philadelphia. One of these had its beginnings in 1826 when Samuel C. Atkinson and Charles Alexander (also founders of the *Saturday Evening Post* in 1821) launched the *Casket: Flowers of Literature, Wit and Sentiment.* The *Casket* was bought by George R. Graham in 1839, who merged it with *Burton's Gentleman's Magazine* a year later to form *Graham's Magazine*. Short fiction, poetry, essays, biography, travel sketches, and literary reviews were solicited from a list of contributors including William Bryant, James Cooper, James Paulding, James Lowell, Lydia Sigourney (the widely popular "Sweet Singer of Hartford"), Henry Longfellow, Nathaniel Willis, and Edgar Allan Poe. Poe served as literary editor for fifteen months in 1841 and 1842. He was succeeded by Rufus Wilmot Griswold, another transplanted New Englander, now infamous as Poe's hostile literary executor and biographer and throughout the period as an influential literary editor. In 1842 Graham launched his policy (which he took pains to publicize) of offering liberal payments to well-known authors: up to $50 a poem to Longfellow, $11 a page to Willis and $1,000 to Cooper for a series of biographies of naval commanders. Poe, less of a draw, received from $4 to $5 a page, and in 1842, Hawthorne was offered $5 a page. Griswold was paid $1,000 a year for his editorial services. In the late 1840s Graham encountered serious financial difficulties, brought on by bad outside investments, and he was forced to sell out his interest in 1853. *Graham's Magazine* had by then in any case lost much of its original popularity, but in the early 1840s its success was nothing short of astonishing. In its first year circulation increased from 5,500 to 25,000 (at a standard subscription rate of $3 a year), and Graham was soon able to claim 40,000 subscribers. The *North American Review*, in the same period, had managed to achieve a fairly stable circulation of 3,000.

Graham's most successful Philadelphia rival was Louis A. Godey. During the Panic of 1837 Godey purchased the *Ladies' Magazine*, founded in Boston in 1828 by Sarah Josepha Hale, and hired Hale as literary editor of its Philadelphia successor, *Godey's Lady's Book*. *Godey's* contents consisted mainly of verse, short fiction, travel sketches, and book reviews (but no discussions of politics) by such writers as Sigourney, Catharine Sedgwick, Willis, Harriet Stowe, Paulding, Ralph Emerson, Longfellow, Oliver Holmes, Hawthorne, and Poe. But the hallmarks of the magazine were fashion plates, watercolored by hand, and copperplate engravings of famous or original works of art, and it included recipes, essays on fashion, domestic advice, and other "women's" features. Godey also soon adopted Graham's policy of paying top rates to the most popular writers (but nothing to unknowns), and his successes more than matched Graham's. By 1839 he was predicting a circulation of 25,000 (also at $3 a year). By 1850 he had amassed a list of 50,000 subscribers, and the figure rose to 150,000 before the Civil War. The success of *Godey's* spawned a host of imitators—most notably *Peterson's Lady's Magazine,* founded in Philadelphia in 1842—and it also had a pronounced influence on the content and format of many more general literary magazines, for whom it identified both a large audience and a set of strategies for winning and holding this audience's allegiance.

New York, in the meantime, was making its own innovations in the business of magazine publication. These innovations involved not the promotion of native writers but the blatant piracy of their British contemporaries. Such piracy had always been a staple of American magazines. In 1836 Horace Greeley, who would found the *New York Tribune* in 1841, started the *New-Yorker,* whose contents consisted mainly of reprinted (and uncompensated) foreign literature, and the title of Willis's *Corsair* (1839–40) revealed his purposes quite clearly; in fact he originally planned to call it, even more frankly, the *Pirate.* In New York in the late 1830s and early 1840s, literary piracy was undertaken on a new scale—a scale that briefly threatened to bring the fledgling book-publishing industry to its knees.

The story begins in 1839, when Park Benjamin and Rufus Griswold founded *Brother Jonathan.* They called it a newspaper to secure low postal rates, and its large-page format aided the deception, but its contents consisted almost entirely of serials of pirated British novels. When Benjamin and Griswold lost control of *Brother Jonathan* in 1840, they immediately founded a nearly-identical rival, the *New World.* These journals and their imitators were soon dubbed "Mammoth Weeklies." There was still the problem, however, that full copies of the novels these Mammoths were pirating were available from book publishers long before the serials had run their courses, and readers were willing to pay the higher book price for a full novel. So in 1841 the *New World* inaugurated a new technique: it began issuing complete novels as "extras"—still in large-page, multicolumn format, still distributed as newspapers, and selling for fifty cents an issue. *Brother Jonathan* and others immediately followed suit, competition rapidly drove the price down as low as six cents, and book publishers were forced to slash their own prices. By 1843 the market was becoming glutted; even the *New World* and *Brother Jonathan* were feeling the pinch of low prices. Then, in April, the Post Office ruled that the Mammoths could no longer enter the mails at newspaper rates, bringing this curious episode to a close. *Brother Jonathan* sold out to the *New World* early in 1844, and the *New World* itself folded a year later, but the effects of the episode were long-lasting. Although competition and price-cutting were brought under control, the standard price charged by book publishers for a novel, previously one to two dollars, now stabilized at fifty cents. It was this change, as has already been noted, that forced Cooper and others into overproduction in the 1840s.

New York also had its share of more conventional literary magazines. Foremost among them (along with the *Mirror,* which continued to appear throughout the period) was the *Knickerbocker Magazine,* founded in 1833. It was edited, in brief succession, by Charles Fenno Hoffman, S. D. Langtree, and Timothy Flint, but it achieved stability only in 1834, when it was purchased by Clement Edson and Lewis Gaylord Clark, with Clark serving as editor through the 1850s. The magazines' affection for Irving was indicated frankly by its title, and from 1839 to 1841 Irving himself served as a regular contributor at a munificent salary of $2,000 a year. Other contributors included Cooper, Bryant, Paulding, Hoffman, Willis, Benjamin, Longfellow, Whittier, Holmes, and Hawthorne. What distinguished the magazine, however, were its self-styled Rabelaisian humor and Clark's opinionated "Editor's Table," a standard feature of every issue. By 1837 circulation had increased (at a subscription rate of $5 a year) from something like 500 to more than 5,000.

The *Knickerbocker* never approached the commercial success of *Graham's* or *Godey's,* but it was influential nonetheless, and it came to play an important part in the so-called literary wars that erupted in New York in the 1840s. On one side were Clark's *Knickerbocker* and Morris's *Mirror,* which were Whig in politics and urbane and cosmopolitan (which is to say generally Anglophile) in their literary sentiments; it was not irrelevant that the *Knickerbocker* took its name from Irving. On the other side was a group of writers and editors loosely allied under the rubric Young America, including such figures as Cornelius Mathews, William A. Jones, and the brothers Evert and George Duyckinck—and, more peripherally or briefly, William Gilmore Simms, Edgar Allan Poe, and Herman Melville. Young America was generally Democratic in politics, nationalistic in literature, and committed among other things to the search for an original "American Genius" (which Clark and his circle ridiculed) and the battle for an international copyright law (which Clark and his circle opposed).

More will be said shortly about these literary wars of the 1840s; what needs to be noted here is that Young America also conducted its campaigns in magazines. Mathews and Evert Duyckinck edited *Arcturus* from 1840 until it failed in 1842, this failure resulting largely from their serialization of Mathews's incoherent satirical novel *The Career of Puffer Hopkins,* which Clark lambasted with gusto in the *Knickerbocker. Arcturus* also printed contributions from such writers as Hawthorne, Longfellow, and Lowell. Young America received some support (and space) in John Louis O'Sullivan's *United States Magazine and Democratic Review*, founded in Washington in 1837 and moved to New York in 1840 when the Whigs won the national election. O'Sullivan was a close friend of Hawthorne (he was the godfather of the Hawthornes' first daughter, Una), and many of Hawthorne's tales appeared in the *Democratic Review*. Charles Frederick Briggs, the founder of the *Broadway Journal* in 1845, was a Whig, but Poe soon forced Briggs out and devoted the *Broadway Journal* to his ongoing attacks on Longfellow's alleged plagiarisms and more generally on the supposed imitative Britishism of literary Boston. From 1847 to 1853, the *Literary World* provided another outlet for Young America's literary opinions (and its attacks on Clark and the *Knickerbocker*), especially after 1848, when the magazine was purchased by Evert and George Duyckinck. Evert Duyckinck was among Melville's first literary mentors, until *Moby-Dick* cooled his enthusiasm. Melville's nationalistic appreciation of Hawthorne, "Hawthorne and His *Mosses*" (1850), was published in the *Literary World*.

There were also influential literary magazines in other centers, in the South and West. The most notable was the *Southern Literary Messenger*, founded in Richmond, Virginia, in 1834 by Thomas W. White and now best known because Edgar Allan Poe was a frequent contributor and served as assistant editor from 1835 to 1837 (at a salary of $15 a week). Other journals sought like the *Messenger* to tap the cultural pride of specific regions, but northern cities—Boston and especially New York and Philadelphia— clearly dominated magazine publishing in the 1830s and 1840s. Even within the southern market, for instance, the *Messenger* never matched the sales of its northern rivals, and its total circulation never greatly exceeded 4,000 (at a subscription rate of $5 a year). In any case, major magazines did not, for the most part, confine themselves to local contributors, or even to local editors. The same names kept appearing in the contents pages of magazines from Boston, New York, Philadelphia, Richmond, and elsewhere: such figures as Bryant, Sedgwick, Hawthorne, Lowell, Longfellow, and, above all, N. P. Willis and Lydia Sigourney, the last claiming to have placed her work in as many as three hundred American journals.

Boston may have had no enduring popular literary magazine before 1857, but contributions by Boston authors had by the 1840s become staples of the magazines published elsewhere, and a significant number of the period's most influential magazinists (Sarah Hale and Willis, for example) had emigrated from Boston. Among editors, some had decidedly local identities (for instance, Lewis Gaylord Clark), but more had strikingly peripatetic careers. Poe edited magazines in Richmond, Philadelphia, and New York, and Griswold was active in both New York and Philadelphia. The homogeneity of American literary magazines is not surprising. These magazines were competing for the same national reading public—still not so much a "mass" readership as an audience of educated, middle-class readers, often women—wherever they lived in the United States. Editors inevitably sought to woo this audience with the kinds of writing that had brought success to other magazines, more often than not with the same writers.

The influence of the rise of magazines on the development of American literature in the second quarter of the nineteenth century can scarcely be exaggerated. Cooper and Irving achieved fame in the 1820s as authors of books, but by the 1840s new native writers were far more likely to appear first in magazines. Such magazines as *Graham's* and *Godey's,* with circulations of 40,000 to 50,000, reached a far broader public than Irving and Cooper could have dreamed of only two decades earlier. It would not be until the late 1840s and early 1850s that publishers of books by native authors would begin to capture this audience. In the meantime the most popular and successful American books of fiction tended increasingly to be works by writers who had won their fame in the magazines, and more than a few of these books simply reprinted material that had already appeared in magazines. More and more the tastes of magazine readers—for gentle humor, sentiment, and light entertainment—were coming to determine the kinds of literature that appeared in books, and many of the most successful magazine writers seldom even bothered to reissue their writings in book form. The Mammoth Weeklies had generated sales of up to 30,000 copies by reprinting book-length novels, but the most significant trend of the 1840s was in precisely the opposite direction. Writers of novels and story collections were imitating the literature of the magazines, where the most successful of these writers, in an era of fallen book prices, were earning the bulk of their literary incomes.

Fiction in the 1830s and 1840s

Magazines, Mammoth Weeklies, and the aftermath of the Panic of 1837 radically transformed both the American literary marketplace and the nature of American fiction in the 1840s. In the 1830s there were some indications of the coming changes, but the decade's most obvious trends were not transitional but conservative, even reactionary. This is especially true of the emergence in the 1830s of what one might call the "school of Cooper," as American novelists and publishers, encouraged by Cooper's success, attempted to exploit the presumed market for regional historical novels. By the mid-1830s, the most prolific American historical novelists were almost exclusively male, and they were supported by the most influential publishing houses. American historical fiction was only a decade old, but new writers and established publishers seemed to assume that the mode of Cooper was the appropriate, even the inevitable, fictional expression of national character and serious literary vocation.

The most important and professionally consistent of these new writers was William Gilmore Simms of South Carolina, but Simms had a good deal of literary company. Henry William Herbert (1807–58), a British-born writer who would achieve his greatest fame writing on field sports under the pseudonym Frank Forrester, published the first of his many historical romances, *The Brothers, a Tale of the Fronde*, in 1835. Boston's John Lothrop Motley (1814–77), who would become famous as a historian in 1856 with *The Rise of the Dutch Republic,* wrote two New England historical romances in the late 1830s: *Morton's Hope* (1839) and *Merry-Mount* (which was not published until 1849). New Yorker Charles Fenno Hoffman (1806–84), the brother of Washington Irving's fiancée Matilda, achieved considerable success in 1840 with *Greyslaer: A Romance of the Mohawk,* but his literary activities, like Paulding's, were rather miscellaneous (including satire, travel letters, verse, and the editing of newspapers and magazines in New York), and they were cut short by the onset of mental illness in 1849. Vermont's history entered American literature in 1839 when Daniel Pierce Thompson (1795–1868) published *The Green Mountain Boys,* which had gone through fifty editions by 1860. Although Thompson continued to produce works of historical fiction, he never again matched this initial success.

Robert Montgomery Bird (1806–54) turned from drama to historical fiction when Edwin Forrest refused to share the enormous profits he was making from performances of *The Gladiator* (1831). Bird's first historical novel, *Calavar,* deals with Cortéz's sixteenth-century exploitation of Mexico; it was published in 1834 by Philadelphia's House of Carey (doing well, at the time, with Cooper's historical fiction), and it was still being reprinted in the 1840s. In 1835 Bird published *The Infidel,* another Mexican historical romance, and *The Hawks of Hawk-Hollow,* set in the Delaware Valley of Pennsylvania at the end of the American Revolution. Bird's most interesting historical novel, *Nick of the Woods; or, the Jibbenainosay. A Tale of Kentucky,* was published in 1837 (still by Carey). Overtly dissenting from Cooper's vision of the nobility of American Indians (and perhaps more personally from Forrest's endless successes with John A. Stone's *Metamora*), *Nick of the Woods* is dominated by the character Nathan Slaughter, a mild Quaker by day who secretly and brutally kills Indians by night, more or less at random, to avenge the family he lost to an Indian massacre. This novel achieved considerable success, and Bird published two more books (a collection of Mississippi River sketches and a picaresque novel) in 1838 and 1839, but his health collapsed in 1840, prematurely ending his literary career.

The 1830s also saw the belated entry of the South into the annals of American historical fiction. William Alexander Caruthers (1802–46) (whose contemporary epistolary novel *The Kentuckian in New York* had appeared in 1834) published *The Cavaliers of Virginia*, a historical novel about Bacon's Rebellion, in 1835, and a second historical work, *The Knights of the Horseshoe*, in 1845. Nathaniel Beverly Tucker (1784–1851) published both *George Balcombe* and *The Partisan Leader: A Tale of the Future* in 1836. The first of these, a regular historical romance, was issued by the Harpers in New York. The second, a fantasy of the future of the South, supposedly from the vantage point of 1856, was published in Washington; it was clearly not aimed at a national audience. A third Tucker novel, *Gertrude*, was serialized in the *Southern Literary Messenger* in 1844–45. But the most important of the new southern historical novelists were John Pendleton Kennedy and especially William Gilmore Simms.

That this first literary "southern renaissance" was belated is hardly surprising; the South had no publishing centers on the scale of New York or Philadelphia. And it may be a bit misleading to describe this belated outpouring of historical fiction as a southern renaissance at all. There can be no doubt that the economic, political, cultural, and intellectual traditions of the South were significantly different from those of the North, but (with the exception of purely sectional works like Tucker's *Partisan Leader*) these differences did not manifest themselves all that notably in the production and distribution of southern historical fiction in the 1830s. Even in the South, we recall, the circulation of regular literary magazines was far surpassed by national journals produced in the North, and Simms and Kennedy more or less automatically turned to northern book publishers in their pursuit of a national audience.

What matters here is not simply that the South did not control its own literary market, although this does matter; more important is the fact that southerners like Simms and Kennedy conceived of their audience in national, not regional, terms. Although their novels deal with the customs and history of the South, such regionalism was after all the dominant quality of most historical fiction in the 1830s—at least the fiction inspired by the example of Cooper. The careers of Simms and Kennedy were in any case by no means harbingers of secession, of southern cultural separatism; they were, rather, expressions of a nationalism (at once political and literary) that fell apart in the 1840s as sectional conflict loomed larger and as the example of Cooper became increasingly irrelevant to the realities of the literary marketplace. Kennedy and Simms ended up taking different sides on the issue of secession, but the approach of civil war affected both of them in much the same way. It destroyed the assumptions upon which they, and many of their southern contemporaries, had undertaken the vocation of literature.

John Pendleton Kennedy (1795–1870), the son of a prominent Baltimore merchant who moved his family to Virginia when his business failed, began practicing law in Baltimore in 1816, but he gradually turned to literature and politics. *Swallow Barn,* a volume of fond sketches of Virginia life published (as were all of Kennedy's works) by the House of Carey, appeared in 1832. *Horse-Shoe Robinson,* a historical romance of the Revolution in Virginia and the Carolinas, appeared in 1835 and was compared favorably to the work of Cooper. *Rob of the Bowl* (1838), set in colonial Maryland, was less popular; the Panic of 1837 was having its effect on literary sales. In any case, Kennedy, who was elected to Congress in 1838, was becoming increasingly involved in Whig politics. *Rob of the Bowl* was his last work of historical fiction; his subsequent writings were mainly political and polemical. Moreover, as Simm's career would demonstrate more clearly, the growing crisis over slavery was beginning to make untenable the position of the white southern writer who wished to appeal to a national audience through northern publishing centers while remaining loyal to his or her native region. In the 1850s Kennedy, whose ideals in both literature and politics had always been national, took the Union side in the sectional conflict; he opposed secession in 1860 and voted for Lincoln in 1864. After the war, however, he advocated conciliatory treatment of the South by the North. He died in Newport, Rhode Island, in 1870 and was buried in Baltimore.

Cooper's most successful rival among his American contemporaries was also the most successful southern writer before the Civil War. William Gilmore Simms (1806–70) was widely read and widely praised. For example, in 1844, Poe declared that although "Mr. Simms has abundant faults. . . . Nevertheless, leaving out of question Brockden Brown and Hawthorne, (who are each a *genus* [*sic*],) he is immeasurably the best writer of fiction in America. He has more vigor, more imagination, more movement and more general capacity than all our novelists (save Cooper,) combined." Simms was also, as the conditions of the literary marketplace increasingly demanded, extraordinarily productive. During his long career he published eighty-two volumes of poetry, fiction, and nonfiction, including thirty-four novels or story collections. At the same time he contributed regularly to periodicals, was actively involved in politics, and edited a number of newspapers and magazines.

Although it has become a commonplace of literary history that Simms turned to writing to overcome his supposed exclusion as an impoverished outsider from the patrician society of Charleston, South Carolina, there is abundant evidence that Simms was in fact, and not just in aspiration, at home in the plantation-based aristocracy of his native region. In any case, insider or outsider, his early years were clearly traumatic enough to help explain the single-mindedness of his later dedication to literature. When he was only two years old, his mother died in childbirth and his distraught father departed for the Southwest, leaving Simms in the care of his maternal grandmother. Eight years later his father's attempt to regain custody ended up in the courts, and when the decision was left to the ten-year-old boy, he chose (and one assumes the choice was painful) to stay with his grandmother. Simms would later recall his childhood as a time of mourning and isolation, which he relieved as best he could through voracious reading. By the age of sixteen he was publishing verse in the Charleston papers, and in 1825, after a year traveling with his father on the Southwest frontier of Mississippi, Alabama, and Louisiana, he returned to Charleston to combine literary activities with the study of law. He was married in 1826, at the age of twenty, and admitted to the bar a year later.

Literature, however, soon won out over the law. Simms published five volumes of poetry in Charleston, was coeditor of the *Southern Literary Gazette* in 1828–29, and in 1830 purchased a Jacksonian daily newspaper, the *Charleston City Gazette,* in whose pages he vigorously supported the Union side in the virulent Nullification controversy. This stand cost him subscribers, and in 1832, after the death of his wife (leaving Simms with the care of their daughter), he sold the paper at a loss and left Charleston with a packet of unpublished literary manuscripts to seek his literary fortunes in the North, ending up in New York. Here his *Atlantis: A Story of the Sea,* a long poem published in 1832 by the Harpers, was a great success. He was back in New York in the summer of 1833, and from then on, until the Civil War intervened, he normally spent his summers in the North, where he was very much a part of the New York literary scene, and the rest of the year in the South.

The Harpers brought out *Martin Faber,* a crime novella and Simm's first published volume of fiction, in 1833, and the edition was exhausted in four days. *Guy Rivers,* set on the Georgia frontier, appeared in 1834 and was hugely successful; a second edition was required by the end of the year, the book was reprinted in London in 1835, and reviews were almost universally favorable. Although his subject matter was southern, Simms was by now in every other respect a national writer. In 1835, at what would turn out to have been the peak of his career, he published two historical romances. *The Yemassee: A Romance of Carolina* dealing with the destruction of an Indian tribe by white civilization in the early eighteenth century and was a literary sensation. The first edition of 2,500 copies were sold in three days, there were two more editions in 1835, and the book was reprinted and praised in England. American reviews were laudatory, and in the *New-England Magazine,* Park Benjamin, himself on the point of departing for New York, went so far as to declare that "the Yemassee is superior, in plot, style, and execution, to the Last of the Mohicans." In the fall of the same year Simms published *The Partisan*—the first of a series of seven romances of the Revolution on the Carolina frontier that would ultimately come to include *Mellichampe* (1836), *The Kinsmen* (1841, later renamed *The Scout*), *Katharine Walton* (1851), *The Sword and the Distaff* (1852, later renamed *Woodcraft*), *The Forayers* (1855), and *Eutaw* (1856). In 1835 Simm's earnings from his writing amounted to $6,000, a figure nearly equal to Cooper's average of $6,500 a year in the heyday of the 1820s.

After 1835 Simm's productivity seldom slackened (and hurried composition left its mark on all his works), but circumstances were becoming more complex and less auspicious. The Harpers were especially hard hit by the Panic of 1837; they were reluctant to risk new ventures and even had difficulty paying Simms any of the $1,300 he was owed on account. So in 1838, with *Richard Hurdis; or the Avenger of Blood,* Simms moved to Philadelphia's House of Carey, which—with Cooper, Bird, Kennedy, and now Simms on its list of native novelists—was gaining clear dominance in American fiction. Still, the economic instability of the literary marketplace continued, and the drop in prices fueled by competition and the Mammoth Weeklies drove even Simms, for a time, from the novel. In the 1840s he turned to biography, criticism, and tales for magazines and annuals. This move did not necessarily indicate a decline in popularity—in terms of sales the most popular of all his works was a biography of the Carolina revolutionary hero Francis Marion, published in 1844—but increased sales, as we have already seen, no longer translated into increased earnings or even sustained earnings. "My income from Literature," Simms lamented in 1847, "which in 1835 was $6000 per annum, is scarce $1500 now, owing to the operation of cheap reprints which pay publishers and printers profits only & yield the author little or nothing."

Cheap reprints were hardly Simm's only problem. In New York he became embroiled in the literary wars between Young America and the Whig writers gathered around Lewis Gaylord Clark's *Knickerbocker* magazine and George Pope Morris and N. P. Willis's *Mirror.* In the late 1830s, for reasons now somewhat obscure, Simms and Clark became enemies, and Simm's Democratic politics and his nationalistic stance in his critical writings—some of which were later collected as *Views and Reviews in American Literature, History and Fiction* (1846, 1847)—naturally allied him with Young America. The members and allies of this group defended him, hence Poe's lavish praise in 1844, in John Louis O'Sullivan's *United States Magazine and Democratic Review.* But from 1838 on, the attacks in Whig papers and journals became increasingly vicious.

In 1836 Simms married again and thenceforth made his southern home at Woodlands, his father-in-law's plantation seventy miles inland from Charleston. By the late 1840s, with sectional controversy on the rise and Young America in growing disarray, he was identifying himself more and more as a specifically southern writer, in opposition to the politics and literary culture of the North. In the presidential election of 1848 he broke with the Democratic Party to support the Whig candidate, Mexican War hero General Zachary Taylor, a slaveowner from Louisiana. He returned to historical fiction in 1850, when *Katharine Walton* (published in book form in 1851) was serialized, but by the 1850s the old Scott-derived formulas of historical romance—placing a genteel love story against the backdrop of historical events and legends—had become something of an anachronism. In any event, the intersection of regional and national interests that had made Simms's success possible in the 1830s had long since collapsed under the weight of political and literary controversy. His historical fiction was no longer a regional component of a national enterprise; it was rather a partisan defense of his native land against its enemies. Although Simms was still visiting New York in 1856, he was now there to lecture in defense of slavery, and he vigorously supported secession in 1860. In 1866, when he returned to New York in the aftermath of the war, he was welcomed by his friends, but his efforts to revive his northern publishing connections proved unsuccessful. He died four years later in Charleston.

Although serious historical and regional fiction in the mode of Scott and Cooper dominated American book publishing in the 1830s, its dominance was by no means uncontested. For instance, a few women writers were following the example of Catharine Sedgwick's domestic fiction—and in the process laying the groundwork for the extraordinary outpouring of best-sellers written by and for women that would distinguish the early 1850s. These women wrote in the context of the reigning ideology now referred to as the Cult of True Womanhood or the Cult of Domesticity. A woman, for instance, was not to concern herself with politics; "woman's sphere" (to use a phrase in wide circulation during this period) was the home, and a woman was to work through loving and submissive influence, not worldly ambition. The Cult of Domesticity confronted aspiring women authors with a profound and potentially unsettling problem, for was not the pursuit of literary fame a form of "unfeminine" ambition? "There is a delicacy . . .," wrote Nathaniel Hawthorne in an 1830 discussion of women writers, "that perceives, or fancies, a sort of impropriety in the display of woman's natal mind to the gaze of the world . . .; and woman, when she feels the impulse of genius like a command of Heaven within her, should be aware that she is relinquishing a part of the loveliness of her sex, and obey the inward voice with sorrowing reluctance."

Hawthorne had obvious reasons for wishing to discourage authors with whom he was in direct competition, but what matters is that in pre–Civil War America such sentiments were widely shared, even and perhaps especially by literary women. Sarah Josepha Hale, soon to become one of the most influential literary women of her era, insisted in 1829 that "the path of poetry, like every other path in life, is to the tread of woman, exceedingly circumscribed. She may not revel in the luxuriance of fancies, images and thoughts, or indulge in the license of choosing themes at will, like the Lords of creation." Few women writers openly or even privately contested this assumption. Catharine Sedgwick wrote in her journal in 1835, at the height of her fame, that her "*author's* existence always seemed something accidental." Thus could a successful woman neutralize guilt about inappropriate ambition by denying ambition altogether (even overt literary intention), and many women writers adopted this rationale. Many also published anonymously or adopted euphonious pseudonyms. Moreover, many women turned to literature as a profession only when their husbands or fathers died or became incapable of providing necessary support. Such women were not forsaking but fulfilling their domestic duties by writing; they had to feed their families. And if woman's proper sphere was the home, women writers could make the home, the domestic lives of women, their subject. After all, this subject was the familiar experience of the great majority of the American reading public for fiction, women to whom Natty

Bumppo and Chingachgook were bound eventually to become a bit tiresome. In any case, the body of assumptions underlying the Cult of True Womanhood determined both the public stance of many American women writers and the subject of much of the fiction they produced.

The phenomenon of best-selling domestic novels still lay in the future, but works by two writers of the 1830s—Hannah Farnham Lee (1780–1865) and Emma Catherine Embury (1806–63)—foreshadow the concerns of such later best-sellers as Susan Warner's *The Wide, Wide World* (1850) and Maria Cummins's *The Lamplighter* (1854). The death of Hannah Lee's husband in 1816 left her a widow at age thirty-six, with three daughters to support. It was presumably financial necessity that led her to take up the pen in 1830, and by 1854 she had published more than twenty novels, all anonymously. She scored her first great success with *Three Experiments in Living* in 1837, chronicling the financial and spiritual hardships of the once-prosperous Fulton family, hardships brought on by living beyond their means. The book was reprinted at least thirty times in America and England and was immediately followed by a sequel, *Elinor Fulton,* in which a strong-willed Fulton daughter assumes the moral leadership of her mother and siblings, teaching them to accept the error of their former extravagance while the father seeks the basis of a new living in the West. If Elinor recalls Catharine Sedgwick's exemplary heroines, she also anticipates Susan Warner's Ellen Montgomery and Maria Cummin's Gertrude Flint.

The same sort of exemplary female success story underlies Emma Embury's most popular work of fiction. Embury (1806–63) grew up in New York, married the president of a Brooklyn bank, and made her home a literary salon frequented by Poe and other New York literati. Her first publication was a poetry collection issued in 1828, but she was most widely known for her fiction, especially for *Constance Latimer; or, the Blind Girl, With Other Tales,* a collection published by the Harpers in 1838. Like Lee's Fultons, the Latimers of Embury's title story fall suddenly from prosperity; scarlet fever kills their son and blinds their daughter, Constance, and then they lose their fortune in the Panic of 1837. But Constance, in spite of her blindness, provides the moral example and the financial assistance that rescue her family from the destitution her father could not evade. In the works of Lee and Embury—and of Catharine Sedgwick, who was still the best-known American woman fiction writer in the 1830s—a tradition of women's fiction was indeed beginning to emerge, domestic in subject matter, didactic in intention, and demonstrating again and again the power of an exemplary (but neither bitter nor defiant) heroine to triumph over the evils of both immoral extravagance and family hardship. Embury continued to produce tales and collections until she was permanently disabled by illness in 1848.

The 1830s and early 1840s also saw the emergence in print of the vernacular American humor that would culminate in Mark Twain's *Adventures of Huckleberry Finn* (1884). In Maine, in 1830, Seba Smith (1792–1868) began publishing humorous Yankee-dialect letters attributed to "Major Jack Downing"; collected in 1833 as *The Life and Writings of Major Jack Downing of Downingville*, they went through nine editions in two years. In 1835, in Augusta, Georgia, Augustus Baldwin Longstreet (1790–1870) published a collection of sketches called *Georgia Scenes, Characters, Incidents, Etc., in the first Half Century of the Republic.* It was picked up by the Harpers in 1840 and regularly reprinted during the next decade, establishing the vogue of what came to be known as Southwestern Humor. This vein was also worked successfully by Longstreet's friend William Tappan Thompson (1812–82), whose *Major Jones's Courtship,* first published in 1843, was reprinted (in an expanded version) by Philadelphia's Carey and Hart in 1844 and was followed by *Chronicles of Pineville* (1845) and *Major Jones's Sketches of Travel* (1848). The ranks of the Southwestern Humorists also included such writers as George Washington Harris (1814–69), creator of "Sut Lovingood"; Johnson Jones Hooper (1815–62), creator of "Simon Suggs"; and Thomas Bangs Thorpe (1815–75), now best known for his short story "The Big Bear of Arkansas" (first published in 1841). American historical romances, usually running to three volumes, were conceived and published as *books.* In the case of southwestern humor, book publishers like the Harpers and Carey and Hart were turning to a mode conceived and produced, first of all, for newspapers and magazines—notably, in the 1840s, for William Trotter Porter's *The Spirit of the Times,* published in New York.

More and more of the new fiction in the 1830s and early 1840s was magazine fiction, and many writers, including Poe and Hawthorne, pursued their vocations primarily in and for magazines. Magazines were particularly hospitable to literary women. For instance, Eliza Leslie (1787–1858) was for two decades an active magazinist in Philadelphia, both as popular contributor and as editor, including *Miss Leslie's Magazine* in 1843. She had made her first success with a cookbook, published in 1827 and consistently reissued and expanded thereafter. Leslie also wrote children's literature and etiquette books and formally entered the Philadelphia literary world in 1832 when her story "Mrs. Washington Potts" won a prize from *Godey's.*

She produced only one novel, *Amelia; or, a Young Lady's Vicissitudes* (1848), but issued a number of collections, including three volumes of *Pencil Sketches; or, Outlines of Characters and Manners,* published by Carey, Lea, and Blanchard in 1833, 1835, and 1837. It is important to recognize how different Leslie's career was from the careers of such male writers, also published by the House of Carey, as Simms, Bird, and Kennedy.

Caroline Howard Gilman (1794–1888) moved from Boston to Charleston, South Carolina, when she married in 1819 and turned to literature to supplement the meager income of her husband, a Unitarian minister. She founded a children's magazine, the *Rose-Bud,* in 1832, for which she wrote much of the material. It became the *Southern Rose-Bud* in 1833 and then the *Southern Rose* in 1835, by which time it had evolved from a juvenile miscellany into a general family magazine. Gilman edited it until it failed in 1839, a belated victim of the Panic of 1837. In 1834 the Harpers, in New York, published her first popular book, *Recollections of a Housekeeper* (later *Recollections of a New England Housekeeper*), in which the wife of an ambitious Boston lawyer describes her domestic duties and frustrations, the latter having mainly to do with servants. This was followed in 1838 by *Recollections of a Southern Matron,* which was more nearly a novel or story but still basically a plantation version of its predecessor and included an argument for the beneficence of slavery. Gilman's third novel, *Love's Progress,* appeared in 1840. Although both volumes of *Recollections* were quite popular, their author earned surprisingly little money from their success. The Harpers paid her a mere $50 for *Recollections of a Housekeeper* in 1834, and a sale of 2,000 copies of *Recollections of a Southern Matron* in six months in the post–Panic year of 1838 netted Gilman only $200. For the most part she was compelled to rely on the magazines, in which she published not only fiction but poetry and essays.

Caroline Kirkland (1801–64) did not begin as a magazine writer. Born and raised in New York City, she moved with her husband to Detroit in 1835. Her *A New Home—Who'll Follow? Or Glimpses of Western Life* was published in New York in 1839. A vaguely fictionalized collection of essays and sketches on the life of the western frontier, it had gone through four editions by 1850. *Forest Life,* a semifictional account of a tour of Michigan, followed in 1842, and *Western Clearings,* in which Kirkland was turning increasingly to the short story, appeared in 1845. A year later Edgar Poe described Kirkland as "unquestionably . . . one of our best writers" and singled out her "*freshness* of style" and "verisimilitude" for special praise. Meanwhile, the Kirklands had returned to the East in 1843. When William Kirkland died three years later, leaving his widow with four children, she supported them by editing and writing for magazines in New York City.

The New York literary scene in the 1830s and early 1840s was dominated by magazines and magazinists and by their public feuds, especially by the literary wars between the Anglophiles of the *Knickerbocker* group and the literary nationalists of Young America. This feud was reflected in the fiction produced by both camps. Nathaniel Parker Willis (1806–67), popular magazinist and foe of Young America, perfected his Irvingesque stance during a five-year sojourn in Europe and produced such Crayon-like collections as *Inklings of Adventure* (1836), *Loiterings of Travel* (1840), and *Dashes at Life with a Free Pencil* (1845). Also for a time coeditor of the *Mirror* was Theodore Sedgwick Fay (1807–98), a collection of whose early *Mirror* pieces was issued in 1832 with the Irvingesque title *Dreams and Reveries of a Quiet Man*. Fay's subsequent travels in Italy inspired a highly melodramatic novel, *Norman Leslie: A Tale of the Present Times*, published by the Harpers in 1835; a second edition was soon required, a stage adaptation had some success in New York, and the book continued to be reprinted during the next half-dozen years.

Norman Leslie's concern with American characters in a gothically mysterious Italy might be seen as foreshadowing Hawthorne's *Marble Faun* (1860), but the book's most immediate impact grew out of the extraordinarily hostile mockery it elicited from Edgar Poe in the *Southern Literary Messenger*. "The plot," Poe wrote, after summarizing it in cruel and hilarious detail, " . . . is a monstrous piece of absurdity and incongruity." Attacking Fay, Poe was attacking the whole Whig literary circle gathered around the *Mirror*, and he knew it: his review repeatedly mentions that the author of *Norman Leslie* is an "Editor of the New York Mirror"; it speaks of the title character's decision "to go a-Willising in foreign countries"; it remarks that even this character, "goose as the young gentleman is," is not "silly enough to turn travelling correspondent to any weekly paper"; and it finally explains the books' stylistic infelicities (after providing copious examples) by speculating that Fay himself has been abroad "so long as to have forgotten his vernacular language." Poe patched up his quarrel with Willis, who in any case well understood the importance of sensationalism and controversy to the self-publicizing world of magazines and who may have appreciated the humor of the performance from the beginning. But other members of the Whig literary circle, particularly Lewis Gaylord Clark, were permanently alienated. The *Norman Leslie* review began the process that eventually made Poe, if only by default, an ally of Young America.

Other members of the New York literary scene were seeking to produce an American fiction outside the traditions of both Irving and Cooper. Charles Frederick Briggs (1804–77)—an independent-minded ally of the Whigs, who would found the *Broadway Journal* in 1845 and then be forced out a year later by his coeditor, Poe—published *The Adventures of Harry Franco: A Tale of the Great Panic* in 1839. The book was popular and was followed by *The Haunted Merchant* in 1843 (the first and only number of a projected series of *Bankrupt Stories*) and by *Working a Passage; or, Life in a Liner* in 1844. In 1846, in the *Mirror*, Briggs began serializing *The Trippings of Tom Pepper*, a Dickensian picaresque novel set in New York including thinly disguised caricatures of various New York literary figures. The first volume was published in book form a year later, but the story was not completed until a second volume appeared in 1850, and this was Briggs's last novel. In 1853 he became an editor of *Putnam's Monthly Magazine*.

One of the principal targets of the satire of *Tom Pepper* (in which he appears as "Mr. Ferocious") is Cornelius Matthews (1817–89), who in the 1840s was disastrously promoted by Young America (particularly by Evert Duyckinck) as its great hope for a new, original "American Genius." Matthews's first novel, *Behemoth: A Legend of the Mound-Builders* (1839), is set in the prehistoric Mississippi Valley. It was followed by *The Career of Puffer Hopkins* (1842), an incoherent tale of contemporary New York City, and by *Big Abel and the Little Manhattan* (1845), an allegorical fantasy in which a white man and a descendant of the Indian chief who sold Manhattan to the Dutch wander around New York. In one sense Matthews fulfilled the hopes of his supporters: he was certainly new and original, in something like the flamboyant, self-promoting manner of John Neal two decades earlier. That his literary hodgepodges were works of genius was far less evident. His main importance to literary history may be that the efforts of Duyckinck and others to deny his inadequacies helped accelerate Young America's disintegration.

What was finally at stake in the New York literary wars of the 1830s and early 1840s was Young America's creation or discovery of an American fiction free of the oppressive influence of both Irving and Cooper. Many literary historians have seen the works of Poe, Hawthorne, and Melville as the ultimate outcome of this struggle. All three writers had ties to Young America and had works published in the "Library of American Books" Duyckinck edited for New York's Wiley and Putnam: Poe's *Tales* and *The Raven and Other Poems* in 1845 and Hawthorne's *Mosses from an Old Manse* and Melville's *Typee* in 1846. But in 1845—with Poe's *Tales* selling only about

1,500 copies, with Hawthorne still regarded in most quarters as a writer of minor stories and sketches, and with Melville as yet unpublished—such an outcome for the ambitions of Young America was far from clear. Nor, for that matter, was this outcome any clearer a decade later, when Hawthorne, though far better known, was still by no means a best-seller, when Melville, after brief fame, was on his way back to obscurity, and when Poe, like Young America itself, was long since dead. We should be careful about reading our own ideas of literary value and the literary canon back into the pattern of literary history; in 1845, it would seem, the nature and future of American fiction were as unclear as they had been in 1830.

If there were significant trends emerging in the profession of fiction writing by 1845, they had rather little to do with Poe, Hawthorne, and Melville—or even with Simms and Cooper or with Fay, Briggs, and Matthews. The most obvious developments were taking place elsewhere. In 1844, for example, George Lippard (1822–54) began issuing as a series of pamphlets *The Monks of Monk Hall* (later called *Quaker City*), which he described as "an illustration of the life, mystery, and crime of Philadelphia." For all its lurid sensationalism and stylistic sloppiness, *Quaker City* is a fascinating picture of urban depravity, and Lippard was quite sincere in his horror at the exploitation of the lower classes in supposedly democratic America. But the book's appeal clearly derived from its sensationalism, and what makes it matter most immediately to the literary historian is its astonishing commercial success. When the first two-thirds of the pamphlets were bound together as a "book," 48,000 copies were sold in six months; an edition of the whole book sold 60,000 copies in 1845; and by 1850 Lippard had issued twenty-seven more editions, running from 1,000 to 4,000 copies each. One should recall that Simm's *The Yemassee*, only ten years earlier, had become a sensation by selling out a first edition of 2,500 copies in three days. In 1845, with the phenomenal success of *Quaker City*, the age of the American best-seller was on its way.

Lippard was not the only American in the 1840s to write sensational pamphlet-novels aimed at a large, mainly lower-class audience. Such cheap mass fiction soon came to constitute almost a separate industry. Oddly enough, given our current notion of the literary tone of New England, much of this cheap literature was published in Boston. A writer named George Thompson produced such works as *City Crimes; or, Life in New York and Boston* and *Venus in Boston: A Romance of City Life* (both in 1849). Joseph Holt Ingraham (1809–60), who had tried out various fictional modes in the 1830s, turned himself into a kind of fiction factory in the 1840s, publishing rapidly written "novels" of fifty to a hundred pages; in 1846 he boasted to Longfellow that he had produced twenty such works in the previous year, earning $3,000. Timothy Shay Arthur (1809–85)—magazinist, editor, and temperance writer—was equally prolific. His *Ten Nights in a Bar Room* (1854) would become one of the great American best-sellers of the 1850s, its sales surpassed only by those of *Uncle Tom's Cabin*. Arthur had no comparable success in the 1840s, but it is worth noting that in 1843 he published thirteen separate volumes of fiction. When Cooper and Simms complained about "cheap" competition in the 1840s, they were talking about pirated editions of foreign novels. What the successes of Lippard's *Quaker City* indicated was that the "cheap" fiction of the 1850s might be more likely to be of domestic manufacture. A distinctively American mode in fiction was perhaps emerging, but such market-oriented mass production was hardly what the nationalists of Young America had in mind.

At the end of the 1840s, both American fiction and the conditions of professional literary vocation in America were approaching a watershed. Cooper, through his own works and by influence and example, had held sway over the previous three decades. But Cooper, who would die in 1851, was at the end of his career, and Scott-derived historical fiction was on the wane, as Simms's attempt to revive the mode in the 1850s would demonstrate. Poe, whose book sales had never been impressive, died in 1849. But Melville was at the height of his fame at the end of the 1840s, as the author of *Typee* (1846), *Omoo* (1847), and *Redburn* (1849). And Hawthorne's most productive years were immediately ahead of him; between 1850 and 1853 he would publish *The Scarlet Letter*, *The House of the Seven Gables*, and *The Blithedale Romance*, as well as three books for children, two collections of stories (one a new edition of an earlier collection), and a campaign biography of Franklin Pierce. Melville, in the same period, would produce three more novels, including his masterpiece, *Moby-Dick* (1851). What lay ahead, this is to say, was the first *true* American renaissance. This is the literary history to which we have long been accustomed, for good reasons.

From the point of view of the literary marketplace, however, the story looks a bit different, in terms both of significant trends and of major players. Hawthorne's extraordinary literary activity in the early 1850s did not produce a great deal in the way of earnings; his total *lifetime* income from American sales of *The Scarlet Letter*, for instance, amounted to a mere $1,500. And Melville, of course, would fail as a professional author; at the end of the 1840s *Mardi* (1849) was already providing a taste of the inclinations that would soon cost him his audience, and our sense that *Moby-Dick* is a masterpiece was not shared by many of Melville's contemporaries. So from the point of view of the marketplace the most significant portents of future developments may not have been the prospects of writers like Hawthorne and Melville but such things as the rise of authorial mass production on the part of such writers as Joseph Ingraham and Timothy Arthur, the emergence of an increasingly distinct "women's fiction" in the work of such writers as Catharine Sedgwick, Hannah Lee, and Emma Embury, and the phenomenal sales of George Lippard's *Quaker City*. Developments in the later 1840s were beginning to suggest the existence of two potentially large and quite different audiences for fiction. There was a mostly urban, lower-class audience, presumably the main consumers of sensational pamphlet fiction. And there was a national, middle-class audience, apparently consisting mainly of women, the principal readers of literary magazines. This second audience was to prove the most important for the early 1850s, producing a renaissance in American fiction quite different from the one represented by Hawthorne and Melville. It is to this renaissance that we now turn.

5 Women's Fiction and the Literary Marketplace in the 1850s

Let us begin our consideration of the 1850s by returning to F. O. Matthiessen's classic 1941 study, *American Renaissance: Art and Expression in the Age of Emerson and Whitman.* Matthiessen commences by observing "how great a number of our past masterpieces were produced in one extraordinarily concentrated moment of literary expression" in the first half of the 1850s. For Matthiessen the literary masters of this American renaissance are Emerson, Hawthorne, Melville, Thoreau, and Whitman. Noting that "the half-decade of 1850–55" saw the appearance of *Representative Men* (1850), *The Scarlet Letter* (1850), *The House of the Seven Gables* (1851), *Moby-Dick* (1851), *Pierre* (1852), *Walden* (1854), and *Leaves of Grass* (1855), he goes on to declare, "You might search all the rest of American literature without being able to collect a group of books equal to these in imaginative vitality."

In 1940, a year before *American Renaissance,* Fred Lewis Pattee published a quite different account of American literature in the years just before the Civil War, called *The Feminine Fifties.* Emerson, Hawthorne, Melville, Thoreau, and Whitman play a part in Pattee's version of midcentury American literature, but it is a notably subordinate part. Far more important are such writers as Susan B. Warner, Anna Warner, Timothy Shay Arthur, Fanny Fern (the pen name of Sara Payson Willis), Caroline Lee Hentz, Mrs. E. D. E. N. Southworth, Ann Sophia Stephens, Henry Wadsworth Longfellow, Sylvanus Cobb, Jr., Ik Marvel (Donald Grant Mitchell), Grace Greenwood (Sara Jane Clarke), and Fanny Forrester (Emily Chubbuck). What distinguishes Pattee's 1850s from Matthiessen's is his emphasis on writers who were widely popular and commercially successful in a decade when Melville was losing the audience he had won briefly in the late 1840s, when Thoreau and Whitman attracted only very limited circles of readers, and when even Hawthorne's novels fell far short of best-seller status. It is also notable that whereas Matthiessen's writers are all men (he considered calling his book "Man in the Open Air"), the majority of Pattee's are women (hence, in part, the "Feminine" of his title).

Matthiessen admits in his introduction that his "choice of authors" might be considered "arbitrary," that none of their works achieved the popular success of Longfellow's *Hiawatha* (1855), T. S. Arthur's *Ten Nights in a Bar Room* (1854), or Willis's *Fern Leaves from Fanny's Portfolio* (1853). (Oddly enough, Matthiessen's introduction does not mention the most famous bestseller of the 1850s, Harriet Beecher Stowe's *Uncle Tom's Cabin,* which is acknowledged only once in *American Renaissance*—as having reached a wider audience than Emerson.) The popular "feminine" literature of the 1850s, Matthiessen writes in his introduction,

> still offers a fertile field for the sociologist and for the historian of our taste. But I agree with Thoreau: "Read the best books first, or you may not have a chance to read them at all." And during the century that has ensued, the successive generations of common readers, who make the decisions, would seem finally to have agreed that the authors of the pre–Civil War era who bulk largest in stature are the five who are my subject.

Matthiessen's standards for determining and canonizing literary excellence are a bit curious. The "best" writers are apparently the biggest, those "who bulk largest in stature," yet the power implied by this image hardly seems consonant with the fact that, in market terms at least, Matthiessen's five masters were by no obvious quantitative standard among the "biggest" writers of the 1850s. And if the "one common denominator" linking these five writers was, as Matthiessen writes, "their devotion to the possibilities of democracy," it seems somewhat paradoxical to dismiss other writers because they were widely popular. Moreover, Matthiessen seems here to argue, again rather paradoxically, that whereas popular writers failed of greatness because they only reflected public "taste," it is nevertheless precisely the taste of "generations of common readers" that guarantees or legitimizes *his* canon. If readers' taste is in both cases the standard, it is more than a little difficult to understand why *contemporary* popularity should be an index of literary inferiority.

One should note that Pattee, for all the difference of his emphasis, does not finally disagree with Matthiessen's devaluation of popular American

writing in the 1850s. He intends the "Feminine" of his title mainly as a pejorative epithet—synonymous, as he puts it, with *"fervid, fevered, furious,
fatuous, fertile, feeling, florid, furbelowed, fighting, funny."* He presents
himself, in Matthiessen's phrase, as a "historian of our taste," a taste that he
considers to be (like the "feminine") cute but inferior. And in any case,
whatever disagreement there is between Matthiessen and Pattee about the
midcentury literary canon, it would seem to have been settled very much
in Matthiessen's favor. *The Feminine Fifties* has long been out of print,
but *American Renaissance* has been bought, read, and admired consistently since 1941. Matthiessen gave the literary 1850s a name still in use,
the "American renaissance," and his canon is still, for the most part, our
canon—although we have, in recent years, been adding to it.

Matthiessen's influence is understandable; his interpretations of his five
authors are brilliant, and these authors produced a kind of writing that literary "modernism," especially in academic circles, had by 1941 legitimized as
central and valuable: complex, ironic, often self-reflexive, and concerned
with national political issues and questions of American identity, of empire,
and abuse of empire. Except for *Uncle Tom's Cabin,* fiction by women in the
1850s seldom touched on political questions, and self-reflexive complexity,
then as now, was an unlikely ingredient of successful popular writing. There
is surely nothing wrong with devoting attention to writers only modestly
popular or even unknown among their contemporaries; one would hardly
wish to dismiss Emily Dickinson, for instance, because her works came to
the attention of the public only after her death. But to suppress a large body
of popular literature in order to assert the "stature" of five male writers is to
suppress what may be *the* crucial fact about American literature in the
1850s. Not only were most *readers* women (who cared not at all for Melville
and Whitman, and whose enthusiasm for Hawthorne was, in commercial
terms, rather moderate); the most successful *writers,* especially of fiction,
were also by and large women, women now mostly forgotten. More recent
critics—for instance, Ann Douglas in *The Feminization of American Culture* (1977), Nina Baym in *Women's Fiction* (1978), Mary Kelley in *Private
Woman, Public Stage* (1984), and Jane Tompkins in *Sensational Designs*
(1985)—have begun the essential task of rediscovering these "lost" writers.
Responsible literary history, whether feminist or not, should no longer conspire to ignore them.

The point of this rediscovery is not to determine which group of writers
is "better." Indeed, one benefit of the debate over the midcentury American

literary canon has been to make us more aware of the political and gender biases, the usually unspoken ideological assumptions, underlying many determinations of literary "value." Faced with assertions that particular works or writers are "good," we have learned to ask what they are "good" *for.* Nor does one turn to the popular literature of the 1850s in order to substitute it for the current canon. The point, rather, is to recognize the simultaneous existence of *two* literary traditions in the 1850s—and, what may be more important, to recognize their interconnectedness.

All of these writers—women and men, popular and unpopular—were competing in the same literary marketplace, and their awareness of this competition is clear in many of the texts they produced, particularly in the texts produced by Matthiessen's "masters." In fact Matthiessen's impulse to suppress the "feminine fifties" might be traced to a similar impulse in the writers he canonizes. Male writers, threatened (successfully) by the market power of women readers and writers, had every reason to try to marginalize them, to advertise their supposed inconsequence. We should also recognize that these competing traditions, for all their apparent differences (man in the open air, woman in the home), shared a good deal of common ground. Both the open air and the home were above all refuges from a nineteenth-century present viewed as increasingly complex, unmanageable, and incomprehensible. It is in this sense that both literary traditions of the 1850s are allied with the intellectual movement we now call Romanticism. But to understand either tradition, we need first to attend to the context in which both had their being: the expanding market for literature in the 1850s.

The Marketplace in the 1850s

The growth of American book and magazine publishing from the 1820s through the 1840s has already been described. Book publishing, by the 1840s, had consolidated in dominant firms in major cities, notably the House of Carey in Philadelphia and the House of Harper in New York, and increased capitalization and efficiencies of production and distribution had made an increasingly national market available to native writers. By the late 1840s two new firms were contesting the hegemony of Carey and Harper. In New York, in 1840, George Putnam became a partner of John Wiley; he began publishing on his own in 1847, his ventures including highly successful uniform editions of Carlyle, Irving, and Cooper. And in Boston, James T. Fields turned the business of William D. Ticknor (in which he became a partner in 1843) into New England's first major literary publishing house;

they published Tennyson, Longfellow, Holmes, and Whittier, and their list of New England writers would be joined by Hawthorne in 1850, when Ticknor and Fields issued *The Scarlet Letter.* Meanwhile, a large national reading public, consisting mainly of women, had been developed by the most successful literary magazines, notably *Graham's Magazine* and *Godey's Lady's Book* in Philadelphia. By the end of the 1840s, the magazine writer had become perhaps the most characteristic American literary figure, and the tastes of magazine readers were coming to determine the most characteristic modes of American literature.

Not all was prosperity for American literary magazines in the 1850s. The Panic of 1857 wiped out a number of ventures, and at the end of the decade the onset of the Civil War not only raised costs for ink and paper but deprived national, northern magazines of their southern readers. Indeed, the 1850s saw the demise of several of the most influential magazines of the 1840s, including *Graham's,* O'Sullivan's *United States Magazine and Democratic Review,* and Morris and Willis's *New York Mirror.* Among the dominant literary periodicals of the 1840s, only *Godey's Lady's Book* retained its position through the 1850s. Still, a new postal regulation of 1852, reducing magazine rates and for the first time allowing the publisher rather than the recipient to pay postage, created a more favorable commercial climate, and new popular magazines soon replaced or surpassed their declining predecessors.

In 1850, for example, New York's House of Harper launched *Harper's New Monthly Magazine,* whose contents consisted mainly of reprints from British periodicals and serialized British novels (including Dickens's *Bleak House* and *Little Dorrit* and Thackeray's *The Newcomes* and *The Virginians*). Although some American materials were included—for instance, short stories by such writers as Caroline Cheesebrough, Herman Melville, Elizabeth Stuart Phelps, and Rose Terry—the emphasis was always on reprinted British literature, and this emphasis paid off. In the magazine's first six months, circulation (at $3 a year) rose from 7,500 to 50,000; by 1860 it had reached 200,000. Detractors could question the Harpers' patriotism but hardly their success. In 1853, in part as a direct challenge to *Harper's,* George Palmer Putnum founded *Putnam's Monthly Magazine,* edited by Charles F. Briggs (with George William Curtis and Parke Godwin) and dedicated to the publication of works by American writers. Contributors included Longfellow, Cooper, Lowell, Thoreau, and Melville—the last contributing a number of stories and the novel *Israel Potter* as a serial. *Putnam's* published many of the writers now in the literary canon, and it is worth noting that this strategy did not at the time prove successful. Circulation, which started in 1853 at 20,000, declined steadily from that figure, and Putnam sold the magazine to another publisher in 1855. It failed two years later, in the Panic of 1857, although it was revived after the Civil War.

The year of the Panic also saw the founding of an important and enduring new literary magazine: Boston's *Atlantic Monthly*, published by Moses Phillips and edited by James Russell Lowell. When Phillips died in 1859, the magazine was purchased by Ticknor and Fields, and Fields succeeded Lowell as editor in 1861. The *Atlantic* rapidly became an influential vehicle for New England writers, many of them veterans of *Putnam's;* the first issue included contributions from, among others, Emerson, Longfellow, Holmes, Lowell, John Lothrop Motley, Rose Terry, and Harriet Beecher Stowe, and the New England focus remained dominant, sometimes to the irritation of writers in other regions. Moreover, Lowell's strong antislavery position (as contrasted with the avoidance of politics in *Harper's*) alienated potential southern readers. The new magazine nevertheless survived; following the Civil War, under the editorship of William Dean Howells, it was to become extraordinarily influential. Yet the *Atlantic* was hardly a typical popular literary magazine of the 1850s. *Godey's*—still edited by Sarah Josepha Hale and still featuring engraved fashion plates, domestic advice, and sentimental fiction and verse—remained far more popular, with growing competition for the "ladies" market from its Philadelphia imitator, *Peterson's Lady's Magazine*. The same market was tapped from New York by *Frank Leslie's Illustrated Newspaper,* a weekly containing both news and light literature (with copious illustrations) founded in 1855 by Henry Carter. By 1858 *Leslie's* was claiming a circulation of 100,000 and by 1860 more than 160,000.

But the most spectacular and sensational success of the 1850s was the *New York Ledger,* edited and published by an enterprising Irish-born New Yorker named Robert Bonner. In 1850 Bonner, a printer, invested his meager savings in a commercial journal, the *Merchant's Ledger and Statistical Record,* which he gradually made over into a literary weekly. In 1853, for instance, he began including verse by Lydia Sigourney, and in 1855 he transformed the magazine dramatically—dropping the commercial features, changing the title to the *New York Ledger,* and hiring newly famous "Fanny Fern" (Sara Payson Willis) at the extraordinary rate of $100 a week for a regular column. Bonner promoted the *Ledger* by advertising lavishly, by publishing early portions of serials in other magazines and newspapers (only to announce at the end of a suspenseful installment that the story would be continued exclusively in the *Ledger*), and above all by paying high rates to secure the contributions of popular or famous writers. Fanny Fern ended up earning $5,000 a year for her contributions, and Mrs. E. D. E. N. (Emma Dorothy Eliza Nevitte) Southworth, who became an exclusive *Ledger* author in 1857, came to earn at least that amount. Bonner also managed to secure a year's worth of weekly columns from Boston's Edward Everett, hardly one to succumb to pecuniary enticement, by offering to donate $10,000 to Everett's pet project, the Mount Vernon Association. Everett, Bryant, Longfellow, and Tennyson gave the *Ledger* an aura of culture, but its staple remained serialized popular fiction, especially works by Southworth and Sylvanus Cobb, Jr., who was signed on in 1856 and whose contributions to the *Ledger* would ultimately include about one hundred and thirty serial novels (notably, in 1859, the widely popular *Gunmaker of Moscow*). Bonner's promotional strategies were highly successful; by 1860 the *Ledger* had achieved a circulation (at $2 a year) of 400,000, a figure unmatched by any other American literary magazine of the time.

The *Ledger*'s 1860 circulation had already been matched and surpassed, however, in book publishing as America entered its first great "age of bestsellers." The story of this age begins in 1850, when an unknown author submitted a novel manuscript to George Palmer Putnam. The author, Susan B. Warner, was the daughter of a New York lawyer who had lost his fortune in the Panic of 1837. The burden of supporting the family had fallen on Warner and her sister, and she had turned to literature out of financial necessity. Her manuscript had already been turned down by a number of New York publishers (the Harpers, for example, had dismissed it as "Fudge") and Putnam was not initially inclined any more favorably. But he took it home and gave it to his mother, asking if she thought it worth publishing. "If you never publish another book, George," she responded after reading Warner's novel and being moved to tears, "publish this." "Providence," she later insisted, "will aid its sale." The book appeared in December under the pseudonym Elizabeth Wetherell, and Mrs. Putnam's prophecy was soon fulfilled. *The Wide, Wide World,* chronicling the trials and triumphs of an orphan named Ellen Montgomery, went through thirteen editions in the next two years, outselling any previous novel by an American author and ultimately selling more than half a million copies in the United States. It was also widely popular in England.

The Wide, Wide World inaugurated an extraordinary decade in American book publishing. In 1851, Harriet Beecher Stowe began serializing *Uncle Tom's Cabin* in Washington's *National Era* magazine. Readers were enthralled, and Boston's John P. Jewett offered Stowe a contract for book publication. The book appeared in two volumes in March of 1852 and sales were spectacular: 20,000 copies in the first three weeks, 75,000 in the first three months, 305,000 in the first year. By 1857 *Uncle Tom's Cabin* had sold 500,000 copies and was still being bought at the rate of 1,000 copies a week. No other American writer matched Stowe's success in the 1850s, but several came close. Sara Payson Willis's collection of sketches *Fern Leaves from Fanny's Portfolio* (1853) sold 70,000 copies in its first year; a collection of sketches for juveniles and a sequel to *Fern Leaves* (both also attributed to Fanny Fern) appeared in 1853 and 1854, and combined sales of the three volumes in the United States and England reached 180,000. In the same year Maria Cummins's *The Lamplighter* created another sensation, selling 40,000 copies in eight weeks and 70,000 in its first year. Other women—for instance, Augusta Evans Wilson, Mrs. Southworth, and Ann Sophia Stephens—were soon to join the ranks of best-selling authors.

Not all the best-selling writers of the 1850s were women. The most popular book in the 1850s after *Uncle Tom's Cabin* was *Ten Nights in a Bar Room* (1854), a temperance tract by Philadelphia author and magazine editor Timothy Shay Arthur. *Reveries of a Bachelor* (1850), a collection of sentimental sketches written by Donald Grant Mitchell under the pseudonym Ik Marvel, sold 14,000 copies in its first year and continued to sell for decades. In 1855, while the first edition of Whitman's *Leaves of Grass* remained largely unread, Longfellow's *Song of Hiawatha* sold 11,000 copies in its first month and 30,000 in its first five months; in 1860 it was still being bought at the rate of 2,000 copies a year. Nevertheless, a clear majority of the most successful writers were women—as were the overwhelming majority of readers, the readers who made Arthur, Mitchell, and Longfellow (along with Warner, Stowe, Fern, and Cummins) successful. For instance, in 1852, Ik Marvel's *Reveries of a Bachelor* was devoured eagerly in Amherst by Emily Dickinson, who would write of Whitman ten years later, "I have never read his book, but was told that it was disgraceful." Longfellow became a best-seller by tailoring his poetry to the tastes of the largely feminine reading public. Thus both as writers and as readers women were at the cen-

ter of the phenomenal growth in book sales in the 1850s. And of the popular
American writing of the 1850s, the most interesting is the fiction written by
women for women.

Fiction by Women

The success of the best-selling American women novelists in the 1850s was
unprecedented. Susan Warner's *The Wide, Wide World* sent a signal to
women writers and male publishers in 1850 analogous to the signal sent in
1821 by the success of Cooper's *The Spy*. And the new signal was considerably more precise, identifying not only a specific subject (women's domestic
experience) but a specific (and large) audience. Moreover, novels like *The
Wide, Wide World, Uncle Tom's Cabin,* and *The Lamplighter* achieved sales
far beyond what Cooper, in his prime, could even have dreamed of. Nevertheless, the women novelists of the 1850s, their commercial success
notwithstanding, were as deeply influenced as their predecessors had been
in the 1830s and 1840s by nineteenth-century assumptions about woman's
proper sphere—by the Cult of Domesticity, or Cult of True Womanhood.

Women writers, however successful, were never to proclaim worldly
ambitions, or even admit it to themselves, and the popular women novelists
of the 1850s all disclaimed such ambition. Woman's place, they agreed, was
in the home rather than the marketplace, and although commercial success
seemed therefore by definition "unfeminine" (as many a male novelist
protested), several factors served to exonerate these women writers in their
own eyes and in the eyes of others. They were writing to support their families or children (often after the death or bankruptcy of a father or husband);
they were thus not competing with men but fulfilling their "feminine" duties. Nor were they flaunting their success as a form of personal self-assertion; many went so far as to insist that their books virtually wrote themselves
(or at least were not produced with conscious deliberation). Most also protected personal privacy and "feminine" delicacy by assuming pseudonyms
or by publishing anonymously. Finally, if woman's place was in the home,
the home—the domestic life of women—was the great subject of these
writers, and the values rewarded in their novels are almost uniformly "feminine" and "domestic." *Uncle Tom's Cabin* might seem an exception to the
assumption that women were not to concern themselves with politics (exclusively, it was generally agreed, a province of *man's* sphere), but from her
title to the final scene of her novel, Stowe deals with politics very much under the guise of domesticity.

Both in their public stances as authors and in their novels, then, these writers in different ways advertised their conformity to contemporary ideas of woman's proper sphere, and it may well have been this very forswearing of ambition and the masculine world that guaranteed their success in the supposedly masculine competition of the marketplace. The primary consumers in this marketplace, after all, were also women. For them the home *was,* by definition, the world, a world with which only other women could claim full familiarity—hence the rising vogue of "ladies' magazines" in the 1830s and 1840s. The Cult of Domesticity did not, then, only or even mainly constrict the novelists who embraced it, at least in commercial terms. It made these novelists, writing out of their own experience, particularly well situated to appeal to the experience of their readers.

The outpouring of women's fiction in America in the 1850s is impressive not only because of the huge sales of particular best-sellers but also because of the growing number of women producing best-sellers, in some cases long series of best-sellers. One could devote many pages simply to chronicling these women and the novels they produced—from Susan Warner's *The Wide, Wide World* in 1850 through Mrs. Southworth's *The Curse of Clifton* (1852) and *The Hidden Hand* (1859) and Augusta Evans Wilson's *Beulah* (1859) and, to look beyond 1860, her extraordinarily popular *St. Elmo* (1867), whose publisher, only four months after the book was issued, claimed that it had been enjoyed by one million readers. It seems wiser, however, to concentrate in more detail on three of these writers and their most popular novels: on Susan Warner and *The Wide, Wide World,* on Maria Cummins and *The Lamplighter,* and on Fanny Fern and *Ruth Hall.* The career and writings of Harriet Beecher Stowe are the subjects of a separate section.

Susan Warner (1819–85) was born in the same year as Walt Whitman, Herman Melville, George Eliot, and John Ruskin. Her father, Henry Warner, was a successful New York lawyer. Susan was raised in something approaching luxury and educated by her father and by private tutors in a wide range of subjects. When Susan's mother died in 1827, Henry Warner's unmarried sister, "Aunt Fanny," moved in to take charge of the house and children. Susan's young sister, Anna, who would also turn to fiction writing in the 1850s, later recalled in Susan "a strong temper, an impervious will, a masterful love of power that very ill brooked curbing," but the personal journal Susan began keeping at the age of twelve reveals an equally strong current of self-doubt, of guilty dedication to possibly irrelevant duties. An elite young woman in America in the 1820s and 1830s had few if any outlets for "impervious will" and "love of power."

In the spring of 1837, when Susan was seventeen, the Warners' privi-
leged status collapsed. Bad investments forced Henry to sell much of his
property, including his New York town house, and the family retired to a
farmhouse on Constitution Island, near West Point on the Hudson River,
where they had planned to build a country estate and where they now eked
out a precarious living in growing poverty and almost total isolation. "It has
been a long time," Susan confided in her journal in 1839, "since we were
used to seeing many people." Whatever her education had been preparing
her for was now no longer a possibility. Moreover, her father's inept efforts
to improve the family's condition through further speculation only made
things worse, and Susan turned more and more to reading for consolation.
But the need for money became increasingly acute; there were repeated
threats of eviction, and the family lived at times without furniture. The
daughters would have to compensate somehow for the father's failures.

Late in 1846 Anna designed and sold a "Natural History" card game to
help make ends meet, and then Aunt Fanny announced to the older sister:
"Sue, I believe if you would try, you could write a story." "Whether she
added 'that would sell,'" Anna wrote later, "I am not sure; but of course that
is what she meant." The result of this urging was *The Wide, Wide World,* attributed to "Elizabeth Wetherell." Its success, once it finally found a publisher, has already been described. It was followed in 1852 by *Queechy,*
nearly as popular, and by Anna's *Dollars and Cents* (attributed to "Amy
Lothrop"), and Elizabeth Wetherell and Amy Lothrop would ultimately
produce, separately or in collaboration, a total of twenty-one novels, along
with books of domestic advice and religious instruction. This furious literary
activity never restored the family's affluence; much of what Susan and Anna
earned went to pay their father's debts and legal costs, and the need for
ready money forced the sisters to sell most of their copyrights rather than
wait for royalties on sales. Still, from 1851 on, Susan and Anna were supporting the family, and in six months in 1853, *The Wide, Wide World,* whose
copyright Susan had not sold, earned royalties of $4,500.

The Wide, Wide World also, of course, brought fame, but Susan Warner
took pains to hide herself behind her pseudonym. To a male editor who had
discovered her identity and asked permission to reveal it to the public, she
replied in 1851: "I had no mind in the first place to have my real name
known at all, and though that is now beyond my control, I do certainly never
wish to see it in print." "Mere personal fame," she explained, "seems to me
a very empty thing to work for." Later in the same year she was a bit clearer
in her journal about the reasons for her privacy: "fame," she wrote, "never

was a woman's Paradise, yet." Although Elizabeth Wetherell's real name was soon revealed anyway, Susan Warner continued to live in personal seclusion. She remained loyal to the doctrine of woman's circumscribed sphere, even minimizing her own agency in producing her best-selling novels. "I do not deserve your commendations,—not in anywise," she wrote in 1852 to Dorothea Dix, who had praised *The Wide, Wide World.* "You say 'God bless me' for what I have done,—nay but say "Thank him for it," and I wash my hands of all desert in the matter." Such self-effacement was typical of the best-selling American women writers of the 1850s, and self-effacement and the acceptance of women's limited roles also lie at the heart of Warner's first and most popular novel.

The Wide, Wide World is explicit enough about the powerlessness of women and even about the cruelty that often exploits and sustains this powerlessness. At the outset, ten-year-old Ellen Montgomery learns that she is about to be separated from her invalid mother. Her father, Captain Morgan Montgomery, has imperiled his fortune (like Warner's father) through obscure business dealings. He must relocate from New York to Europe, and his wife must accompany him, supposedly for her health. He insists, however, that he cannot afford to take Ellen along; she is to live in the country with his unmarried half sister, Fortune Emerson. This opening suggests an intriguing set of subterranean connections. It is as if the mother's illness were somehow caused by the father's inept financial dealings, or even as if he had designed it all to break up the intense relationship between Ellen and her mother. In any case, his overt cruelty and insensitivity are quite clear: he is almost never at home with his wife and daughter, he refuses to pay for his wife's parting presents for Ellen (instead, she sells a gold ring given her by her own mother to raise the money), and, when arrangements have finally been made for Ellen's trip to her Aunt Fortune's, he prevents his wife from waking her early, thus denying them their last moments together. Ellen is quite conscious of Captain Montgomery's meanness; her sorrow at parting from her mother, we are told, was "perhaps . . . sharpened by a sense of wrong and a feeling of indignation at her father's cruelty." For all her sorrow, however, she does go. She has no choice, and neither does her mother; they are both male property.

For the rest of her story Ellen is victimized, more or less, by various people chosen by her absent father to serve as her legal guardians. The snobbish family with whom she travels to her Aunt Fortune's home neglects and humiliates her. Aunt Fortune herself provides food and shelter but no love, and she delights in such petty torments as dyeing Ellen's white stockings gray-brown and withholding letters to Ellen from her mother. The girl nevertheless finds warm friends and supporters: the farmer who works for Aunt Fortune, a well-educated young woman named Alice Humphreys, Alice's clergyman brother, John, and others. Alice and John provide comfort when the news arrives that Mrs. Montgomery has died abroad, and they lovingly see to the education Aunt Fortune has neglected. When Alice reveals that she too, like Ellen's mother, is dying, Ellen moves in with her, and she stays on to care for Alice's bereaved father and brother. This arrangement seems fairly stable, because news had arrived a year earlier that Captain Montgomery had been lost at sea. Alice and John have claimed Ellen as their "little sister," but this adoption unfortunately has no standing in law; in *The Wide, Wide World* legal relationships are rigorously distinguished from those based on love and communal feeling.

After a year at the Humphreys' Ellen discovers that Aunt Fortune has been concealing a letter written by her father before his death and announcing that her mother's wealthy family, the Lindsays, are living in Edinburgh, that they wish to take Ellen in, and that he has placed her in their custody. So Ellen goes to Scotland to become the property of yet another set of legal guardians. Her uncle Lindsay insists that she forget America and the Humphreys, that she call him "father," that she call herself Ellen Lindsay. He is loving on his own terms, but these terms are, to say the least, peremptory. Although Ellen is only fourteen when she arrives in Edinburgh, one detects in her relationship with this guardian/uncle, who changes her name to his, Warner's figuration of the conditions of nineteenth-century marriage. "When Mr. Lindsay clasped her to his bosom," we are told, "Ellen felt it was as *his own* . . . ; in his whole manner love was mingled with as much authority." "It was singularly pleasant," Ellen reflects on her life in Scotland; "she could not help but enjoy it all very much; and yet it seemed to her as if she were caught in a net from which she had no power to get free." This picture of Ellen's status as pampered property could scarcely be more stark. No doubt many a reader of *The Wide, Wide World* responded in sympathy, and no historian should ignore the profound social significance of Mrs. Putnam's tears—or of the novel's extraordinary sales.

The book's brief and rather perfunctory conclusion—in which John Humphreys appears at the Lindsays', impresses them with the strength of his character, and reestablishes his relationship with Ellen—only barely overcomes the stark picture of her condition. One assumes that Ellen will return to America eventually and marry John (she is now almost sixteen), but marriage somehow does not seem a fully adequate solution to her predicament. Ellen has earlier reflected, contrasting Mr. Lindsay's love with John's, that John's was not only "a higher style of kindness" but also "a higher style of authority." Her best possible conception of freedom is based on the assumption that she must in any event be governed, owned. This assumption, it should be noted, inevitably controlled the lives of Susan Warner and of most of her readers.

The Wide, Wide World has often been dismissed, at least by modern readers, as sentimental or melodramatic. "Melodramatic," according to *Webster's,* refers to literature that is "sensational, violent, and extravagantly emotional"; the label also tends to get applied to works in which character is radically simplified along moral lines, to works populated mainly by paragons of virtue and monsters of vice. "Sentimental" is the term more often used to denigrate *The Wide, Wide World* and other works of American women's fiction. Among *Webster's* definitions of the term the most pertinent in this context would seem to be "influenced more by emotion than reason; acting from feeling rather than from practical and utilitarian motives," and the values of many popular women novelists of the 1850s (and of many of the writers we now call Romantics) would indeed seem to be "sentimental" in this sense. But modernist standards of taste have made "sentimental" a pejorative, and not simply a descriptive, term. To be "sentimental," we have been assured through much of the twentieth century, is to be insincere and unrealistic. The only genuine emotion is that which remains unexpressed, or at least understated, and the emotion in "sentimental" literature is therefore false and excessive. Or so we have been led to believe.

Why, then, is *The Wide, Wide World* now generally dismissed as "sentimental" or "melodramatic"? Nothing could be more "realistic" than Ellen Montgomery's sense of the limitations on her freedom, and much of the charm of her story grows out of Warner's "realistic" notation of country customs and domestic routines. Moreover, compared, for instance, to Charlotte Brontë's *Jane Eyre,* which had appeared in 1847, *The Wide, Wide World* is relatively unmelodramatic. In Ellen Montgomery's world there are no gothic mysteries, and those who claim to own her are by no means the villains of melodrama. Mr. Lindsay and Aunt Fortune behave decently enough on their own terms—they are a far cry from Brontë's Reed family—and Ellen, unlike Jane Eyre, is always able to find friends. Modern readers have complained about Ellen's frequent fits of crying, of which there are a great many, but tears are clearly her only permissible means for expressing her unhappiness, and she soon learns to cry in private. Nor is Warner's novel notably damper, in this respect, than much of Dickens.

The deepest problem for modern readers of *The Wide, Wide World* is Ellen Montgomery's *responses* to her constricted situation: her rejection of rebellion for Christian submission. "Her passions," we are told early on, "were by nature very strong, and by education very imperfectly controlled." What happens in *The Wide, Wide World* is that Ellen learns to control these passions. "Remember, my darling," her mother tells her while explaining that they must soon part, "who it is that brings this sorrow upon us—though we *must* sorrow, we must not rebel." She is referring not to Captain Montgomery but to God. Again and again Ellen's mentors—Alice Humphreys, John Humphreys, and others—insist that Ellen recognize God's love in her own sorrows. She is to be weaned from earthly affections—parted from her mother, from Alice, from John—so that she may recognize the superior love of Christ. In short, she must learn to submit, and to the modern reader (to whom it seems clearly to be Captain Montgomery who "brings this sorrow upon us") such submission may well seem offensive. To some contemporary feminist critics, novels like *The Wide, Wide World* simply seem to urge women to conspire in their own subjection.

Others reply that Warner, whatever her message, nonetheless does present a stark and potentially subversive picture of Ellen's situation. Yet Ellen's mentors repeatedly warn her against the implications of even this sort of subversive "realism," and Warner provides no hint whatsoever that their admonitions are to be regarded ironically. "Take care, dear Ellen," Alice Humphreys cautions her, "don't take up the trade of suspecting evil; you could not take up a worse; and even when it is forced upon you, see as little of it as you can; and forget as soon as you can what you see." This is precisely what Ellen learns to do, and her self-effacement is presented as an admirable achievement. Readers who prefer Ahab's defiance in Melville's *Moby-Dick* can only be annoyed; but then these readers, who are not sailing on the *Pequod,* are not obliged to bear the consequences of their preference. Warner and her enthusiastic audience knew well the conditions of their own voyage, and to object to their accommodation, to their desire to discover the possible pleasures of their circumscribed condition, smacks of something very close to easy condescension.

The Wide, Wide World certainly has its faults, especially in plotting. For instance, an "old gentleman" who befriends Ellen in New York and then sends a barrage of gifts to her mother and whose identity is kept shrouded in tantalizing secrecy is never identified. (It might be noted that *Moby-Dick*, in which the sailor Bulkington simply disappears after a spectacular introduction, fares little better on this score). But those who deplore Susan Warner's response to Ellen Montgomery's situation should at least recognize that Warner fully understands the limits of this situation. They should also attend to the gifts given to Ellen by her mother during a joint shopping expedition before their separation. First of all, Ellen chooses a Bible from an elaborate display of possibilities. "Such beautiful Bibles," we are told, "she had never seen; she pored in ecstasy over their varieties of type and binding, and was very evidently in love with them all." Warner here seems oddly enough to propose a kind of spiritual consumerism as an antidote to woman's status as male property, and it is certainly disconcerting to have a display of Bibles described as "so many tempting objects." But this dissonant note is not sustained; what finally matters about the Bible given to Ellen by her mother is that it helps her—like a hymnal given her by a kind stranger and a copy of *Pilgrim's Progress* presented by John Humphreys—to learn the discipline and gratification of Christian submission.

It is also significant that these lessons come from books and that Mrs. Montgomery's second gift to her daughter, again elaborately chosen, is a writing desk complete with paper, envelopes, pens, and ink. *The Wide, Wide World* is filled with warnings against the dangers of fiction, and Warner was disturbed when the book was described as a "novel"; she herself preferred to call it a "story." Still, many of the most important relationships in *The Wide, Wide World* are sustained by reading and writing, and the cruelty of Ellen's legal guardians often takes the form of interfering with these relationships. Thus Aunt Fortune withholds letters to Ellen from her dying mother, and her uncle Lindsay seizes and hides her copy of *Pilgrim's Progress*. Alice and John Humphreys, by contrast, encourage Ellen's literary development; in fact ten-year-old Ellen first speaks to John, at a Christmas house party, to request his assistance with a piece of writing. Finally, the point of John's successful intervention with the Lindsays, at the close of the novel, is to secure permission for him to correspond with Ellen from America. Reading and writing, books and private correspondence, may not seem much of a response to a legal system that defines women as male property, but one should recall that Susan Warner began a private journal when she was twelve, that she turned more and more to reading after the collapse of her father's fortune, and that writing ultimately rescued her family from poverty. One should recall, too, the extraordinary circulation of *The Wide, Wide World* in nineteenth-century America. If reading and writing about shared experience testified to a community that transcended or at least helped compensate for the strictures of legal subjugation, Susan Warner's novel revealed that this community was very large indeed—and potentially very powerful, at least in its own sphere.

If the labels "sentimental" and "melodramatic" seem finally inappropriate to *The Wide, Wide World,* they are rather more justly applied to *The Lamplighter,* published in 1854. In fact, it was this first and most popular of Maria Cummins's novels that inspired Nathaniel Hawthorne's famous declaration, in an 1855 letter to his publisher William Ticknor, that "America is now wholly given over to a d——d mob of scribbling women." "I should have no chance of success," Hawthorne complained, "while the public taste is occupied with their trash—and should be ashamed of myself if I did succeed. What is the mystery of these innumerable editions of the Lamplighter, and other books neither better nor worse—worse they could not be, and better they need not be, when they sell by the 100,000." Behind Hawthorne's exasperation one detects clear envy. In the same letter he estimates the total value of his copyrights on all the books he had published since 1837, together with his Concord real estate, at $5,000. By the end of 1854, sales of *The Lamplighter* had earned Maria Cummins something like $7,000. Whatever the "mystery" was, Hawthorne could not understand it, and by 1855, two years into his political appointment as American consul at Liverpool, he had at least temporarily given up writing fiction.

Unlike most of the popular American women novelists of the 1850s, Maria Susanna Cummins (1827–66) did not write out of financial necessity. Her father, David Cummins, whose antecedents went back to colonial Ipswich, was a successful lawyer who ultimately became judge of the Court of Common Pleas of Norfolk County, Massachusetts. Maria was born in Salem, the first of four children by David Cummins's third wife, Mehitable Cave Cummins (there were four older children from his first two marriages). The family moved to Springfield and then to a comfortable home in Dorchester, where Maria, who never married, would live until her early death at the age of thirty-nine. David Cummins provided his daughter with a solid education at home and then sent her to the Young School in Lenox, Massachusetts. This school was run by Mrs. Charles Sedgwick, sister-in-law of the famous novelist Catharine Maria Sedgwick, who lived nearby and visited frequently.

All of Maria Cummins's novels were published anonymously. Like Susan Warner, she carefully insulated her personal privacy from her public fame, and in Dorchester she was less a literary celebrity than an exemplary citizen, admired for her devotion to the Unitarian church. Nevertheless, she did keep writing: *The Lamplighter* was followed in 1857 by *Mabel Vaughan;* then came *El Fureidis* in 1860 and *Haunted Hearts* in 1864. Cummins's value to her publishers, as indicated by the royalties they paid her, rose steadily. Boston's John P. Jewett, also the publisher of *Uncle Tom's Cabin,* paid a royalty of 10 percent on her first two novels, but overexpansion to handle the sales of Stowe's and Cummins's best-sellers weakened his business, and it failed in the Panic of 1857. Cummins took *El Fureidis* to Ticknor and Fields, who offered a royalty of 15 percent. For *Haunted Hearts,* finally, J. E. Tilton paid a royalty of thirty cents a copy. Still, none of the later novels matched the sensational success of *The Lamplighter,* which provides the clearest index of the "mystery" that so baffled Hawthorne.

At the beginning of *The Lamplighter,* its eight-year-old heroine, an orphan named Gerty, is living in poverty in Boston. The unsympathetic woman, Nan Grant, with whom she was left at the age of three when her mother died and with whom she still lives has not revealed the mother's identity or even Gerty's last name. Gerty's situation recalls that of Warner's Ellen Montgomery, living with her unsympathetic Aunt Fortune, and *The Lamplighter* is indebted in many ways to *The Wide, Wide World,* but here at the opening, as everywhere else, Cummins is far more melodramatic than Warner. When Gerty spills a pail of milk, she is "scolded, beaten, deprived of the crust which she usually got for her supper, and shut up in her dark attic for the night." She is befriended by the lamplighter of the title, an old man significantly named Trueman Flint, who gives her a kitten. When Nan discovers the kitten, she throws it into a large pot of boiling water, where it dies in agony, and Gerty, when she reacts violently, is thrown into the street. Rejected by Nan, Gerty is taken in by the lamplighter, who says of what he can offer her: " 't ain't much . . .; but it's a *home*—yes, a *home;* and that's a great thing to her that never had one." Gerty is also befriended by True's neighbors, Mrs. Sullivan and her son Willie, and by an exemplary and wealthy young blind woman named Emily Graham, and with the benefit of these "home" influences she prospers.

Part of what happens to Gerty in the course of her story is that, like Ellen Montgomery, she learns Christian forbearance; she learns to suppress "her ungoverned and easily roused nature." "Who can be happy?" she asks Emily. "Those only, my child," Emily replies, "who have learned submission; those who, in the severest afflictions, see the hand of a loving Father." But the truer significance of Gerty's growth lies elsewhere. "I ain't good,"

she complains to Emily; "I'm real bad!" "But you *can be good*," Emily as-
sures her, "and then everybody will love you." Emily's assurance effectively
summarizes the story of *The Lamplighter*: Gerty's goodness does bring her
love and glowing admiration. When her "Uncle True" suffers a stroke, she
cares for him and nurses him, earning almost universal public admiration.
After True's death, Emily becomes her guardian. At the Graham house,
Gertrude (as she is now called) is persecuted by the housekeeper, but she
resists the impulse to anger and leaves the housekeeper with "a stinging
consciousness of the fact that [the girl] had shown a superiority to herself."
Gertrude has done nothing deliberately to call attention to this superiority,
and although she never mentions the housekeeper's behavior to Emily,
Emily learns of it anyway, so that her protégée's self-effacing reticence has
the effect of producing an even more perfect self-promotion. Willie Sullivan, meanwhile, has left for India to pursue his fortune—not for himself but
so that he can support his mother and his grandfather, Mr. Cooper.
Gertrude, by now fourteen, has promised to care for Mrs. Sullivan and Mr.
Cooper in Willie's absence.

Four years later Gertrude leaves the Grahams' suburban summer home
for Boston to fulfill her promise to Willie (whose mother and grandfather
are now ill) and to support herself by teaching. Emily's father objects, insisting that Gertrude is now in his power, but Gertrude defies him—not, of
course, out of self-assertion but out of duty. "I see in the sacrifice you are
making of yourself," declares an admiring Emily, "one of the noblest and
most important traits of character a woman can possess." For Gertrude, as is
far from the case with Ellen Montgomery, "feminine" self-sacrifice is thus
rather directly transmuted into a form of personal power, even autonomy
and freedom, the trick being that this transmutation is never intentional. In
Boston, Gertrude nurses Mr. Cooper and Mrs. Sullivan until they die and
also provides for Nan Grant, who has rather miraculously reappeared, until
she dies. And the more she is good, as Emily prophesied, the more others
come to love and admire her.

At this point, less than halfway through *The Lamplighter*, all the conflicts involved in the story of Gertrude's growth have pretty much been resolved. She has learned to control her early rebelliousness, and through her
self-sacrificing benevolence she has overcome the stigma associated with
her early poverty and obscure origins. The rest of the novel defies summary.
There are excursions into the terrain of Dickens: an eccentric old woman
named Patty Pace, whose outlandish clothes are matched by her orotund
diction; a mysterious Byronic stranger named Mr. Phillips, who seems

wracked by melancholy remorse and who follows Gertrude and Emily on their travels. There are excursions, too, into the realm of Jane Austen: for instance, a love triangle in which an idle young man forces his attentions on a young woman named Kitty Ray in order, as he supposes, to arouse Gertrude's jealousy. There is also considerable cultivation of one of the favorite themes of Catharine Sedgwick and other American women writers of the 1830s and 1840s: the contrast between the frivolous life of fashion and the solid virtues of domestic competence.

Through all of this Gertrude marches triumphantly. She returns to the Grahams to care for Emily. On a burning Hudson River steamboat, she risks her own life to save that of an idle young woman of fashion whom she supposes to be her rival for the love of Willie Sullivan (now returned from India). She learns that Mr. Phillips is in fact Phillip Amory—and that he is both Emily's former beloved and Gertrude's own father! She then learns, of course, that Willie has loved her all along. "What is there," he has already exclaimed to Phillip Amory, whom he turns out to have rescued from Bedouins years before in the deserts of Arabia,

> in the wearisome and foolish walks of Fashion, the glitter and show of wealth, the homage of an idle crowd, that could so fill my heart, elevate my spirit, and inspire my exertions, as the thought of a peaceful, happy home, blessed by a presiding spirit so formed for confidence, love, and a communion that time can never dissolve, and eternity can but render more serene and unbroken?

Gertrude and Willie finally come to an understanding in a rural cemetery, over the graves of Willie's family and Gertrude's lamplighter. At the conclusion they are married—as are Emily and Phillip Amory, the latter now cured of his Byronic despair. "Through the power of a living faith," we are told on the final page, "he has laid hold on eternal life."

Although *The Lamplighter* is clearly something of a hodgepodge, especially following the deaths of Trueman Flint, Nan Grant, and Willie Sullivan's family, the reasons for its appeal to contemporary readers are also clear. It advertises the virtues of domesticity, of what Willie calls the "peaceful, happy home," far more consistently and extravagantly than does *The Wide, Wide World*. And it persistently turns submission and self-sacrifice into unconscious triumph. Gertrude never *intends* to triumph, and she never calls attention to her own virtue or to her mistreatment by others, but both the reader and the characters, compelled alike into the role of admiring spectators, are repeatedly reminded of her superiority. This superiority is singularly uncomplicated. As has been noted, Cummins draws for much of the plot of the later portions of *The Lamplighter* on the kinds of romantic misunderstanding central to the plots of Jane Austen, yet Gertrude (unlike, for instance, Austen's *Emma*) is never in the wrong. Moreover, Gertrude's superiority, unlike that of Warner's Ellen Montgomery, is relentlessly rewarded.

The basic messages of *The Lamplighter* must have been clear to the novel's many readers and must have been consoling. Domesticity is not confinement to the home but liberation from the idle extravagance of fashion. Self-sacrifice and adherence to duty lead not to suffering but to happiness, including worldly happiness. All of this is a far cry from the abiding sense of at least worldly constriction and limitation one encounters in *The Wide, Wide World*, even in its conclusion. In *The Lamplighter*, in other words, *The Wide, Wide World*'s sense of Christian self-sacrifice gets secularized. If Ellen Montgomery's story seems meant to recast the progress of Bunyan's pilgrim Christian in "feminine" terms, Gertrude's story seems more nearly a "feminine" foreshadowing of the progress from rags to riches of the heroes of Horatio Alger.

On a deeper level, though, what is most interesting about these two books is what they have in common. Like so many nineteenth-century novels, both tell the stories of orphans, and yet there is in them little abiding sense of the alienation and guilt associated with orphanhood in the works of Dickens or the Brontës or in Melville's *Redburn* and *Moby-Dick*. Ellen, and especially Gertrude, learn rather rapidly to suppress their antisocial anger and to find ideal substitute families; neither blames society in general for her own situation, so that orphanhood is for them less a general symbol than an unfortunate personal condition. They welcome love when they get it, and they both do get it; love is their sure reward for "feminine" virtue and forbearance.

In both novels, too, love is so fully subsumed into the home, so thoroughly equated with domestic relationships, that all true relationships become in effect family relationships—between ideal pseudoparents and pseudochildren or between ideal pseudosiblings—and it is often difficult to distinguish parent-child relationships from sibling-sibling relationships or to distinguish either from sexual, or "romantic," relationships. Gertrude's extended adoptive family consists of her "Uncle" True, Mrs. Sullivan (who functions as her mother), Willie (her adoptive brother), and Emily Graham (her adoptive older sister, a role assumed by Alice Humphreys for Ellen Montgomery). But these relationships are far from stable. After True's stroke we are told that "the cases are quite reversed"; the "robust man" who had been to little Gerty both "a father and a mother" is now "feeble as a child," and Gerty, "with the stature of a child, but a woman's capacity," becomes *his* mother. As Emily comes to depend on Gertrude, their relationship also tends to get reversed, as Gertrude comes to function as *Emily's* mother, and the introduction of the mysterious Mr. Phillips abets the confusion. His indeterminate age (he looks like a young man with prematurely gray hair) and his increasingly fervent attentions to Gertrude lead us to believe that he is her suitor, and the revelation that he is actually her father and Emily's former beloved scarcely diminishes the oddity of the family romance implicit in *The Lamplighter,* especially since Phillip Amory was originally Emily's stepbrother, and they were raised (like Willie and Gertie) as brother and sister. It is as if Gertrude's and Emily's ties to this father/brother/suitor were both displacements of some deeper tie, an implication reinforced at the close when Gertrude, having proved her virtue by playing "mother" to most of the characters in the book, marries *her* "brother" Willie.

The symbolic family situation in *The Wide, Wide World* is not quite so complicated as in *The Lamplighter,* but its deepest implications are significantly similar. Alice and John Humphreys adopt Ellen Montgomery as their "little sister." When Alice learns that she is dying, she says to Ellen: "You must come here and take my place, and take care of those I leave behind." That this charge should lead, as the book's conclusion strongly hints, to Ellen's eventual marriage to her "brother" John should not seem entirely surprising; in fact, the tie between John and Alice has all along seemed more like the passion of lovers than the affection of siblings. When John is absent at seminary, Alice pines for him with the melancholy of the Romantic heroine, and when he returns home just in time for her death, they embrace passionately. "Are you happy, Alice?" he asks. "Perfectly," she replies. "This was all I wanted. Kiss me, dear John." "As he did so," the narrator continues, "again and again, she felt his tears on her cheek, and put up her hands to his face to wipe them away; kissed him then, and then once again laid her head on his breast." In this embrace Alice dies, and the intensity of the scene suggests what it might mean for Ellen to fully take her place.

One does not necessarily wish to argue that there is some sort of secret incest theme in *The Wide, Wide World* and *The Lamplighter.* There may well be, but what matters most is that we recognize how something like incest, however displaced or confused, may be the inevitable result of setting up the home and its web of domestic relationships as the alternative to a world dominated by masculine power, including masculine sexual power.

Paradoxically enough, if the family or ideal pseudofamily is divorced from
the realm of sex and is presented as a refuge from the realm of sex, then sexual relationships or their equivalents can take place only within the family.
And we should recognize in any case that intimacy and sexual attraction are
largely missing from these books, especially from *The Lamplighter.* As
virtue becomes exemplary, relationships become spectatorial, based not on
private intimacy but on the public demonstration and appreciation of right
conduct. Such conduct makes no direct claim to power; it works indirectly,
through the "influence" that was the hallmark of the Cult of Domesticity:
the influence of the ideal mother.

The most passionate image of this influence, in either novel, may be
Mrs. Sullivan's dream, shortly before her death, of flying across the ocean to
lift her absent Willie from the sexual temptations of the world of fashion.
"As we rose in the air," she tells Gertrude,

> my manly son became in my encircling arms a child again, and there rested
> on my bosom the same little head, with its soft, silken curls, that had nes-
> tled there in infancy. Back we flew, over sea and land, and paused not until
> on a soft, grassy slope, under the shade of green trees, I thought I saw my
> darling Gerty, and was flying to lay my precious boy at her feet, when I
> awoke, pronouncing your name.

Gerty's marriage to her "brother" is thus not so much a displaced violation of
sexual taboo as a regression into an ideal childhood (quite different from the
one she actually had), in which she can be at once admiring sister and admired mother. Willie later reveals that he *was* saved from temptation and
preserved pure for Gerty by "the recollection of my pure-minded and
watchful mother," by "the consciousness of her gentle spirit, ever hovering
around my path, saddened by my conflicts, rejoicing in my triumphs." Even
in the world of spirits, this is to say, virtue is exemplary, and relationships are
spectatorial. At the beginning of *The Lamplighter,* little Gerty is discovered
at her window, gazing out in wonder as Trueman Flint lights the lamps along
her street. At the close, Gertrude and Willie are gazing out another window,
the window of their new home, as the gas-man lights the lamps of a mod-
ernized and efficient Boston. "Dear Uncle True!" Gertrude sighs, "his lamp
still burns brightly in heaven, Willie; and its light is not yet gone out on
earth."

In 1855, a month after complaining to William Ticknor about "these innumerable editions of the Lamplighter, and other books neither better nor

worse," Nathaniel Hawthorne sent another letter to his publisher, announcing an exception to the "vituperation" he had bestowed "on female authors." "I have since been reading 'Ruth Hall,'" he wrote, "and I must say I enjoyed it a good deal. The woman writes as if the devil was in her. . . . Can you tell me anything about this Fanny Fern? If you meet her, I wish you would let her know how much I admire her." Although few other contemporary male readers were inclined to admire a woman for writing "as if the devil was in her," it was clear to all that *Ruth Hall* (1854) was markedly different from such books as *The Wide, Wide World* and *The Lamplighter*. And the life of the author of *Ruth Hall*—which by 1855 had included two marriages, with the second ending in divorce, and which would lead to another marriage in 1856, to James Parton—had been equally different from the lives of Susan Warner and Maria Cummins. Yet in at least one significant respect the career of Sara Payson Willis Eldredge Farrington Parton (1811–72) resembled that of Susan Warner and most other American women writers of the 1850s. She had turned to literature as a profession only rather late in her life (at the age of forty) and only under the pressure of acute financial hardship.

Sara Payson Willis was born in 1811, in Portland, Maine, the fifth of nine children. The family soon moved to Boston, where Sara's father, "Deacon" Nathaniel Willis of Boston's Park Street Church, founded *The Recorder*, a religious weekly, in 1816 and *The Youth's Companion*, a children's weekly that he would edit for thirty years, in 1827. Three of his sons, most notably Nathaniel Parker Willis, would follow him into the world of magazines. Even as a girl of twelve, Sara helped with the *Youth's Companion*, although she was of course not encouraged to contemplate a literary career. She was well-educated nonetheless, attending, among other institutions, Catharine Beecher's Hartford Female Seminary. Harriet Beecher, who at the time was both a student and a teacher at her sister's school, would later recall Sara Willis as a "laughing witch of a half saint half sinner." Sara returned to Boston at eighteen, and eight years later, in the Panic year of 1837, she married Charles Eldredge (known as "Handsome Charlie").

The marriage was apparently happy and produced three daughters, but in the mid-1840s the happiness turned sour. In 1844 Sara Eldredge's mother, whose influence Sara would later credit for her own poetic inclinations, died, and in 1845 Sara's oldest daughter, Mary, died. Then, in 1846 Charles Eldredge died, and the claims of his creditors left nothing to support his widow and her two surviving children. She received only minimal and grudging support from her father and parents-in-law, and early in 1849 she was more or less forced into a disastrous second marriage with a widower named Samuel Farrington. Two years later she left him, and they were subsequently divorced. Her first husband's parents had taken responsibility for her older surviving daughter, Grace, but only on the terms that the mother have no control over her, and both her father and the Eldredges used the scandal of her separation as an excuse for refusing Sara further support. Left completely on her own, she sought to support herself by teaching (she passed the Boston teachers' examination but was unable to get a teaching job) and then by sewing (never earning more than seventy-five cents a week).

It was at this point that Sara Willis Eldredge Farrington turned to writing for a living. In June of 1851 she published, pseudonymously, her first piece in Boston's *Olive Branch*, and she was soon producing five to ten pieces a week (for a total of only six dollars) for the *Olive Branch* and for Boston's *True Flag*. In September she settled on the pseudonym Fanny Fern. She had sought help from her influential brother Nathaniel, but he had refused her contribution to the *Home Journal* (where he was advancing the careers of other women writers), he had ridiculed her writing, and he later even refused to allow his editor, James Parton, to reprint pieces by her that had appeared elsewhere. Parton, incensed, resigned. Meanwhile, in 1852, another New York magazinist, Oliver Dyer, solicited her contributions for his *Musical World and Times*, doubling the fee she was receiving in Boston. "Fanny Fern," in spite of the hostility of her famous brother (whose relationship to her was in any case not publicly known), was becoming popular, and in 1853 New York publisher James Derby brought out the first collection of her newspaper sketches, *Fern Leaves from Fanny's Portfolio*, whose instant success has already been described. *Fern Leaves* also demonstrated its author's growing business acumen. Offered the choice of a flat fee of something like $1,000 or a royalty of ten cents a copy, she chose the latter; as a result, sales earned her close to $10,000 in less than a year, and she was soon earning even more from *Little Ferns for Fanny's Little Friends* (1853) and from a second series of *Fern Leaves* (1854). By the summer of 1853 she was doing well enough to move to New York and to reclaim her daughter Grace.

In 1856 she married James Parton, eleven years her junior; their marriage agreement guaranteed her control of her own property and income. In the same year she began her career as an exclusive columnist in Robert Bonner's *New York Ledger*, to which she would contribute faithfully until her death from cancer in 1872. Bonner originally offered her $25 for each weekly column; she held out for $100, a fee Bonner then proceeded to advertise widely. By the mid-1850s the former Sara Willis was known as Fanny even to her friends and to her husband. As Fanny Fern, author of sometimes sentimental but far more often colloquial, humorous, and satirical newspaper sketches, she had become a nationally known celebrity, a star, and her literary earnings enabled her to buy comfortable homes first in Brooklyn and later in Manhattan.

Although Fanny Fern was by 1854 already a best-selling writer, her ultimate celebrity was to some extent a result of the scandal produced by the publication of *Ruth Hall* at the end of that year. Thinking herself protected by her pseudonym, she produced in her first novel (*Rose Clark* followed in 1856) a very thinly veiled version of her mistreatment by the world and by members of her own family—a version that included a clearly recognizable dandy named "Hyacinth Ellet," editor of the "Irving Magazine." The true identity of the author of *Ruth Hall* was revealed in print shortly after the book appeared, and she was widely condemned for "unfeminine" indelicacy and vindictiveness. Although this public exposure was deeply embarrassing, the scandal only helped sales, which soon reached 70,000; and to Fanny Fern, who had turned to literature for support only after her family had refused to help her, such sales must have been doubly satisfying. The Christian submission and "feminine" self-sacrifice advertised pseudonymously or anonymously by such writers as Susan Warner and Maria Cummins were not central to the repertoire of Deacon Willis's daughter, and the story of *Ruth Hall* is the story of a woman who, rather than accepting her circumstances, overcomes them to achieve economic and psychological autonomy—albeit, still, in order to fulfill her duties as a mother.

The book opens on the eve of Ruth Ellet's marriage to Harry Hall. Unlike Sara Willis, who married at the age of twenty-six, Ruth is only eighteen when she marries, and just returned from the boarding school where she had been sent following her mother's death. She is now glad to be leaving "her father's roof, (for her childhood had been anything but happy,)," but she wonders apprehensively if "that craving heart of her's [had] at length found its ark of refuge?" That is, she is not seeking freedom but only a more benign dependency, to be guaranteed by the "love" she never received as a child. Although Harry gives her this love, her worries turn out to have been well-founded. Her parents-in-law, with whom the newlyweds at first live, subject Ruth to an unending series of petty cruelties and humiliations. When Ruth and Harry move to their own house in the country, following the birth of their daughter Daisy, Dr. and Mrs. Hall move into a house nearby ("for Harry's sake," as his jealous mothers puts it), and they continue to torment their daughter-in-law. Then little Daisy dies of croup, and Dr. Hall comments to a neighbor on Ruth's sorrow: "Now that proves she didn't make a sanctifying use of her trouble. It's no use trying to dodge what the Lord sends." This sounds very much like the advice Alice Humphreys gives Ellen Montgomery in *The Wide, Wide World* when Ellen learns of her mother's death, but in *Ruth Hall* such declarations are motivated mainly by self-centered hypocrisy.

Eight years later Ruth and Harry are staying at a seaside hotel, with two new daughters, Katy and Nettie. There Harry dies of typhoid fever (the disease that killed Charles Eldredge) and Ruth's real troubles begin. Although both the Halls and Mr. Ellet have money to spare, they provide Ruth with less than she needs for subsistence, and she and her children end up living on a meager diet of bread and milk in a shabby urban boardinghouse where Ruth sews late into the night to try to support them. Her wealthy cousins, the Millets, find her poverty so embarrassing that they ask her to keep Katy and Nettie from acknowledging them in public. Mr. Millet also votes against her when she applies for a teaching job at a school on whose board he sits. Eventually, Mrs. Hall even gets Katy away from her and subjects the child to treatment that recalls Ellen Montgomery's life with Aunt Fortune.

In her preface to *Ruth Hall,* Fanny Fern insists that she does not dignify her "story . . . by the name of 'A novel.'" "There is no intricate plot," she explains, "there are no startling developments, no hair-breadth escapes." All of this is clearly true. Unlike *The Lamplighter,* for instance, *Ruth Hall* makes no use of tantalizing mystery and surprising discovery, and there are no reunions with lost relations at the close; after all, Ruth's relations are precisely her problem. The account of Ruth's troubles might be called melodramatic; it is certainly the case that there is almost no form of petty nastiness that her persecutors do not commit. But these persecutors are less villains than comic buffoons, and the tone with which they are treated has less in common with melodrama than with satire. For instance, Ruth's brother Hyacinth, at Harry's deathbed, is concerned only with Ruth's unattractive appearance (she has fainted). "Somebody ought to tell her, when she comes to," he comments, "that her hair is parted unevenly and needs brushing sadly." And the point of the accounts of Mr. Ellet's stingy and unloving meanness to his daughter is mainly to satirize the hypocrisy of those for whom religion consists only of maintaining "correct" doctrine and a "Christian" reputation.

The first half of *Ruth Hall* might be described as sentimental, although this term also distorts the actual effect. The book proceeds by brief chapters, many running to little more than a page; we shift from scene to scene, with little narrative comment or expository connection. On occasion the narrator does intrude with the full, flowery language of "sentiment." For example, while Ruth, newly married, suffers in silence at the home of the Halls, the narrator exclaims: "Oh, love! that thy silken reins could so curb the spirit and bridle the tongue, that thy uplifted finger of warning could calm that bounding pulse, still that throbbing heart, and send those rebellious tears, unnoticed, back to their source." In the next paragraph, however, the tone shifts from indulgence to indictment: "Ah! could we lay bare the secret history of many a wife's heart, what martyrs would be found, over whose uncomplaining lips the grave sets its unbroken seal of silence." Although the language in this second paragraph is equally "sentimental" (and the parallelism is clearly deliberate), the effect is now to parody the rhetoric of "feminine" submission by revealing the actual conditions its masks.

There is also an ecstatic narrative effusion on the birth of little Daisy: "Joy to thee, Ruth! Another outlet for thy womanly heart; a mirror, in which thy smiles and tears shall be reflected back; a fair page, on which thou, God-commissioned, mayst write what thou wilt; a heart that will throb back to thine, love for love." But we are then immediately informed (with no comment on the irony of the juxtaposition) that "Ruth thinks not of all this now, as she lies pale and motionless upon the pillow." She has passed out from the pain of childbirth. Fanny Fern hardly dismisses the "joy" of motherhood, but throughout *Ruth Hall* the conventional language of sentiment is deftly balanced and qualified by an ironic sense of actual circumstance.

Eight years after little Daisy's death, we discover Ruth in her room, weeping over cherished tokens of her departed daughter: a little shoe and a lock of Daisy's golden hair—the latter, surely, a reference to the famous scene in *Uncle Tom's Cabin* during which little Eva, dying, dispenses countless locks of *her* golden hair to those she will be leaving behind. Little Katy Hall interrupts her mother's sentimental reverie. "Daisy's in heaven," she comments. "Why do you cry, mamma? Don't you like to have God keep her for you?" Then she adds: "*I* should like to die, and have you love *my* curls as you do Daisy's, mother." This declaration startles Ruth out of her self-absorbed reverie. Recognizing both the excesses and the potential cruelty of her sentimental indulgence, she cuts a lock of Katy's brown hair and places it next to Daisy's. Then Katy, in a wonderful touch on Fanny Fern's part, gives her mother one of her own shoes. This is a "sentimental" moment, to be sure, but the sentiment is fully human, and not without humor.

Ultimately, Ruth responds to her predicament with neither "feminine" self-sacrifice nor sentimental self-indulgence; instead, she asserts her own power to compete, and succeed, in the marketplace that has made no provision for her. She comes to no overt recognition of the political conditions that have made her predicament possible, but a series of increasingly surreal scenes and interpolated stories expresses her growing understanding— her disillusionment with the "love" on which she has been taught to depend. There is the comic story of her landlady, Mrs. Skiddy, and her henpecked husband, who is obsessed with the dream of escaping to California. These characters are drawn from Dickens (who is mentioned twice in the course of their story), but the outcome enforces a very un-Dickensian point. Mr. Skiddy finally makes his escape and our sympathies are with him, even when he writes back to say that California has been a failure and to request passage money to return home. Then both sympathy and valuation are suddenly reversed. "Drawing from her pocket a purse well filled with her own honest earnings," Mrs. Skiddy "chinked its contents at some phantom shape discernible to her eyes alone; while through her set teeth hissed out, like ten thousand serpents, the word 'N – e – v – e – r!' "

Then, with Katy (not yet captured by Mrs. Hall), Ruth visits a hospital for the insane. "There," we are told, "was the fragile wife, to whom *love* was breath—being!—forgotten by the world and him in whose service her bloom had withered, insane—only in that her love had outlived his patience." Ruth sees a woman, chained in a cell, whose husband has left her and, with full support of the law, has taken their child with him. The Ruth views the body of a former friend, Mary Leon, confined in the hospital by her husband with the full connivance of his close friend, the hospital's male superintendent. Mary has left a note for her: "I am not crazy, Ruth, no, no— but I shall be; the air of this place stifles me; I grow weaker—weaker. I cannot die here; for the love of heaven, dear Ruth, come and take me away." Her last words, Ruth learns, were, "I want to be alone." The asylum visit, by 1854, had long been a staple of sentimental fiction, in both America and England, but here the visit is not an occasion for the indulgence of feeling (Ruth's reaction is scarcely reported) but a surreal image of the imprisonment of women not only by masculine power but by the compensatory rhetoric of "love."

Ruth, in any case, turns to writing for the newspapers, and the story of her eventual triumph (closely paralleling the life of her author) dominates the final chapters of *Ruth Hall*, which carefully detail the consequent humiliation of the relatives, who now try, unsuccessfully, to take credit for the triumph of "Floy" (Ruth's nom de plume). One of her Millet cousins complains, in a letter to his parents: "How could *I* tell she was going to be so famous, when I requested her not to allow her children to call me 'cousin John' in the street?" Ruth's brother Hyacinth has taken pains to impede her advancement, but, as before, the point is not so much to accentuate his melodramatic villainy as to score satiric points—in this case on the corruption of the world of American literary magazines. For instance, Hyacinth's subeditor Horace Gates (based on Fanny Fern's future husband, James Parton) remembers Hyacinth's insistence that the "Irving Magazine" provide only a neutral "notice" of "Uncle Sam's Log House" (i.e., *Uncle Tom's Cabin*) "for fear of offending southern subscribers." What matters most, however, is that Ruth does triumph; her first collection, "Life Sketches" (i.e., *Fern Leaves*), is a tremendous financial success and enables her to rescue Katy from the Halls and to move to another city (i.e., New York) and live in welcome comfort and independence. And the accent is very much on independence; the conventional "happy marriage" plays no part in the happy ending of *Ruth Hall*.

What saves all this from the charge of "unfeminine" egotism (a charge Fanny Fern obviously knew she was risking) is that Ruth triumphs not for herself but for her children. She masters the business of writing and publishing and then beats her various male oppressors at their own game in order to feed Nettie and recover custody of Katy. " 'Floy' scribbled on," we are told, "thinking only of bread for her children." Moreover, it is not Ruth but John Walter, a male editor who befriends her, who explicitly denounces the way she has been treated. Ruth herself never boasts of her achievements. When she reads one of her stories to little Nettie, her daughter asks, "when I get to be a woman shall I write books, mamma?" "God forbid," Ruth replies, to herself; "no happy woman ever writes. From Harry's grave sprang 'Floy.' " Even Ruth's apparent ambition, this is to say, is really a fulfillment of her duties as wife and mother. When a correspondent requests a portrait bust of "Floy" for a young lady's parlor, Ruth says to herself: "No, no, . . . better reserve the niche destined for 'Floy' for some writer to whom ambition is not the hollow thing it is to me." Instead, she focuses her attention on another letter, expressing gratitude for the effects of her moral influence.

Nevertheless, Ruth Hall clearly (and justly) glories in the fruits of her labors, both financial and psychological. When Nettie expresses her unwillingness to forgive Grandmother Hall, Ruth responds with the appropriate Christian message, but with a special twist. "She has punished herself worse than anybody else could punish her," she explains. "She *might* have made us all love her, and help to make her old age cheerful; but now, unless she repents, she will live miserably, and die forsaken, for nobody can love her with such a temper." Human vengeance is unnecessary because the Lord, apparently, will work his own vengeance in the here and now, and we never learn that Mrs. Hall or any of Ruth's persecutors *have* repented. On the morning she decides to try writing for the newspapers, Ruth recognizes that she will face long and difficult struggles. *"Pride,"* she tells herself, "must sleep!" "But," she continues, glancing at her sleeping children, "it shall be *done*. They shall be proud of their mother." "Pride," in other words, will not sleep forever; it must only be deferred in order to be perfected. In the next-to-last chapter of the novel, John Walter presents Ruth with a certificate for one hundred shares of bank stock, her first investment of the surplus earnings from "Life Sketches." "Now confess," he urges, "that you are proud of yourself." Ruth remains modestly silent, but Nettie chimes in, "We are proud of her, . . . if she is not proud of herself."

It is not easy to name Fanny Fern's literary descendants. One perhaps finds traces of her irony and humor in the work of Dorothy Parker, in the twentieth century, but Fanny Fern exhibits none of Parker's self-destructiveness. *Ruth Hall's* reliance on brief scenes and ironic contrast rather than authorial exposition and her often parodic use of the language of sentiment foreshadow similar qualities in the work of Stephen Crane, another writer who would have his beginnings in the mode of the newspaper sketch. One might also see affinities between *Ruth Hall* and Kate Chopin's *The Awakening* (1899), which also portrays the condition of women and the ideology of "feminine" submission with telling irony. Nevertheless, *Ruth Hall* is finally a singular book. For all its overt adherence at least to the letter of the Cult of Domesticity, it is mainly an anomaly among the best-selling works of American women's fiction in the 1850s.

Harriet Beecher Stowe

Uncle Tom's Cabin, published in book form in 1852, made Harriet Beecher Stowe (1811–96) a national and international celebrity, the most famous American novelist of the 1850s and perhaps the most famous American woman of the nineteenth century. The book's phenomenal sales, described earlier, provide only a limited sense of its full impact. There was widespread praise and also condemnation, especially from the South, including counternovels portraying slavery and plantation life as wholly beneficent. To an astonishing extent, between 1852 and 1860, the national debate over slavery became a debate over the truth or falsity of Stowe's fictional picture of life in the South. And in the years following the Civil War, Stowe's story, increasingly drained of its abolitionist message, became a staple of American popular culture, in songs, giftbooks, card games, souvenir plates, and above all in plays, theatrical spectacles, and even in traveling minstrel shows.

Stowe's personal celebrity set her apart even from such widely popular women writers as Susan Warner and Maria Cummins. For one thing, although Stowe's "literary" merit has often been questioned, she has never been forgotten; *Uncle Tom's Cabin* has remained in print consistently since it was published in 1852, and it is now quite solidly entrenched in "American literature" as that literature is defined by the academic curriculum. Moreover, in her own time Stowe departed in a number of significant ways from the postures and practices of contemporary American women writers. With *Uncle Tom's Cabin* she directly confronted the principal political controversy of her day, and in the wake of that novel's success she embraced the role of public figure with relish. She toured Scotland and England in 1853 as a celebrity, expressed her strong opinions on such political matters as the struggle over "Bloody Kansas" in a weekly newspaper column, and even, in the early years of the Civil War, took public issue with the policies of President Lincoln.

This penchant or compulsion for outspokenness would eventually lead to a major scandal. In 1869, responding to an attack on Lord Byron's widow (with whom she was acquainted), Stowe came to the woman's defense with "The True Story of Lady Byron's Life." Here she made public the story that Byron had committed incest with his sister. Both Calvin Stowe (her husband) and Stowe's publisher, James R. Osgood, protested, but a writer of Stowe's reputation and determination was not easily opposed, and the piece appeared in the *Atlantic Monthly* in Boston and in *Macmillan's* in England. Public discussion of slavery was one thing; discussion, especially by a woman, of incest was quite another; and the reaction to this scandalous violation of the Cult of Domesticity—and to the book-length version, *Lady Byron Vindicated,* that followed in 1870—was swift and overwhelming. *Atlantic Monthly* readers canceled their subscriptions in droves, Stowe was repeatedly attacked in public, and the incident ended up undermining much of her undisputed eminence.

Nevertheless, Stowe's departure from the Cult of Domesticity was not quite as complete as this evidence might suggest, at least not in the case of *Uncle Tom's Cabin.* Stowe indirectly acknowledged the possibly "unfeminine" implications of her plan to write a story protesting the evils of slavery when she wrote to the editor of the *National Era* in 1851: "Up to this year I have always felt that I had no particular call to meddle with this subject, and

I dreaded to expose even my own mind to the full force of its exciting power. But I feel now that the time is come when even a woman or a child who can speak a word for freedom and humanity is bound to speak." Only the intensity of the moral crisis, that is, could lead her to transgress the boundaries of "woman's sphere." Nor did Stowe present herself as contending with men in the realm of *artistic* endeavor. Looking back on *Uncle Tom's Cabin,* after it had made her famous, she declared that she "no more thought of style or literary excellence than the mother who rushes into the street and cries for help to save her children from a burning house, thinks of the teachings of the rhetorician or the elocutionist." There is a dig here, to be sure, at the political or moral irrelevance of those who concern themselves with "literary excellence," but in forswearing all "thought of style," Stowe was conforming rather precisely to the standard rationale adopted by most American women writers of the 1850s, and it is surely significant that ambition is here transmuted into a manifestation of maternal duty—domesticity animated to action only by a child-threatening emergency. Equally conventional, and equally "feminine," was Stowe's famous and oft-repeated declaration that it was not she, but God, who wrote *Uncle Tom's Cabin.* It should also be recognized that Stowe's controversial political writing of the 1850s, although it accounts for her widespread fame, represents only an episode in the story of her full career as a highly successful professional writer. *Uncle Tom's Cabin,* although it is a clear and sincere expression of Stowe's character and beliefs, is by no means representative of her full oeuvre.

Harriet Esther Beecher was born in 1811 in Litchfield, Connecticut, into an extraordinary family. Her father, Lyman, was a Presbyterian minister and was one of the most famous preachers in America and a dominant influence on his children. His seven sons all followed him into the ministry, and one of them, Henry Ward (1813–87), would become at least as famous as his father. Daughters, of course, could not enter the ministry, but Harriet's older sister (and oldest sibling), Catharine, would become an influential proponent of education for American women. For many years, Harriet Beecher hardly seemed the most likely candidate for ultimate distinction in this distinguished family. By the age of eleven she had become shy and retiring, with a passion for solitary reading. At the age of thirteen she was enrolled in the Hartford Female Seminary, established by sister Catharine. When Catharine discovered that Harriet was secretly writing a long verse tragedy, Stowe later recalled, she "pounced down upon me and said that I must not waste my time writing poetry." More serious writing, however, was by no means forbidden. Harriet had already earned her father's praise in Litch-field for a prize-winning school essay entitled "Can the Immortality of the Soul Be Proved by the Light of Nature?"

In 1832, Lyman Beecher accepted an offer to become president of Lane Theological Seminary, a new Calvinist divinity school in Cincinnati, and Catharine and Harriet both joined the family crusade to spread the Gospel in the West. In Cincinnati Catharine established a new school, the Western Female Institute, where Harriet also taught, and here, in a somewhat desultory fashion, Harriet Beecher launched her literary career. In 1834 she began publishing stories in Judge James Hall's *Western Monthly Magazine,* and one of these stories won a prize of $50, teaching its author the important lesson that literature could provide a source of at least supplemental income. The need for such income would soon become pressing. In 1836 Harriet Beecher married Calvin Ellis Stowe, a widower and Lane professor whose circumstances were far from prosperous. "I was married when I was twenty-five years old," she wrote in 1853, "to a man rich in Greek and Hebrew, Latin and Arabic, and, alas!, rich in nothing else." It was impossible to support their growing family, eventually including seven children, on his professor's salary, so that whatever Harriet Beecher Stowe could earn from her writing was not only welcome but essential, and she pursued literature with a solid professional sense. In 1842, when she had written enough sketches to constitute a collected volume, she traveled to New York to negotiate with the House of Harper; she clearly knew where to look for national distribution. "On the whole, my dear," she wrote to Calvin from New York, "if I choose to be a literary lady, I have, I think, as good a chance of making profit by it as any one I know of." "My dear," Calvin replied, "you must be a literary woman." "If I am to write," his wife responded, "I must have a room to myself, which shall be *my* room."

The result of this mutual enthusiasm was *The Mayflower,* published by the Harpers in 1843, but its impact was far from sensational, and it is not recorded whether Harriet Beecher Stowe, at this time, actually got a room of her own. In any case, she hardly had the time or physical well-being to pursue a serious literary career. Between 1836 and 1850 she gave birth to seven children, she suffered at least two miscarriages, she was frequently prostrated by her pregnancies and recoveries, and when she was well enough to write, there was a growing family to care for. "I am but a mere drudge," she wrote to a friend in 1838, "with few ideas beyond babies and housekeeping," and in 1838 the press of duty and illness had hardly reached its peak. "I am determined," she wrote in 1839, explaining her need for literary income, "not to be a mere domestic slave, without even the leisure to excel in my duties." All of this climaxed in 1846–47, in a year of isolation and hydrotherapy in Brattleboro, Vermont.

Other circumstances were filling in the background of *Uncle Tom's Cabin.* In 1836, in Cincinnati, antiabolition mobs had threatened the office of James G. Birney, editor of the abolitionist *Philanthropist.* "I wish he would man it with armed men," Stowe wrote to her husband, who was in Europe buying books for the Lane library, "and see what can be done. If I were a man, I would go, for one, and take good care of at least one window." The mob prevailed, and Birney left Cincinnati, but the incident had its effect on Stowe and on her younger brother Henry Ward Beecher, now also in Cincinnati. Thirteen years later, in 1849, a virulent cholera epidemic killed one-year-old Samuel Charles Stowe. In 1853 his mother wrote:

> It was at his dying bed that I learned what a poor slave mother may feel when her child is torn away from her. In those depths of sorrow which seemed to me immeasurable, it was my only prayer to God that such anguish might not be suffered in vain. . . . I felt that I could never be consoled for it unless this crushing of my own heart might enable me to work out some great goods to others.

The tension between the sense that domesticity was "duty" and the sense that it was "slavery" was beginning to crystallize into the complex metaphor that would enable Harriet Beecher Stowe to transform the Cult of Domesticity into a political weapon.

In 1849 Calvin Stowe was offered an appointment at Bowdoin College, and in 1850 the Stowes moved from Cincinnati to Brunswick, Maine. But this liberation also entailed an obligation. Calvin was to be paid a salary of only $1,000 a year at Bowdoin; Harriet Beecher Stowe would need to make more money from her writing. She became a regular contributor to the *National Era,* an abolitionist journal that had been founded in Washington in 1847 by Gamaliel Bailey, who had succeeded James G. Birney in 1836 as editor of Cincinnati's *Philanthropist.* Meanwhile, the new federal Fugitive Slave Law, part of the legislative package known as the Compromise of 1850, aroused strong protest and resistance in the North. "Hattie," Stowe's sister-in-law wrote to her, "if I could use a pen as you can, I would write something that will make this whole nation feel what an accursed thing slavery is." Stowe, after reading the letter aloud to her children, declared: "I *will* write something. I will if I live." Then, in February of the following year, while taking communion, she had a vision of a slave being flogged to death on the orders of his vicious master and forgiving his persecutors as he died—a vision that would become Chapter 40 of *Uncle Tom's Cabin*. When Stowe insisted that "the Lord himself wrote" *Uncle Tom's Cabin*, that she "was but an instrument in His hand," she was being perfectly sincere. She now knew where her story would end, and she had only to imagine the events leading up to this climax. Her story began appearing in the *National Era* as a serial in June, its length ultimately far exceeding anything Stowe had had in mind when she started.

When Stowe visited the White House in 1862, President Lincoln is supposed to have said: "So this is the little lady who made this big war?" Whatever effect *Uncle Tom's Cabin* may have had on American politics, it soon made its author a major spokeswoman for antislavery opinion, and it transformed the finances of the Stowe household. In July 1852 the Stowes moved to Andover, Massachusetts, where Calvin joined the faculty of Andover Theological Seminary. In the same month Harriet received her first royalty check from John P. Jewett—for $10,300 (more than ten times the annual salary Calvin had been paid at Bowdoin). From now on she was not just supplementing family income; she was the principal source of family income, and she also took charge of financial decision making. She and her family could now live in comfort. In 1863, content to live on his wife's ample income, Calvin retired, and the Stowes moved from Andover to Hartford. There were still domestic trials. In 1857 the Stowes' son Henry, a freshman at Dartmouth, drowned while swimming in the Connecticut River. Another son, Fred, enlisted in the Union army, was wounded at Gettysburg, and emerged from the war an incurable alcoholic; in 1870 he would flee to California and disappear. But from 1852 on, Harriet Beecher Stowe's days of poverty and domestic drudgery were over. Magazine editors and book publishers now competed for her writings, whatever the subject, and it has been estimated that her literary income, for at least the next two decades (i.e., until the Byron scandal of 1870), averaged something like $10,000 a year.

Stowe did not immediately return to fiction. Her next book, *A Key to Uncle Tom's Cabin* (1853), was an effort to demonstrate the factual accuracy of her best-seller, and in the midst of the controversy over *Uncle Tom's Cabin* it sold 90,000 copies in its first month. *Sunny Memories of Foreign Lands* (1854) described Stowe's European tour of 1853. There were newspaper and magazine articles, an abridged version of *Uncle Tom's Cabin* for children, and a reissue of the 1843 collection of stories and sketches. Stowe's second abolition novel, *Dred: A Tale of the Great Dismal Swamp*, did not appear until 1856. This time, to guarantee British royalties, Stowe traveled to England to publish the book there before it was issued in the United States. Although reviews were disappointing, the novel did well commercially, selling about 165,000 copies in England and about 150,000 in America in its first year.

Dred is considerably more violent—or, we might say, more "militant"— than its predecessor, and it is also a good deal less coherent. It is, in fact, a bit of a mess. The title character, supposedly a son of Denmark Vesey, lives in hiding with a band of followers, where he advocates not Christian submission, like Uncle Tom, but violent rebellion. Yet Dred never leads his uprising, he is finally rather pointlessly killed, and at the end of the book even the few good white southerners, those who free their slaves, are compelled to flee to Canada along with the black fugitives. One can hardly blame Stowe for her inability to produce a successful abolition novel in 1856, and one suspects that the violence and incoherence of *Dred* owe something to her recognition that *Uncle Tom's Cabin,* although it had brought her fame and professional success, had done very little to advance the prospects of abolition and sectional understanding.

Dred has much more in common with the popular American women's fiction of the 1850s than *Uncle Tom's Cabin* did. The novel begins by introducing Nina Gordon, a seventeen-year-old orphan-heiress just returned to her family's plantation from a northern boarding school. As the book proceeds, we follow Nina's conversion from frivolous coquetry to Christian charity, self-sacrifice, and submission. Nina proves herself worthy of her noble and Byronic suitor, Edward Clayton, who is trying to overcome the evils of slavery on his own plantation. In *Dred,* then, Stowe is attempting to adapt the story of the exemplary orphan, or of the orphan who learns to be exemplary, to *structure* an abolition novel. Two-thirds of the way through the book, however, this attempt is rather summarily abandoned. Nina, who has perhaps been reminding us of Susan Warner's Ellen Montgomery or even of Maria Cummins's Gerty, suddenly turns into little Eva and dies in a cholera epidemic, and it is at this point that what little coherence the novel has had is more or less completely dissipated. Nor does Nina's death have much to do with *Dred's* message. Although Eva is killed pretty much directly by the evils of slavery, which shock her sensitive nature, Nina seems to die mainly because her author cannot figure out what else to do with her. Still, Stowe is here drawing, in a way she was not in *Uncle Tom's Cabin,* on the central formula of popular American women's fiction, and the story of the exemplary heroine, in one form or another, would continue to be important as a structural device in her novels.

Thus *The Minister's Wooing*, set in Newport toward the end of the eighteenth century, focuses on the trials and ultimate triumph of a young woman named Mary Scudder. This novel, first serialized in Boston's new *Atlantic Monthly*, appeared in book form first in England and then in the United States, in 1859. Unlike *The Wide, Wide World* or *The Lamplighter*, *The Minister's Wooing* is a historical novel; it is concerned with the amelioration of the Calvinism of Jonathan Edwards and even features an appearance by Edwards's famous grandson, Aaron Burr. At the center of the book, however, is the exhibition of Mary Scudder's exemplary piety and virtue. She loves her cousin, James Marvyn, who goes to sea (like Willie Sullivan in *The Lamplighter*). When James is reported drowned, with no evidence that he was converted beforehand, his mother collapses, but Mary is reconciled. She even agrees, out of a sense of duty, to become engaged to the Calvinist minister, Dr. Samuel Hopkins (another historical character). Then, when James reappears, not only undrowned and prosperous but also converted, Mary chooses duty over love. But she is spared the consequences of her choice when a local gossip, Miss Prissy Diamond, explains the situation to Hopkins, who renounces his claim to Mary and frees her to marry her cousin.

We are told that Dr. Hopkins "scarce ever allowed a flower of sacred emotion to spring in his soul without picking it to pieces to see if its genera and species were correct," whereas Mary, by contrast, "had the blessed gift of womanhood—that vivid life in the soul and sentiment which resists the chills of analysis, as a healthful human heart resists cold." Yet Mary is no mere advocate of feeling and the heart; a true daughter of the Puritans, she saves her French friend, Virginie de Frontignac, from the wiles of Aaron Burr, and in the moment of crisis she is willing to submit her own desires to what she sees as her Christian duty. What perhaps distinguishes Stowe from such writers as Susan Warner and Maria Cummins is that she to some extent criticizes Mary's submissive self-denial. But Mary herself never acts on such a criticism; it takes the common sense of Miss Prissy to save her from her potential fanaticism. In the end Mary is as lavishly rewarded for her virtue as was Cummins's Gerty: by marriage, wealth, and family.

Stowe's expenditures rose at least as rapidly as her literary income, forcing her to take on more and more literary tasks to keep up with her obligations, and in 1861 she was publishing two novels as serials: *Agnes of Sorrento* in monthly installments in Boston's *Atlantic Monthly* and *The Pearl of Orr's Island* as a weekly in the New York *Independent*. Both were published as books, by Ticknor and Fields, in 1862. Stowe had a high opinion of *Agnes,* set in Italy, but most readers (including James T. Fields, who published it rather reluctantly in the *Atlantic*) have disagreed, preferring *The Pearl of Orr's Island.*

In one sense the story of Mara Lincoln, the "Pearl" of the title, is as sentimental and melodramatic as anything Stowe wrote. Mara is orphaned at birth and, in what may be a reference to one of Lydia Sigourney's better-known poems, baptized at the double funeral of her parents. She is raised by her grandparents on the Maine coast, and there, when Mara is three, a storm washes up a dead woman holding a live male child. This child is named Moses and is also raised by Mara's grandparents. There are mysteries and secrets: for instance, the local minister, Theophilus Sewell, recognizes Moses' dead mother, whom he loved and lost years earlier. But the main story turns on the relationship between Mara and Moses. She is devoted, he is selfish, yet finally, years later, they are engaged, just before Moses sails for the first time as master of his own ship. Mara then becomes ill, as suddenly as Nina Gordon before her, and Stowe intrudes quite overtly to answer the complaint of readers who "want to read only stories which end in joy and prosperity." "We wished in this history," she replies, "to speak of a class of lives formed on the model of Christ, . . . which . . . have this preciousness and value that the dear saints who live them comes nearest in their mission to the mission of Jesus." Mara dies, but not before her "mission" is accomplished. She brings her careless neighbor, Sally Kittridge, to Christ, and Moses, who returns shortly before her death, is also ultimately converted by her example. Four years later, we are told, Moses and Sally are married.

Such a summary, however, provides little sense of the flavor of this book, which depends less on plot or story than on descriptions and evocations of country customs and dialect. Already in *The Minister's Wooing* the first four chapters were devoted to the conversation and behavior at a country tea party, and the final wedding was described in a long dialect letter from Miss Prissy Diamond to her sister, "Lizabeth," in Boston. In *The Pearl of Orr's Island,* Miss Prissy is replaced by a pair of old, unmarried sisters, Roxy and Ruey Toothacre, who function far less for comic relief than as guardians or avatars of folk wisdom and of the communal spirit. They are constantly telling dialect stories, as is Captain Kittridge, Sally's father. For long stretches the novel's plot functions mainly as a framework for description and anecdote so that, oddly enough, this tale of Mara's Christ-like renunciation of the world ends up being most memorable for evoking the very world Mara renounces.

Stowe's growing emphasis on community came to fruition in the last novel she published before the Byron scandal. *Oldtown Folks* (1869) is not, however, without clichéd and melodramatic plot devices. We have a pair of mysterious orphans (Harry and Tina Percival), who come into their rightful fortune at the close; we have a haunted mansion with a secret chamber, and an elegant rake named Ellery Davenport (like Aaron Burr, a grandson of Jonathan Edwards). The main character and narrator, Horace Holyoke, is male rather than female, but Tina Percival (whose first name recalls that of Nina Gordon in *Dred*) goes through a number of the stages of the standard career of the exemplary heroine. When Tina is forced, early on, to live with a strict and unsympathetic old woman, Stowe is fairly clearly drawing on the Aunt Fortune episode of *The Wide, Wide World,* and by the end Tina's charity is in full flower, setting all problems aright.

These devices do little more, however, than provide a loose structure around which Stowe arranges descriptions of "Oldtown" (Natick, Massachusetts, where Calvin Stowe had grown up) at the end of the eighteenth century, with brief excursions to Boston and to "Cloudland" (Stowe's native town of Litchfield, Connecticut). There are loving descriptions of funerals, of small-town Sundays, of religious controversies, of New England Thanksgivings, and so on. Above all, there are dialect stories told by the town gossip, Sam Lawson, stories Stowe had learned from her husband. His object in writing, Stowe's narrator explains, is "to show how the peculiar life of old Massachusetts worked upon us [i.e., upon himself, Harry, and Tina], and determined our growth and character and destinies." But these "destinies" for the most part take a back seat to "the peculiar life of old Massachusetts." Toward the end of the book, for instance, when Horace tells of having learned that his beloved Tina was planning to marry Ellery Davenport, we might expect a detailed account of his sorrow; instead, we get a long chapter in which Ellery, in company, draws out the loquacious Sam Lawson. And at the beginning of the next-to-last chapter, after apologizing for the "minuteness" of the narrative thus far, Horace simply begins summing up the final twelve years of his story, devoting only one short paragraph to his own eventual marriage to Tina.

The Byron scandal severely damaged Stowe's reputation, but it hardly ended her career as a professional writer. She continued to write and publish, her works coming to include two more volumes of New England fiction, *Sam Lawson's Oldtown Fireside Stories* (1872) and *Poganuc People* (1878). She continued to earn royalties from earlier works. And she was a significant influence on younger women writers, most notably, perhaps,

Sarah Orne Jewett. "You must throw everything and everybody aside at times," Jewett wrote in 1899, three years after Stowe's death, "but a woman made like Mrs. Stowe cannot bring herself to that cold selfishness of the moment for one's work's sake, and the recompense for her loss is a divine touch here and there in an incomplete piece of work." Yet Jewett learned a great deal from Stowe all the same, and Stowe's most immediate importance in the development of American literature in the nineteenth century, beyond the sheer magnitude of her accomplishment as a successful professional writer, probably lay in her cultivation or invention of the New England "local-color" writing that Jewett, Mary Wilkins Freeman, and others would develop, perhaps more completely, in the 1880s and 1890s.

However atypical it may be of her writing as a whole, *Uncle Tom's Cabin* remains Stowe's masterpiece—and an American classic. It has been charged with plenty of faults, and although these charges usually involve applying contemporary standards of taste retroactively, they do identify significant qualities in the book. With its overt and frequent appeals to feeling, including the closing declaration that what "every individual can do" about slavery is "see to it that *they feel right*," *Uncle Tom's Cabin* is clearly sentimental, in the most literal sense. Complaints that Stowe relies too much on melodrama seem less persuasive. Few of the novel's characters, Eva and Simon Legree being the most obvious exceptions, are wholly virtuous or vicious, and the rest are rather notably mixed. There are moments of high excitement, such as Eliza's famous crossing of the ice, but for the most part readers who complain about the melodrama of *Uncle Tom's Cabin* are really complaining about the melodramatic violence of slavery, which is of course just what Stowe wished them to object to.

Uncle Tom's Cabin* clearly perpetuates a number of sexist and racist character stereotypes. Stowe's good women rely on "feeling," and most of her men are misled by "judgment." Men are naturally forceful and energetic, and women are naturally submissive. As for blacks, we are told that they have "naturally fine voices," that cooking is "an indigenous talent of the African race," that "the negro mind" is innately "impassioned and imaginative," and that "there is no more use in making believe to be angry with a negro than with a child." And this is only a very selective catalogue. Stowe's sexist and racist stereotypes are in fact fairly identical: that is, the "masculine" characteristics of white males are consistently contrasted with the "feminine" qualities not only of white and black women but of black men. Thus Uncle Tom possesses "the gentle, domestic heart" that, we are told, "has been a peculiar characteristic of his unhappy race," and we are told that blacks, again like women, "are not naturally daring and enterprising, but home-loving and affectionate." George Harris, a slave who openly defies slavery, might seem an exception to this stereotype, but Stowe's explanation only confirms her racism: George has inherited his "European features" and his "high, indomitable spirit" from his white father.

These sexist and racist stereotypes are by no means incidental to Stowe's novel; they are quite central to its meaning. The story begins at the Shelby plantation in Kentucky, with a marriage characterized principally by the contrast between husband and wife. "Feel too much!" Emily Shelby responds to her husband, who is in the process of selling Tom and Eliza's son Harry in order to cover his debts. "Am I not a woman,—a mother?" yet Emily Shelby does not defy her husband's corrupt authority; the contrast between masculine power and feminine feeling does not emerge as open conflict. Rather, what happens in *Uncle Tom's Cabin* is that we move through a succession of homes that present different aspects of this opening domestic situation, variations on the contrast between men who dominate and women who "feel" while submitting. As we move north, with Eliza and then with Eliza and George, each variation is an improvement on its predecessor. Senator and Mrs. Bird, to whose house Eliza first goes once she gets across the Ohio River, are similar to the Shelbys; he is a man of the world and she exerts her influence only in the home. But Senator Bird, unlike Mr. Shelby, is susceptible to such influence, which leads him to help Eliza escape. He allows himself to become, in effect, partly "feminized," and this process of feminization is more or less completed in the next northern variation on the Shelby plantation, the Quaker settlement where Eliza is reunited with George. This settlement is a kind of symbolic domestic, feminine utopia. Its center is Rachel Halliday's immaculate kitchen, from which she presides over community affairs. Her matriarchal authority works effortlessly through "influence," and she is never challenged by any of the Quaker men. Thus to move to the north, for Stowe, is not just to move toward freedom; it is also to move from public to private, from masculine power to feminine influence. And this movement finally brings about the conversion of George Harris from the "high, indomitable spirit" of his white father to the feminine virtues of Eliza and his own black mother.

The movement south, with Uncle Tom, is both more ominous and more strange. The New Orleans home of Augustine and Marie St. Clare is Stowe's most unusual variation on the domestic situation at the Shelby plantation. The length of the St. Clare episode far exceeds any obvious contribution it makes to the plot of *Uncle Tom's Cabin,* and Uncle Tom, in the affairs of this family, is a rather subordinate character. What matters here is that gender roles have gotten reversed: Augustine is sensitive, Marie is selfish. Or, to speak more precisely, gender roles have gotten confused in complex and interesting ways. Marie manipulates the ideas and values by which Emily Shelby sincerely lives. Augustine hides his "feminine" nature—which he has apparently inherited directly from his mother and which he seems to pass on, undiluted, to his daughter, Eva—beneath a veneer of "masculine" rationality and sarcasm. There are other variations on the feminine here: for instance, Eva's world-renouncing sensitivity and Topsy's insubordination. The portrayal of Topsy is likely to seem especially racist and offensive, but we should pay close attention to the precise nature of her misbehavior. We are told that she learns reading rapidly but that "the confinement of sewing was her abomination." Topsy, that is, seems to rebel mainly against "women's work."

Beneath Stowe's overt attack on slavery, then, and implicit in the metaphorical identification of black and female stereotypes lurks a more covert protest against what Stowe called, in 1839, "domestic slavery." This protest comes closer to the surface in the book's final episode, at the plantation of Simon Legree. In the figure of Cassy, at once Legree's mistress and his property, the analogy between marriage and slavery is made quite explicit, and here, finally, the contrast between masculine domination and feminine submission is engaged as conflict. Cassy does not rebel directly; Uncle Tom talks her out of her plan to kill Legree. And Tom's Christian triumph, the scene toward which Stowe had been working all along, seems not to have much effect on Legree. Rather, what brings Legree down is a subversive power at the heart of feminine submission—a power acting through a lock of Eva's hair, through Legree's memory of his mother, through Cassy's manipulation of Legree's superstition. Cassy—like Emily Shelby, Mrs. Bird, and Rachel Halliday—works through "influence," and she maintains it by playing on Legree's guilt. This guilt turns even "things sweetest and holiest," such as the memory of his mother's "dying prayers, her forgiving love," into "phantoms of horror and affright." Thus, "to the soul resolved in evil, perfect love is the most fearful torture, the seal and sentence of the direst despair." What happens at the end of *Uncle Tom's Cabin* is that the Cult of Domesticity becomes a secret weapon, a weapon that need not even be used consciously. The "dying prayers" and "forgiving love" of Legree's mother were perfectly sincere; it is not her fault that they drive her son crazy and, incidentally, permit Cassy to escape with Emmeline.

Although Legree's plantation is in one sense the antithesis of the Shelby plantation, in a deeper sense it reveals the fundamental domestic economy at work from the beginning of the book. Legree is clearly meant to dramatize the true nature, the essential brutality, of slavery as an institution, to reveal what was really going on even at the Shelbys'. And Legree's relationship with Cassy may dramatize the true nature of even the Shelbys' marriage. It is worth noting, in any case, that it is only well into the Legree episode that we learn of Mr. Shelby's death, as if there were some sort of subterranean connection between the fates of the two men. Emily Shelby has not rebelled, but she has triumphed, and when she takes over the plantation, she also proceeds to demonstrate her husband's previous incompetence through her own successful and prudent management. None of this, of course, is as clear as Stowe's attack on slavery, and *Uncle Tom's Cabin* is not a "woman's novel" in the same sense that is an abolition novel—specifically, a Christian abolition novel. But from first to last, and not surprisingly, Stowe's vision of slavery grows out of her experience and understanding of the constricted role of women in mid-nineteenth-century America—just as the cause of abolition allows her to insinuate a vision of women's experience she could hardly have expressed directly. The story of *Uncle Tom's Cabin* has little in common with the stories of Ellen Montgomery, Gertrude Sullivan, or Ruth Hall. But it does share with the works of Warner, Cummins, Fern, and other women novelists of the 1850s a more general subject: a world in which men dominate, often cruelly, and in which women, domestic slaves, have only domesticity itself to protect their severely limited moral autonomy.

Conflicts and Connections

Man in the open air, woman in the home: so might we distinguish the main male and female traditions of American writing in the 1850s. The simplicity of this formulation is quite attractive, but it masks a more complex and messy reality. We might, for instance, understand the distinction between popular women's fiction and the male canon in terms of genre, and with considerable justification. It has long been recognized that the pre–Civil War American fiction writers most often canonized in the twentieth century—Cooper, Poe, Hawthorne, and Melville, all of them men—were more deeply influenced by the tradition of gothic fiction than were most of their British contemporaries (at least, those British writers also canonized in the twentieth century). So we could distinguish between a masculine *gothic* tradition of American fiction and a *domestic* tradition established by American women novelists.

The first complication lurking in this view of things is that gothic fiction in England, first popularized by Ann Radcliffe in the 1790s, was very much a woman's mode, again and again sending a sensitive protagonist (usually a young woman) into an apparently haunted domain (usually a mansion or castle presided over by a threatening male figure). So a major component of the "masculine" American canon grows out of a British *women's* tradition. Moreover, gothic conventions play almost no role in the most popular novels by *American* women in the early 1850s, and the absence of these conventions is a bit curious. In *The Madwoman in the Attic* (1979), Sandra Gilbert and Susan Gubar describe a subversive feminist tradition in nineteenth-century literature by women, mainly British women. Their title refers to Bertha Rochester in Charlotte Brontë's *Jane Eyre,* whose madness indirectly or unconsciously expresses Jane's own rebellion against domesticity and masculine domination. Brontë, this is to say, exploited a useful strategy of women novelists: could not gothic terrors serve as agents of a subversive women's power, a power lurking beneath the pose of submissive self-denial, beneath the Cult of Domesticity? For the most part, however, the American answer to this hypothetical question was no. Best-selling American novelists like Warner, Cummins, and Fern made little or no use of the gothic, even though *Jane Eyre,* adapting gothic for the purposes of the female bildungsroman, had been published in England and America in 1847, just three years before *The Wide, Wide World* made the female bildungsroman one of the most popular fictional modes in America.

One can speculate about the reasons for the divergence of Warner, Cummins, and Fern from the example of Charlotte Brontë. We remember that Warner called her works "stories" rather than "novels"; "novels," for such Christian writers as Warner and Cummins, were immoral and dangerous, and few kinds of fiction were more symptomatic of these dangers than gothic. There is also a crucial difference between Jane Eyre, on the one hand, and Ellen Montgomery or Gertrude Flint, on the other. Whereas Brontë's heroine alternates between self-assertion and submission, Warner's and Cummins's heroines simply submit, eradicating every vestige of private self. There is nothing, in their cases, for a symbolic madwoman to symbolize. Finally, the mystery and secrecy of gothic are antithetical to the kind of exemplary power Ellen and Gertrude achieve, a power that depends absolutely on public performance and public appreciation. One episode in *Ruth Hall*—Ruth's visit to the "insane Hospital," where madness is induced in women by agents of their husbands—comes closer to the conventions of gothic fiction. Indeed, the story of Ruth's friend Mary Leon, who is imprisoned in the hospital and who dies after writing "I am not crazy, Ruth, no, no—but I shall be," anticipates the gothic feminism of Charlotte Perkins Gilman's "The Yellow Wallpaper" (1892). But this episode is hardly typical of *Ruth Hall* as a whole, nor is it particularly relevant to the meaning of Ruth's story. Even here Fanny Fern is far more interested in social criticism than in inspiring terror, and once Ruth has achieved genuine power and autonomy, as the author "Floy," she has no need to impersonate madwomen, or even to visit them. The subversive power of gothic fiction has little to do with royalty checks and stock certificates.

Thus, three of the most popular American domestic novelists of the early 1850s did not exploit the potential intersection of the domestic and gothic modes. This fact sets them apart not only from the gothic tradition of Poe and Hawthorne but equally from the subversive feminist tradition described by Sandra Gilbert and Susan Gubar. Yet one still might be a bit nervous about any rigid generic distinction between gothic and domestic fiction. In both genres, after all, the defining symbolic setting is a house. In domestic fiction we have a "home," ideally protected and presided over by a beneficent maternal influence. In gothic fiction the connotations of the setting are quite different—it is not beneficent but haunted, by some sort of mysterious menace—but the setting is still, usually, some sort of house. And the simultaneous prominence of these two modes in pre–Civil War America created the potential for a kind of generic instability or ambiguity. To know whether one was safe or at risk, protected by domestic influence or menaced by gothic horror, one had to determine what kind of house, what kind of fiction, one was in. One had to determine who was in charge: mother or monster.

In America—at least in the works of such canonized writers as Cooper, Poe, Hawthorne, and Melville—the British gothic formula was modified in significant ways. Since native castles were in short supply, their place was often taken by the terrors of the wilderness. What this means, however, is not so much that men opened up the gothic as that the "open air" of nineteenth-century American fiction often *functions* as a constricted, mysterious, interior space. Also, in the hands of male American writers, the gender implications of gothic (implications that grew directly out of the conventions of the mid-eighteenth-century seduction novel) get inverted. In so-called classic *American* gothic fiction, the sensitive protagonist is more often male than female, and the terrors that confront him are tied not to masculine rapacity but to female sexuality, or to guilty masculine fantasies of female sexuality.

Thus in Hawthorne's "Young Goodman Brown" (1835) the title character heads for a witches' sabbath in the woods shortly after his marriage, the
Devil's list of sins prominently features sexual evils (seductions, husband-
murders, abortions committed by unmarried young women), and Brown's
ultimate revulsion stems from his discovery that his wife, Faith, is present at
the midnight ceremony. Similarly, in story after story, Poe's sensitive male
protagonists are beset by innocent but nonetheless obscurely terrifying
women: Berenice, Morella, Ligeia, Madeline Usher. Indeed, what happens
in "The Fall of the House of Usher" (1839), most essentially, is that a night-
mare version of female "influence" triumphs over male domination, both
literally and symbolically. After Madeline falls upon her catatonic brother, a
widening "fissure" opens in the erect, masculine tower, revealing a "blood-
red moon"; and then all collapses into "the deep and dank tarn." In mid-
nineteenth-century American gothic fiction—as also, much later, in Alfred
Hitchcock's gothic film *Psycho* (1960)—the mother, or the son's fearful and
guilty fantasy of the mother, *is* the monster.

All of which is to say that the symbolic haunted house of American
gothic fiction and the home of the domestic novel are in effect doubles, or
mirror images, of one another; in both, the symbolic inner space is suffused
with feminine influences. The main difference is that this influence, terrifying in gothic fiction, is beneficent in domestic, so that to move from one
mode to the other is to redefine the essential meaning of the house. This
sort of redefinition lies at the heart of what happens at the end of Hawthorne's *House of the Seven Gables*. At the outset the house of the title
seems rather conventionally gothic, symbolizing masculine power and a
masculine curse on that power. At the close, following the death of Judge
Pyncheon, all of this gets explained away in the fashion of Radcliffean, or
"rational," gothic: "Maule's Curse" on the male Pyncheons was simply a
hereditary propensity for apoplexy. But the death of Judge Pyncheon transforms the meaning of the house in a more fundamental way. Suddenly the
posies, whose seeds were brought from Italy by Alice Pyncheon, bloom on
the roof—suggestively, in the angle between the two front gables. Then
Phoebe returns, with "the quiet flow of natural sunshine over her," and two
symbolic transformations, from masculine to feminine and from gothic to
domestic, are brought to completion. Thus, one could describe the ending
of *The House of the Seven Gables* as a domestic revision of the ending of
"The Fall of the House of Usher." In the years following the Civil War, we
have been told again and again, a tradition of "romance" in American fiction
(the tradition of Cooper, Poe, Hawthorne, and Melville) gave way to a tradi-

tion of "realism." These terms and this generalization are inevitably problematic. Nevertheless, one might describe Warner, Cummins, and Fern, in
that they ignore the gothic to elaborate the domestic realities of women's
lives, as harbingers of this development. This description is least plausible in
the case of Cummins; whatever realism there is at the beginning of *The
Lamplighter* rapidly gives way to fantasy. But both *The Wide, Wide World*
and *Ruth Hall* are, in different ways, significantly "realistic." Many of Harriet Beecher Stowe's works, especially her New England novels of the
1860s, also anticipate later works of so-called American realism, and not
surprisingly. Stowe as an *Atlantic Monthly* author, and William Dean Howells, who would lead the battle for realism in the 1880s, got his start on the
Atlantic in the 1860s.

In the final episode of *Uncle Tom's Cabin,* however, Stowe *does* exploit
the gothic possibilities of domestic fiction, or, to speak more precisely, the
possibilities of confusing and combining the gothic and the domestic. She
draws on something like "romance" and for clearly subversive purposes.
Cassy and Emmeline hide in a supposedly haunted room in the attic of
Legree's mansion while Legree searches the swamps. At night, dressed in a
sheet, Cassy visits Legree downstairs to sustain his superstitious fear of the
attic chamber. Eventually, the two women make their escape. Although
Cassy's attic hideout suggests that Stowe has Brontë's madwoman, Bertha
Rochester, very much in mind, the effect seems to be quite different, since
Cassy only pretends to be a ghost. Brontë's true psychological gothic seems
to give way, in Stowe, to gothic hoax, in the manner of Washington Irving's
"Legend of Sleepy Hollow" (1820). Just as Brom Bones impersonates the
Headless Horseman in order to frighten Ichabod Crane (and win the hand
of Katrina Van Tassel), so Cassy impersonates a ghost in order to frighten
Legree (and escape with Emmeline).

In another sense, however, Cassy's masquerade reveals an authentic rebellious power beneath the doctrine of domestic submission and feminine
influence. Legree is Cassy's "owner, her tyrant and tormentor . . .; and yet so
it is, that the most brutal man cannot live in constant association with a
strong female influence and not be greatly controlled by it." Thus, Legree
alternately tyrannizes Cassy and dreads her. As "influence" becomes a cause
of "creeping horror," even little Eva gets turned, briefly but quite literally,
into a kind of Madeline Usher. When Legree takes hold of the lock of hair
Eva gave to Uncle Tom, it twines itself suggestively around his fingers, "as if
it burned him," and we learn that a lock of his mother's hair accompanied
the letter in which, "dying, she blest and forgave him." Then come night-

mares, in which the veiled figure of his mother appears to Legree, and he feels "*that hair* twining round his fingers; and then . . . round his neck." We also learn that the attic room in which Cassy and Emmeline hide is one in which, years earlier, Legree had confined, tortured, and killed a female slave, presumably a prior mistress. So, although Cassy's masquerade may be a hoax, Legree's guilty reaction to it is quite genuine. Cassy acts, in effect, as an avenging angel for all the women Legree has wronged, and her masquerade ultimately kills him.

Legree's death is a kind of gothic inversion of Augustine St. Clare's domestic triumph. "His mind is wandering," says the doctor as St. Clare lies dying. "No!" St. Clare interrupts, "it is coming *home*, at last!" Just before the spirit parted, he opened his eyes, with a sudden light, as of joy and recognition, and said '*Mother!*' and then he was gone." Legree, too, has dying visions of his mother, but they are less joyful: "a cold hand touched his; a voice said, three times, in a low, fearful whisper, 'Come! come! come!' And, while he lay sweating with terror, he knew not when or how, the thing was gone." Legree begins drinking "imprudently and recklessly"; "and, at his dying bed," we are told, "stood a stern, white, inexorable figure, saying 'Come! come! come!' " That this figure turns out to be Cassy in disguise scarcely lessens the significance of what is happening here, for it is Legree's own guilt that turns domestic bliss into gothic terror, "perfect love," as the narrator puts it, into "the most fearful torture."

Uncle Tom's Cabin is, most fundamentally, a Christian novel, and this fact suggests a link between Stowe and such contemporaries as Warner and Cummins. But Stowe is a very different kind of Christian novelist from Warner and Cummins. Christian submission does not, for her, lead to public approbation and worldly success; for example, her two most exemplary Christian characters, Eva and Tom, die. Also, *Uncle Tom's Cabin,* unlike *The Wide, Wide World* and *The Lamplighter,* follows Christian belief into overt protest. Stowe attacks slavery as a *sin,* and the form her novel takes, with all its direct authorial interjections, is finally the form of a sermon. Stowe's Christianity would seem to distinguish her even more clearly from writers like Poe, Hawthorne, and Melville. There is certainly nothing like Tom's "Victory," the climactic event of *Uncle Tom's Cabin,* in the works of any of these men. For Poe, presumably, Tom's death would have mattered mainly as an example of what he called "the human thirst for self-torture," and if we think of the death of Arthur Dimmesdale on the scaffold at the end of *The Scarlet Letter* or of the death of Melville's Billy Budd, we see part of what is distinctive about Stowe: she regards Tom's triumph without any irony whatever.

"Do the worst you can," Tom says to Legree before he is killed, "my troubles'll be over soon; but if ye don't repent, yours won't *never* end!" Modern readers, at least those who do not share Tom's belief in salvation and eternal damnation, may have trouble accepting Tom's (and Stowe's) certainty. Twentieth-century readers are more likely to believe in the reality of unending *psychological* torments, which is one reason the twentieth century has canonized Poe, Hawthorne, and Melville. These writers, in the phrase Henry James applied to Hawthorne, "cared for the deeper psychology," and all three adapted gothic conventions to probe this "deeper psychology." There is nothing like this in Stowe's account of Uncle Tom's triumph. But what happens in the story of *Cassy's* triumph over Legree, the climactic event of the novel's protest against "*domestic* slavery," is that the religious terms of Tom's story get, we might say, gothicized and psychologized. Cassy does not have to wait for divine judgment; her "influence" torments Legree in the here and now. Even Cassy, at the close, is converted and domesticated; the "despairing, haggard expression of her face" gives way to "one of gentle trust" and, secure in "the bosom of the family," she becomes "a devout and tender Christian." Of course, she has no more need to act the madwoman; she and Emmeline are free and, what may be more important, Legree is dead.

In the context of the literary marketplace in the 1850s, the distinction between women's and men's traditions may be even less clear than the generic distinction between domestic and gothic fiction. One thing certainly is clear: Poe, Hawthorne, and Melville never came close to matching the sales achieved by Warner, Stowe, Cummins, and Fern. But sales figures do not necessarily, of themselves, constitute traditions. We should recognize, for instance, that works representing the supposedly distinct traditions of women's and men's writing usually appeared in the same or in similar magazines and were issued by the same book publishers. Between 1853, when it was founded, and 1855, when it was sold, *Putnam's Monthly Magazine* published a number of writers now canonized, including Cooper, Thoreau, and Melville. But George Palmer Putnam had also published Warner's *The Wide, Wide World* in 1850. Boston's *Atlantic Monthly*, founded in 1857, came to publish a number of *Putnam's* authors, and the firm of Ticknor and Fields, which acquired the *Atlantic* in 1859, had been Hawthorne's publisher since *The Scarlet Letter* in 1850. But Hawthorne, like Poe, had published much of his early work in giftbooks and ladies' magazines. Also, when the *Atlantic* was founded, it prided itself on listing Stowe prominently among its contributors, and when John P. Jewett failed in 1857, Stowe moved to Ticknor and Fields. In fact, James T. Fields numbered both Hawthorne and Stowe among his friends. Fern, like Mrs. Southworth, came to publish exclusively in Robert Bonner's *New York Ledger,* a magazine calculated for wide popularity, but Bonner also paid top dollar for works by such writers as Edward Everett, Bryant, Longfellow, and Tennyson. For the most part, then, the people who read Hawthorne and Melville were the same people (or a subset of the same people) who read Warner and Cummins.

We should also recognize that if there was anxiety or antagonism between these male and female "traditions," it flowed almost exclusively in one direction. Writers like Hawthorne and Melville aroused little professional anxiety in popular women writers, and no wonder; neither, after all, had very much of what we would now call market share—not, at least, compared with women like Warner, Stowe, Cummins, and Fern. The male writers who mattered to these women were such popular (mainly British) novelists as, most notably, Charles Dickens. Yet Hawthorne and Melville were clearly threatened by the authors the former called a "d——d mob of scribbling women." Both Hawthorne and Melville discovered their full powers at precisely the time of the rise of the best-selling women writers of the early 1850s, and they were both soon compelled to exercise their powers in the context created or revealed by these best-sellers. Both men tried in the 1850s to appropriate some of the themes (and some of the readers) of popular women's fiction, even as they sometimes subverted or burlesqued the conventions and values of this fiction. And by the end of the decade both men had pretty much abandoned fiction writing.

There is a considerable tradition of what we might call antidomestic American literature, and this tradition is abundantly represented in the version of "American literature" often canonized in the twentieth century. One thinks, for example, of Mark Twain or Ernest Hemingway; Huck Finn and Nick Adams keep running away from precisely the sorts of female-dominated homes and the kinds of feminine "influence" that Stowe idealizes. But Hawthorne, for one, did not respond to female competition by attacking domesticity; quite the contrary. *The House of the Seven Gables* (1851) is as domestic in its setting as in its title; its author was quite deliberately trying—in this, his second novel—to escape from what he called the "gloom" of *The Scarlet Letter*, and he was also clearly seeking to appeal to female readers, with considerable success. After her husband read her the story aloud (a practice that tells us a great deal about his sense of his audience), Sophia Hawthorne praised the "dear home-loveliness and satisfaction" of the conclusion. Phoebe Pyncheon of *Seven Gables* was, for the author of "Rappaccini's Daughter" and *The Scarlet Letter*, a rather new sort of heroine, and this heroine reappeared, in increasingly exemplary forms, as Priscilla in *The Blithedale Romance* (1852) and as Hilda in *The Marble Faun* (1860). Priscilla's curiously self-serving submissiveness suggests an ironic attitude toward the exemplary heroine, but many readers, including quite a few in the twentieth century, have read Priscilla without irony, as the unambiguous moral center of *The Blithedale Romance*. And it is rather difficult to read Phoebe and Hilda, and their affirmations of domestic ideals, in any other way. "Forgive me, Hilda!" pleads the hero, Kenyon, at the end of *The Marble Faun*, after Hilda has expressed "horror" at his speculation on the possibly beneficial acts of sin, "I never did believe it! . . . Oh, Hilda, guide me home!"

It makes more sense to identify Melville with an antidomestic American tradition. After all, such books as *Redburn* (1849), *White-Jacket* (1850), and *Moby-Dick* (1851) avoid women and domesticity almost entirely, and *Pierre* (1852) becomes, among other things, an all-out attack on the domestic. Yet *Pierre* was apparently begun as an effort to court the very audience it ended up alienating. Melville told Sophia Hawthorne in 1852 that the successor to *Moby-Dick* would be "a rural bowl of milk," and he assured his British publisher that *Pierre* would be "very much more calculated for popularity than anything you have yet published of mine." In the event, of course, this prediction proved wrong, even perverse. *Pierre*, however, did not immediately end its author's professional literary career, and the last stage of that career suggests the complexity of Melville's relation to domesticity. In spite of the hostile critical reaction to *Pierre*, and despite the book's dismal sales, *Putnam's* in 1852 asked Melville to contribute to their new monthly, where "Bartleby, the Scrivener" appeared late in 1853. Between 1853 and 1856 Melville placed five more stories and the serialization of *Israel Potter* in *Putnam's* and eight stories in *Harper's*. When he turned to domestic themes in these stories—for instance, in "I and My Chimney" and "The Apple-Tree Table" (1856)—his aggressions were considerably more under control than they had been in *Pierre*. It is also worth noting the dominant influence on many of Melville's magazine stories of the widely popular and far from antidomestic Dickens, whose *Bleak House* had been serialized in *Harper's* in 1852 and 1853.

We should not attribute all concern with the domestic in works by non-canonized male writers to the effort to cash in on or attack the values of women writers and readers. It is hard to imagine a book more sincerely domestic, both in its values and in its details, than Thoreau's *Walden*. Similarly, when Huck Finn and Hemingway's Nick Adams flee civilization, they do so ultimately in order to set up "homes" of their own, on the Mississippi raft or on the banks of the Big Two-Hearted River. In much canonized American literature, men who see themselves as fleeing the domestic or sentimental are often simply running away from women to indulge their own versions of domesticity and sentiment. There is nothing domestic about Ahab's pursuit of the White Whale, but on two major occasions toward the end of *Moby-Dick* a cluster of values we might call both domestic and sentimental emerges in opposition to Ahab's suicidal monomania. First, Ahab invites Pip to share the protection of his cabin, his home—as Uncle True, in *The Lamp-lighter* (published, of course, three years after *Moby-Dick*), takes in the abandoned Gerty. Then, just before the chase begins, Ahab stares into the "magic glass" of Starbuck's "human eye," where he sees "the green land," "the bright hearth-stone," "my wife and child"; and Starbuck exhorts him to abandon his quest. These domestic impulses are rapidly rejected. Unlike, say, Stowe's George Harris, Ahab will not be feminized or domesticated. Yet these are moments of genuine power; they do not mock the emotion they evoke. Of course, one would still never confuse *Moby-Dick* with *The Wide, Wide World* or *Uncle Tom's Cabin;* here there surely *is* a difference between man in the open air and woman in the home. But we should be careful about applying this distinction too generally and too rigidly to American literature in the 1850s; the reality of this literature is more complicated. Even Ahab, as Captain Peleg puts it, "has his humanities," and Ishmael is saved, at the close, by *"the devious-cruising Rachel, that in her retracing search after her missing children, only found another orphan."*

III African-American Writing and the Legacy of the "Protest" Debate

6 African-American Writing, "Protest," and the Burden of Naturalism: The Case of *Native Son*

In 1971, at a Richard Wright symposium at the University of Iowa, Ralph Ellison summarized his views of the achievement of his former friend and early mentor. When he first read *Native Son* "as it came off the type-writer," he recalled, "I was impressed beyond all critical words. And I am still impressed. I feel that *Native Son* was one of the major literary events in the history of American literature." Nevertheless, he added, "at this point I have certain reservations concerning its view of reality" ("Remembering Richard Wright," 210–11). Thirty years earlier, however, Ellison had had no such reservations. In a 1941 *New Masses* essay, he had praised *Native Son*— which had been published to wide acclaim in March, 1940—as the culmi-nation of "a slow but steady movement [in 'recent American Negro fiction'] toward a grasp of American reality." The economic crisis of the past decade, he explained, had discredited the "exoticism and narrow Negro middle class ideals" of the fiction of the 1920s, so that "under the sobering effect of the depression, Negro writing . . . became realistic." And *Native Son* was the crowning achievement of this trend ("Recent Negro Fiction," 11).

There were any number of reasons for the shift in Ellison's opinion of his famous predecessor, and they had emerged long before the 1971 sym-posium. Ellison's political ideas, his understanding of "American reality," had changed significantly since his early days in New York as a *New Masses* author.[1] It had also been a long time since Wright had ruled African-Amer-ican fiction as completely as in the 1940s, and the publication of Ellison's *In-visible Man* in 1952—and the high critical reputation it had rapidly earned its author—had arguably made *him* the preeminent black American man of letters, one who no longer needed to orbit around Wright's axis. Also, and perhaps most important, in the early 1960s Ellison had been pulled into a protracted debate over *Native Son* and the relationship between "art" and "protest"—or, to speak more precisely, over their presumed antagonism—in African-American writing. His position in this debate had placed him publicly at odds with the supposed legacy of Wright's best-known novel.

None of what Ellison wrote in *New Masses* in 1941 was particularly original. Reviewers of *Native Son,* particularly those sympathetic to the left, had been praising the book's "realism" for the past year and a half. And Ellison's idea of "realism" seems to have had less to do with questions of literary form or genre ("realism" as contrasted, say, with literary "romance") than with the political ideas about "American reality" promoted by the Communist Party organ in which he was then publishing—ideas widely shared outside the party as well. Thus he wrote of the "new themes" of "recent Negro fiction," for instance, that they indicated "a broader grasp of American reality and an awareness of the struggling Negro masses." Nevertheless, Ellison's 1941 praise for *Native Son*'s significance did involve at least an implicit claim about literary genre. For while he never used the term, Ellison clearly assumed that Wright's novel introduced a new maturity into "Negro fiction" by appropriating the techniques of literary naturalism. *Native Son,* he declared, "marks the merging of the imaginative depiction of American Negro life into the broad stream of American literature," and he had no doubt about what bed this stream flowed in. While "American Negro literature" before Wright possessed "no background for dealing with such problems as were . . . emerging" in the 1930s, and while it "had developed no techniques for grappling with the deeper American realities," he wrote, "this background was to be found in the work of such men as Dreiser and Upton Sinclair"—in works, this is to say, of literary naturalism ("Recent Negro Fiction," 13, 14, 17).

This assumption, by the summer of 1941, was just as conventional as Ellison's comments about "American reality," and there was surely nothing inaccurate in the oft-repeated association of *Native Son* with naturalism. One of the three books to which reviewers almost compulsively compared Wright's novel (the other two being Steinbeck's *Grapes of Wrath* and Dostoevski's *Crime and Punishment*) was Dreiser's 1925 masterpiece of literary naturalism, *An American Tragedy,* and Dreiser clearly did mean a great deal to Wright. What matters most in Ellison's essay, however, is not his particular assessment of Wright's literary debts but his deeper assumption that for

"Negro American literature" to become "realistic," for it to embrace "the struggling Negro masses," it had to adopt the techniques of naturalism. It was this assumption, perhaps above all, that Ellison would come to question in the argument, in the 1960s, over the relationship between literary "protest" and African-American writing.

The story of the "protest" debate is by now almost tediously familiar, and we are as likely as not, these days, to see the terms of the debate as misleading or even fatuous. The debate no longer dominates discussions of the nature and obligations of African-American writing the way it did in the '60s and early '70s. But it needs to be recalled here not only because it once did dominate such discussions but because at bottom it turned on the literary-historical question with which I am here concerned: the place of literary naturalism in African-American fiction. For beneath the assumption that black writers had to write "protest" fiction lurked the assumption Ellison had at least implicitly endorsed in 1941: that an "American Negro fiction" interested in capturing the "reality" of "the struggling Negro masses" had to adopt the conventions and techniques of literary naturalism.

The "protest" debate erupted because some black American writers, notably Ellison and James Baldwin, began to see in this assumption serious and vexing problems for African-American expression and consciousness— began to believe that the techniques and conventions associated with literary naturalism were perhaps, for the African-American novelist, more a burden than a technique for expressing African-American "reality." Baldwin and Ellison have been seen, in their attacks on "protest," as seeking simply to get out from under Wright's shadow, and there is a good deal of truth to this view, at least in Baldwin's case.[2] But I want to argue that their sense of naturalism as burden was at least as important to them—or to Ellison, anyway—as their sense of Wright's stranglehold on "American Negro fiction." I am even more concerned to argue that Wright himself, as he planned and composed *Native Son*, became increasingly sensitive to the problems and burdens of naturalism as a mode of African-American expression, and that *Native Son* is thus less the monument of naturalist narrative it has been supposed to be than it is a product of Wright's struggle with naturalism's generic imperatives. I wish to show, too, how the very critical discourses that seem largely to have supplanted the debate over "protest"— notably the efforts by Houston Baker, Henry Louis Gates, Jr., and others to theorize a "vernacular" basis for "African-American writing"—have nevertheless perpetuated some of the protest debate's, and naturalism's, deepest assumptions and emphases. And I want ultimately to argue that in re-un-

derstanding *Native Son's* complex relationship to naturalism we may find
ways of re-imagining the complex interaction between African-American
writing and what Ellison, in 1941, called "the broad stream of American literature"—ways of understanding the centrality of such interaction to the
full history of our literature(s).

The "protest" debate began, famously, with two essays Baldwin published
in *The Partisan Review* in 1949 and 1951: "Everybody's Protest Novel" and
"Many Thousands Gone."[3] "Leaving aside the considerable question of
what relationship precisely the artist bears to the revolutionary," he declared in the second of these, "the reality of man as a social being is not his
only reality and that artist is strangled who is forced to deal with human be-
ings solely in social terms" (25). Or as he put it in the conclusion of the earlier essay: "The failure of the protest novel lies in its rejection of life, the
human being, the denial of his beauty, dread, power, in its insistence that it
is his categorization alone which is real and which cannot be transcended"
(17). Baldwin spelled out what he meant by "life" and the "human" in a well-
known passage in "Many Thousands Gone" enumerating the supposed de-
ficiencies and omissions of *Native Son*. What is most important to my
present subject, however, is not Baldwin's account of what he took to be the
proper concerns of African-American writing but his description of the ob-
jectionable "social terms" of protest fiction—his description, that is, of what
he saw as its essential formal qualities or techniques. Thus when he wrote of
the standard fictional embodiment of "the Negro in America" that "he is a
social and not a personal or a human problem," Baldwin explained that "to
think of him is to think of statistics, slums, rapes, injustices, remote violence;
it is to be confronted with an endless cataloguing . . . , as though his continuing status among us were somehow analogous to disease." (18–19)
Baldwin's objection, this is to say, was to a "sociological" fictional mode (supposedly exemplified by *Native Son*) in which the protagonist is constantly
cast as alien other, an object of study viewed from the detached narrative
perspective of the scientist or social scientist—the keeper of "statistics" or
analyst of "disease"—whose version of the "real" relies on "cataloguing" or
"categorization."[4]

   It was not until 1963, more than a decade after the appearance of Baldwin's essays, that Irving Howe entered the fray with a salvo called "Black
Boys and Native Sons." In the brief autobiographical notes that introduce
Notes of a Native Son, the 1955 collection in which his anti-"protest" essays
were collected, Baldwin had written that "one writes out of one thing

only—one's own experience" (4–5). Howe turned this declaration back against its author:

> What . . . was the experience of a man with a black skin, what *could* it be in this country? How could a Negro put pen to paper, how could he so much as think or breathe, without some impulsion to protest, be it harsh or mild, political or private, released or buried? The "sociology" of his existence formed a constant pressure on his literary work and not merely in the way this might be true for any writer, but with a pain and ferocity that nothing could remove.

Against Baldwin's attack on "the school of naturalistic 'protest' fiction that Wright represented," Howe replied with what so many early readers of *Native Son* had assumed at the end of the Depression: that a black novelist true to his experience had to adopt the techniques of this school (168).

Yet Howe insisted on one supposed distinction between *Native Son* and conventional literary naturalism. Like many of the book's early reviewers, he pointed out Wright's debt to Dreiser, "especially the Dreiser of *An American Tragedy*," but he argued that "the comparison is finally of limited value . . . for the disconcerting reason that Dreiser had a white skin and Wright a black one." "The usual naturalistic novel," he explained, "is written with detachment, as if by a scientist surveying a field of operations"; but "*Native Son*, though preserving some of the devices of the naturalistic novel, deviates sharply from its characteristic tone." Why? Again, Howe turned to race: this naturalistic narrative detachment, he said, was "a tone Wright could not possibly have maintained and which, it may be, no Negro novelist can really hold for long." (171–72) In spite of that wonderful "it may be," what is most striking here is Howe's rigid determinism, or at least the determinism he applied to *black* writers—for whom "sociology," we recall his claim, formed "a constant pressure . . . , not merely in the way this might be true for any writer, but with a pain and ferocity that nothing could remove." Which is why the detachment available to white writers like Dreiser was one "no Negro novelist can really hold for long."

This is the strain in Howe's argument that particularly infuriated Ralph Ellison, who responded at the end of 1963 with an essay called "The World and the Jug," and then with a second rejoinder published early the next year.[5] Ellison's essays were pointed and heated, as in his declaration at the conclusion of the first that "I fear the social order [Howe's essay] forecasts more than I do that of Mississippi" (120)—or in his objection in the second to "Jewish intellectuals" who write "as though *they* were guilty of enslaving my grandparents," intellectuals whose "real guilt lies in their facile, perhaps unconscious, but certainly unrealistic, identification with what is called the 'power structure.'" "Negroes," Ellison added dryly, "call that 'passing for white'" (126).[6] But the main point of "The World and the Jug" was to attack Howe's certainty about what the black writer could and could not do. Hence the paragraph leading up to the implicit comparison of Howe to a Mississippi sheriff:

> In his effort to resuscitate Wright, Irving Howe would designate the role which Negro writers are to play more rigidly than any Southern politician—and for the best of reasons. We must express "black" anger and "clenched militancy"; most of all we should not become too interested in the problems of the art of literature, even though it is through these that we seek our individual identities. And between writing well and being ideologically militant, we must choose militancy. (120)

What bothered Ellison was that this white intellectual, from the perspective of his supposedly superior understanding, was telling him what *he,* because he was "black," could and could not do. The white critic got the detachment; the black writer got the determinism.[7]

What would seem to tie the "protest" debate most closely to the conventions of literary naturalism is its concern, at least in the argument between Howe and Ellison, with determinism. But in technical or formal terms, determinism is not the most significant hallmark of naturalism; nor, as June Howard has reminded us in *Form and History in American Literary Naturalism,* is the assertion of determinism really part of the "meaning," of what we might call the "belief system," of American naturalist novels. Determinism certainly seems to govern the lives of the brutal, lower-class characters typical of naturalist novels—figures like Stephen Crane's Maggie, Frank Norris's McTeague, Theodore Dreiser's Carrie. In their inarticulateness, often signaled by vernacular speech, these characters are driven by internal and external forces they have no ability to understand. But the articulate middle-class narrators of naturalist novels are exempt from the determinism that afflicts their characters precisely because they do understand these forces, with an assurance expressed in their own nonvernacular voices through intrusively "scientific" explanatory essays, essays that allow the reader to share their superior wisdom and freedom. In Howard's persuasive account, the formal or stylistic hallmark of conventional naturalism is thus not some group of "philosophical" persuasions but the hierarchical division between the "brute" other and the omniscient, "scientific" narrator.

Even as naturalism makes new forms of life available to the reader as spectacle—particularly the lives of the lower classes, of immigrant masses—it controls and contains these lives by keeping them at a safe distance, by presenting them as alien and exotic.[8]

The relevance of all this to the terms of the "protest" debate is clear. The division between lower-class "brute" and omniscient, "scientific" narrator is precisely the division James Baldwin deplored in "protest" fiction, where the protagonist is cast as alien other, an object of study viewed from the remote narrative perspective of a keeper of "statistics" or analyst of "disease," a social scientist whose version of the "real" relies on "cataloguing" and "categorization." We may also now fully understand the logic at the heart of Irving Howe's curious account of *Native Son*'s "harsh naturalism"—this inevitable naturalism that nevertheless "deviates sharply from [naturalism's] characteristic tone" of narrative "detachment," a tone available only to white novelists like Dreiser. If the African-American writer in Howe's account is compelled by "constant pressure" to fall short of the detachment of the naturalist author, this is because he is uniquely subject to the environmental determinism that afflicts the characters of naturalist novels. For Howe, Wright's Bigger Thomas conforms completely to the behavioral and linguistic features of naturalist other: "brutal and brutalized, lost forever to his unexpended hatred and his fear of the world, a numbed and illiterate black boy stumbling into a murder and never, not even at the edge of the electric chair, breaking through to an understanding of either his plight or of himself." The deepest implication of Howe's essay is that, unlike their white counterparts, black writers—driven by the "sociology" of their experience "with a pain and ferocity that nothing could remove"—are also bound by this stereotype. Thus the description I've just quoted goes on to observe that Bigger "was a part of Richard Wright, a part even of the James Baldwin who stared with horror at Wright's Bigger, unable either to absorb him into his consciousness or eject him from it" (170–72). No more than Bigger Thomas, then, is Howe's Richard Wright able to achieve the distance that would allow him to break through "to an understanding of either his plight or of himself." No wonder Ralph Ellison was infuriated by "Black Boys and Native Sons."

Howe's logic still matters, thirty years after his debate with Ellison, because it reveals the dilemma facing the African-American writer who turned to literary naturalism as his means of literary self-expression, a dilemma Howe himself refused to recognize. On the one hand this choice seemed (perhaps ominously) inescapable. Since naturalism was the ac-

cepted mode for recognizing, for bringing into view, the lives of the dispos-
sessed, surely it was ideally suited to expressing the experience of what Ellison, praising *Native Son* in 1941, had called "the struggling Negro masses."
The problem, though, was that naturalism cast "the Negro" not as author
but as character, not as subjective center of understanding but as object of
detached analysis. How, then, could one turn naturalism's exploitation and
containment of the "brute" and inarticulate other into a mode of self-expression when one was oneself, by naturalist definition, that "brute" and
inarticulate other?

This question points to the deepest reason for Baldwin's and Ellison's attacks on the equation of "black" expression with "protest." What their attacks obscure, however, is the fact that Richard Wright himself would seem
to have wrestled with this question, quite self-consciously, as he planned
and wrote *Native Son.* For all their disagreements, Baldwin, Howe, and Ellison all concur on one thing: that Wright's book is most essentially, for better or for worse, a naturalist novel. But its relationship to the formal
conventions of literary naturalism is in fact a good deal more complicated
and self-conscious (and interesting) than they supposed.

Early in *Native Son*—as Bigger and his friends plan to rob a white shop-
keeper and Bigger, in an attempt to sabotage the plan without admitting his
fear, provokes Gus—the narrator generalizes about his character's behavior:

> Bigger felt an urgent need to hide his growing and deepening feeling of
> hysteria; he had to get rid of it or else he would succumb to it. He longed
> for a stimulus powerful enough to focus his attention and drain off his en-
> ergies . . . All that morning he had lurked behind his curtain of indifference
> and looked at things, snapping and glaring at whatever had tried to make
> him come out into the open. But now he was out; the thought of the job at
> Blum's and the tilt he had had with Gus had snared him into things and his
> self-trust was gone. Confidence could only come again now through action
> so violent that it would make him forget. These were the rhythms of his
> life: indifference and violence; periods of abstract brooding and periods of
> intense desire; moments of silence and moments of anger—like water
> ebbing and flowing from the tug of a far-away, invisible force. Being this
> way was a need of his as deep as eating. He was like a strange plant bloom-
> ing in the day and wilting at night; but the sun that made it bloom and the
> cold darkness that made it wilt were never seen. (471)

Here are the familiar topoi of naturalist narrative: the omniscient language
and style so far beyond the capacities of the character; the tone of distant

generalization ("these were the rhythms of his life"); the lower-class character driven by invisible forces ("invisible," that is, to the character); the
atavistic reduction of motivation to brute instinct ("being . . . was a need . . .
as deep as eating"); the consistent comparison of the character's driven behavior to supposedly "scientific" processes (the moon's gravitational effect
on the tides, the effect of alternating sun and darkness on a blooming plant).

This sort of narrative intrusion was a new development for Wright.
Compare it, for example, to the following passage from the opening of "Fire
and Cloud," a story first published separately in 1937 and then collected in
1938 as the fourth novella in *Uncle Tom's Children:*

> Wistfully he turned and looked back at the dim buildings of the town lying
> sprawled mistily on the crest of a far hill. Seems like the white folks jus er-
> bout owns this whole worl! Looks like they done conquered *everything.*
> We black folks is just los in one big white fog. . . . With his eyes still on the
> hazy buildings, he flexed his lips slowly and spoke under his breath. (355,
> Wright's ellipses)

Here, as in *Native Son* three years later, we have a clear contrast between
the protagonist's dialect and the narrator's "proper" English, but this narrator only describes the protagonist's behavior; his voice does not intrude to
provide detached interpretation, "authorial" judgment, and this procedure
is characteristic of the stories in *Uncle Tom's Children.* Which is to say that
only in *Native Son* did Wright first deliberately adopt the intrusive mode of
naturalist narrative.

But is the passage from *Native Son* really an example of narrative intrusion? It certainly reads and sounds that way, but at the outset, in any case, we
are clearly meant to read the narrator's language as expressing Bigger's own
thoughts: "Bigger felt an urgent need . . . ; he had to get rid of it . . . He
longed for a stimulus." And as the paragraph continues beyond the part
quoted above, we seem to return to Bigger's point of view—or to discover
we have been in it all along—even as we stay with the narrator's language
and what we have assumed to be *his* governing simile: "It was his own sun
and darkness, a private and personal sun and darkness. He was bitterly
proud of his swiftly changing moods and boasted when he had to suffer the
results of them. It was the way he was, he would say; he could not help it, he
would say, and his head would wag" (471–72).

The same strange narrative ambiguity is already evident earlier in *Native Son,* during the opening scene in the Thomas's rat-infested apartment,
as Bigger tries to ignore his family:

Vera went behind the curtain and Bigger heard her trying to comfort his mother. He shut their voices out of his mind. He hated his family because he knew they were suffering and that he was powerless to help them. He knew that the moment he allowed himself to feel to its fullness how they lived, the shame and misery of their real lives, he would be swept out of himself with fear and despair. So he held toward them an attitude of iron reserve; he lived with them, but behind a wall, a curtain. And toward himself he was even more exacting. He knew that the moment he allowed what his life meant to enter fully into his consciousness, he would either kill himself or someone else. So he denied himself and acted tough. (453)

This passage is typical of a good deal of *Native Son,* and the more one attends to it the stranger it comes to seem. Here, too, we have explanatory generalization about Bigger's behavior. But the point of view, even though the language is the narrator's, is clearly Bigger's: we are twice directly told that what we're learning is what "he knew." Where the strangeness comes from is that what Bigger "knows" here is precisely what we're told he *cannot let* himself know: "He knew that the moment he allowed what his life meant to enter fully into his consciousness, he would either kill himself or someone else." We might compare to this moment the account of Bigger's thoughts later, after his fight with Gus:

[H]e knew that the fear of robbing a white man had had hold of him when he started that fight with Gus; but he knew it in a way that kept it from coming to his mind in the form of a hard and sharp idea. His confused emotions had made him feel instinctively that it would be better to fight Gus and spoil the plan of the robbery than to confront a white man with a gun. But he kept this knowledge of his fear thrust firmly down in him; his courage to live depended upon how successfully his fear was hidden from his consciousness. (484)

Again we have a moment in which narrative generalizations about what Bigger does not know—generalization expressed in a style and language unavailable to Bigger and replete with naturalist markers ("confused emotions . . . made him feel instinctively")—are presented as Bigger's knowledge.

It would be easy enough to explain away such moments as mistakes, as instances of inept naturalism; and many of the initial reviewers of *Native Son,* particularly those impressed by the book's stark picture of American "reality," did complain that Wright makes Bigger too self-aware.[9] But the strangeness of point of view in *Native Son*—the seeming attribution to Bigger's consciousness of things only we and the narrator, according to naturalist convention, should know about him—would appear to be quite deliberate; or so, at least, Wright would soon come to claim. Toward the end of "How 'Bigger' Was Born," the essay on the composition of *Native Son* he published shortly after his novel appeared, Wright wrote that while he "tried to keep out of the story as much as possible, for I wanted the reader to feel that there was nothing between him and Bigger," at times "I'd find it impossible to say what I wanted to say without stepping in and speaking outright on my own." "But when doing this," Wright added, "I always made an effort to retain the mood of the story, explaining everything only in terms of Bigger's life and, if possible, in the rhythms of Bigger's thought (even though the words would be mine)" (878–79). Hence the strange moments of narrative indeterminacy in *Native Son*, the "outside" intrusions that seem nevertheless to emanate from Bigger's point of view. These moments are not lapses. They represent, rather, an interesting literary experiment: a deliberate and self-conscious attempt to write in the mode of literary naturalism without succumbing to that mode's rigid and inherently racist division of knowing "white" narrator from ignorant black "brute." And this experiment ended up having a profound effect not only on the novel's narrative form but on its action and outcome.

"How 'Bigger' Was Born" folds together two strikingly different accounts of Wright's motive and procedure in writing *Native Son*—different accounts, ultimately, of his sense of his literary identity and vocation as an African-American writer. For the most part Wright presents himself here in conventional naturalist terms: as distant scientist or social scientist, as outsider generalizing Bigger's meaning from, in effect, observations in the field. Thus we get the account of the five "Bigger Thomases" Wright encountered while growing up in the South, pathological cases through whom Wright came to understand, by recognizing a common "behavioristic pattern" (and the persistent sociologese is important here), "the nature of the environment that produced these men" (857). This account of Wright's growing understanding of the "factors psychologically dominant" in the "Bigger Thomas behavioristic pattern" (859, 862) climaxes in a kind of orgy of scientism:

> Just as one sees when one walks into a medical research laboratory jars of alcohol containing abnormally large or distorted portions of the human body, just so did I see and feel that the conditions of life under which Negroes are forced to live in America contain the embryonic emotional pre-

figurations of how a large part of the body politic would react under stress.

So, with this much knowledge of myself and the world gained and known, why should I not try to work out on paper the problem of what will happen to Bigger? Why should I not, like a scientist in the laboratory, use my imagination and invent test-tube situations, place Bigger in them, and . . . work out in fictional form an emotional statement and resolution of this problem? (867)

With this insistence on *Native Son's* status as *roman expérimental,* Wright bids fair to out-Zola even the French founder of literary naturalism, and it is hard to imagine an account of literary vocation and production that would more radically separate the author from his character.

But as I've said, this portrait of the author as aloof scientist coexists, in "How 'Bigger' Was Born," with a quite different account of how Wright came to produce *Native Son.* For instance when he notes that it was not until he moved to Chicago that he "first thought seriously of writing of Bigger Thomas," Wright does not attribute this fact to some sudden access, in the North, to scientific understanding. Rather, he explains, "being free of the daily pressure of the Dixie environment, I was able to come into possession of my own feelings" (860). This linking of literary inspiration to personal feeling continues through the essay—in a way that comes to stress not observation *of* Bigger but identification *with* him, a way that consequently suggests not so much literary naturalism as a kind of symbolist expressionism, a use of writing *to get rid of* intolerable feelings of personal shame and anger. Thus Wright speaks of his conviction "that if I did not write of Bigger as I saw and felt him . . . , I'd be reacting as Bigger himself reacted," and he speaks of saying to himself: "I must write this novel, not only for others to read, but to free *myself* of this sense of shame and fear." He says of his novel that "the writing of it turned into a way of living for me," and that "my task, as I felt it, was to free myself of this burden of impressions and feelings, recast them into the image of Bigger and make them *true*" (868–69). In this process, he writes, "I had to fall back upon my own feelings as a guide" (871)—feelings like those aroused by his identification with his charges at the Chicago Boys' Club where he had worked, where he had responded to their defiance of the white power structure that did little more than provide Ping-Pong to ameliorate their poverty and constricted expectations. "For a moment," Wright says of these moments of identification, "I'd allow myself, vicariously, to feel as Bigger felt—not much, just a little, just a *little*—but, still, there it was" (874). All of this climaxes not in scientism but in Wright's closing declaration, simply astonishing for a supposed "naturalist," that "the writing of *Native Son* was to me an exciting, enthralling, and even a romantic experience" (880).

The reason these conflicting accounts of authorship in "How 'Bigger' Was Born" matter is that a similar conflict seems to lie at the heart of *Native Son*. Indeed one could describe the novel by saying that it is "about" this conflict, that it is torn between locating the "reality" of Bigger's life in distant generalization and locating that "reality" in identification with Bigger's inarticulate feeling. What might then be said to "happen" in the novel, at least in one way of reading this conflict, is that distant generalization wins out—particularly during the trial, when Bigger's Marxist lawyer, Boris Max, takes over the function of the omniscient naturalist narrator and explicitly expounds the "meaning" of Bigger's story. This is how most of the original reviewers read *Native Son,* and it is the way James Baldwin understood the book—which is why he deplored "its rejection of life, the human being, . . . its insistence that it is his categorization alone which is real and which cannot be transcended." Lately, however, readers have been increasingly inclined to read *Native Son* in precisely the opposite way: as *discrediting* the aloof perspectives of the narrator and Boris Max in order to authenticate *Bigger's* perspective through a kind of irony we might call "unreliable omniscient" narration.[10]

There is a good deal to be said for these ways of reading what happens in *Native Son,* but they both ignore the most distinctive stylistic feature of the novel's actual narrative strategy—that is, the odd indeterminacy of its omniscience. They also ignore, and this omission is more important, the ideal "story" this narrative strategy might be seen as positing or implying, a story having less to do with conflict than with development or even growth. Implicit in the strange way the narrator attributes his own detached "knowledge" to Bigger's suppressed "feelings" is, in a curious collation of Freud and Marx, the assumption that if the repressed contents of Bigger's subconscious were to be brought to the level of conscious thought and made articulate, they would turn out to constitute a socio-political understanding of the mechanism of Bigger's oppression in a capitalist society. Through such articulation, then, the determinism that binds the brutal character would be transmuted into the distant freedom of the knowing narrator. And what ultimately "happens" in *Native Son,* when the novel is read in these terms, is that this ideal story is discredited—or, to speak more precisely, that this story is itself revealed to be a product of unconscious repression, a displacement or sublimation of unacknowledgeable feelings. Unacknowledgeable, that is, to everyone in the novel except *Bigger.* For by the close Bigger has reversed the sequence set forth in his early thoughts about the "shame and misery" of his family's lives: once he *does* "kill . . . someone else," however inadvertently in the first instance, he finally *is* able to allow "what his life meant to enter fully into his consciousness." What it turns out to mean is a far cry from the kind of "scientific" generalization the novel's narrative strategy has encouraged us to expect.

At one point in the second section of *Native Son,* as Bigger is on the run at night, he looks down from the roof of an empty building:

> Directly below him, one floor away, through a window without shades, he saw a room in which were two small iron beds with sheets dirty and crumpled. In one bed sat three naked black children looking across the room to the other bed on which lay a man and woman, both naked and black in the sunlight. There were quick, jerky movements on the bed where the man and woman lay, and the three children were watching. It was familiar; he had seen things like that when he was a little boy sleeping five in a room. Many mornings he had awakened and watched his father and mother. He turned away, thinking: Five of 'em sleeping in one room and here's a great big empty building with just me in it. (676)

The false note of that last sentence threatens everything that had led up to it, substituting a rather banal political observation for emotions that have little if anything to do with politics. What makes the earlier sentences work so well is their Hemingway-esque reticence, evoking the pain of shame-filled memories that still keep Bigger from naming, even in his own mind, the significance of the sensory details: the "quick, jerky movements" and "the three children . . . watching." It would seem that herein his attempt to force his own ideas, "what I wanted to say," into the mind of his character— Wright has simply violated the character's feelings, "the rhythms of Bigger's thought"; this is at any rate how someone like James Baldwin would presumably have read this moment. But we need to recognize that this very violation may be, *for Bigger,* the unconscious point, the desired effect, of such seemingly "authorial" intrusions. Sociopolitical generalization may function for him, finally, as simply another sort of "curtain," another way of blotting out or displacing his feelings of fear and shame and impotent anger even while giving them release and a kind of sublimated expression.

"They going to hate you for trying to help me," Bigger observes to Max before the trial. "Oh, they'll hate me, yes," Max replies. "But I can take it. That's the difference. I'm a Jew and they hate me, but I know why and I can fight" (781). It's not just that knowledge ("I know why") can provide the analytical tools for effective political action—and Max's own fight for Bigger in the courtroom is in fact so spectacularly ineffective as to make the attentive reader wonder if he should have been allowed to serve as a criminal defense attorney in the first place. The deeper implication of Max's reply to Bigger is that knowledge can provide a way out of the kinds of intolerable personal feeling that might otherwise be aroused in Max by, for instance, anti-Semitism. Max is sure his rationality frees him from the emotions that afflict both Bigger and those who would put Bigger to death—frees him, as we might say, from the kinds of "pain and ferocity" that Irving Howe would argue should inevitably drive black writers toward literary "protest." But Max's reply doesn't end this conversation with Bigger; before leaving, he turns and asks: "Bigger, how do you feel?" (781). Bigger isn't able to answer this question until the end of the novel, when he faces execution. His answer then, and especially Max's response to it, reveal the limits of Max's assurance, the fragility of his belief that knowledge has made a "difference" and defused his own individual pain and rage.

In their final conversation, Max urges Bigger to "die free" by "trying to believe" in himself, and then begins to stress, as he stressed in his odd courtroom monologue, the essential identity between Bigger and those who seek to put him to death: "the people who hate you feel just as you feel, only they're on the other side of the fence." This talk of identification remains, however, highly abstract and impersonal—"authorial," we might say—since Max holds aloof from implicating himself in this drama of sympathetic identification, and his refusal of true sympathy soon becomes even clearer when he gets so carried away with his performance as to forget the terminal situation of his audience of one: "On both sides," he hilariously declaims, "men want to live; men are fighting for life." Then—perhaps recognizing, unconsciously, the gruesome inappropriateness of this oration about "life" to a man on the way to the electric chair—Max begins to stutter: "That's why . . . y-you've got to b-believe in yourself, Bigger. . . ." Bigger, in any case, gets the grisly comedy here; he laughs, causing Max's head to jerk up "in surprise." Then he answers Max's much-earlier question about how he feels: "Sounds funny, Mr. Max, but when I think about what you say I kind of feel what I wanted. It makes me feel I was kind of right. . . . I reckon I really didn't want to kill. But when I think of why all the killing was, I begin to feel what I wanted, what I am. . . ." (848–49, Wright's ellipses).

Just as revealing as Bigger's declaration of feeling here is Max's reaction to it. Max "opened his mouth to say something," we're told, "but Bigger

drowned out his voice"; then "he backed away from [Bigger] with com-
pressed lips." Bigger's need "to make Max understand how he saw things
now" shatters Max's verbal composure; it silences him—and not because he
doesn't understand Bigger but because he does. In what are probably *Native Son*'s most famous sentences Bigger declares again, now shouting:
"what I killed for, I *am!* It must've been pretty deep in me to make me kill!"
Max "lift[s] his hand to touch Bigger, but [does] not" (so much for the
abstract insistence on identification) and then, at last, he responds "despairingly" to Bigger's speech: "No; no; no. . . . Bigger, not that. . . ." (849,
Wright's ellipses). The key word here is the pronoun, "that," whose an-
tecedent Max has no need to identify; Bigger's feelings are apparently thoroughly familiar. But Max can't stand this mirroring of his own suppressed
feelings in Bigger any more than Bigger, at the beginning of the novel, could
allow himself fully to admit his own fear and shame. This is why Bigger and
Max, in this final interview, in effect reverse roles, switch places, why power
is suddenly transferred from articulate white lawyer to previously inarticulate black "brute." When Bigger first visited the Dalton mansion, we recall,
his fear forced him into a kind of "shuffle," with eyes downcast and hat in
hand: "he had not raised his eyes to the level of Mr. Dalton's face once," we
learned, "since he had been in the house" (489). Now it is Max who shuffles:
he "grope[s] for his hat like a blind man; . . . [h]e feels for the door, keeping
his face averted" (849).

This role reversal would seem to be the inevitable consequence of
Wright's experiment with naturalist convention, of his attempt to write naturalism without embracing the mode's hierarchical and racist separation of
brutal character, on the one hand, from narrator and reader on the other.
After all, naturalism had enforced this separation for a reason. What it had
always known was that to give the brute his own articulation on his own
terms, to short-circuit through sympathetic identification the convention of
narrative distance, was to let the brute and all he stood for take over the
game. Indeed, as many commentators have noted, it had been in large part
fear of just this triumph by new masses of immigrants that had originally led
to the emergence of naturalism in the United States in the 1890s. The most
important assertion implicit in this naturalism was not so much that class
and racial "others" were brutal but that the middle-class authors and readers, to whose fears and fantasies of such "others" naturalism appealed, were
exempt from brutality. It is this assertion that most closely links, over the gap
of a quarter century, the character Boris Max to the critic Irving Howe. According to Howe, we recall, Bigger Thomas, "brutal and brutalized, lost for-

ever to his fear of the world, . . . and never . . . breaking through to an understanding of either his plight or himself, . . . was a part of Richard Wright, a part even of the James Baldwin who stared in horror at Wright's Bigger, unable either to absorb him into his consciousness or eject him from it." We recall, too, that it was from this paralyzed and fascinated identification that Howe exempted white novelists like Dreiser and, presumably, white critics like himself—who are because of their whiteness supposedly able to write "with detachment, as if by a scientist surveying a field of operations[,] . . . in which the writer withdraws from a detested world and coldly piles up the evidence for detesting it" (170–72). This is the essential pretense exposed by the ending of *Native Son.* "No; no; no. . . . Richard," Wright enables us to imagine Howe saying to him, despairingly; "No; no; no. . . . Richard; not that. . . ."

The specific terms of the "protest" debate no longer dominate discussions of the nature of African-American writing; the way this subject is thought about has been fundamentally transformed, in a kind of paradigm shift, by the development of academic courses, programs, and departments organized around the categories of African-American literature and African-American culture—and by the social and political changes that produced these developments. While Baldwin, Ellison, and Howe were concerned with the question of what form African-American writing should take, that concern soon gave way to the question of what form it has taken, and by the 1980s this question had begun generating important scholarly efforts to theorize African-American writing in poststructuralist terms—most notably, perhaps, Houston Baker's *Blues, Ideology, and Afro-American Literature: A Vernacular Theory,* and Henry Louis Gates Jr.'s *The Signifying Monkey: A Theory of African-American Literary Criticism.*[11] One effect of this paradigm shift, evident in both of these books, was to put the question of *Native Son's* significance back on the terrain where Ellison had placed it in 1941 when he wrote that the novel brought a new maturity to "recent American Negro fiction" by merging that fiction into "the broad stream of American literature": to put it back on the terrain, that is, of literary history. And oddly enough, even as they shifted the ground for understanding this literary history away from the seeming dead end of the "protest" debate, both Baker and Gates, albeit in quite different ways, perpetuated a number of the emphases that had so troubled Ellison in the writings of Irving Howe.

Baker and Gates both theorize African-American writing and its tradition in relation to more general "vernacular" traditions indigenous to

African-American culture—patterns connected to the blues (in Baker's case) or to rhetorical practices (of "signifying") ultimately derived from West Africa (in Gates's). Wright is rather peripheral to *The Signifying Monkey*'s sense of the theoretical underpinnings of African-American writing; Gates's vernacular tradition runs through Zora Neale Hurston and Ellison, the latter of whose *Invisible Man*, Gates argues, "signifies" on Wright in order to stage a "subtle reversal of Wright's theory of the novel as exemplified in *Native Son*." "By defining implicitly in the process of narration a sophisticated form more akin to . . . Hurston's *Their Eyes Were Watching God*," so Gates explains his Bloomian reading of the Ellison-Wright relationship, "Ellison exposed [Wright's] naturalism as merely a hardened convention of representation of 'the Negro problem,' and perhaps part of 'the Negro problem' itself" (106–7). "Unlike Hurston and Ellison," Gates writes,

> Wright sees fiction not as a model of reality but as a representative bit of it, a literal report of it. . . . Wright draws upon empirical social science and naturalism to blend public with private experience, inner with outer history. Rarely does he relinquish what Roland Barthes calls the 'proprietary consciousness,' the constant sign of his presence and of some larger context, which the third-person voice inevitably entails. (184)

One might disagree—as I obviously do and as I will be doing explicitly in a few moments—with this account of Wright's "naturalism," and especially with its assumption that third-person voice "*inevitably* entails" the "constant sign" of authorial "presence." But Gates's position is at least consistent; given his reading of *Native Son*, he *should* see Wright as peripheral or even antagonistic to his vernacular "theory of African-American literary criticism."

Wright is quite central, however, to *Baker's* "vernacular theory" of African-American literature, for clear and important reasons. As the second term in his title indicates, Baker (unlike Gates) wishes to foreground "ideology" in theorizing his version of this literature's "blues" tradition, and no canonized writer has been more directly associated with ideological readings of African-American literature than Richard Wright. But the centrality Baker gives to Wright raises some obvious and interesting difficulties. For one thing, Wright was by all reports insensitive to the blues, and he was quite publicly dismissive of the more general resources of indigenous African-American culture—as in the famous digression, early in his 1945 autobiography, *Black Boy*, on the "essential bleakness" and "cultural barrenness" of "black life" in America, life cut off from "the full spirit of Western civilization" (*Black Boy* [*American Hunger*], 37).[12] Hence Gates's complaint—echoing the earlier complaints of Baldwin and Ellison—that "Wright's class of ideal individual black selves seems to have included only Wright," that in *Black Boy* "Wright's humanity is achieved only at the expense of his fellow blacks" (182).

Baker's recruitment of Wright into his "vernacular theory" also runs up against another famous passage in *Black Boy:* Wright's long account of his discovery of literature and criticism, all produced by white European and American writers—the discovery to which he attributes his own decision to become a writer, the discovery that provided him for the first time, so he claims, with the means for understanding his own experience. "I read Dreiser's *Jennie Gerhardt* and *Sister Carrie,*" he declares, "and they revived in me a vivid sense of my mother's suffering; I was overwhelmed. . . . All my life had shaped me for the realism, the naturalism of the modern novel, and I could not read enough of them" (239). In the conclusion to *Black Boy,* that he added when his publishers cut the part dealing with his Chicago years (the part now known as *American Hunger*), Wright offers his discovery of these writers as the answer to his question: "From where in this southern darkness had I caught a sense of freedom?" "It had been my accidental reading of fiction and literary criticism," he replies, "that had evoked in me vague glimpses of life's possibilities" (*Black Boy: A Record of Childhood and Youth,* 282). How, then, can a writer who traced his inspiration to white influences, and who dismissed the resources of his own culture as "southern darkness," be considered part of a vernacular "blues" tradition of African-American writing?

Baker confronts this question head-on. Against Wright's explicit account of his literary debts he poses the "trope" of Wright as "black hole"— or "Black (W)hole"—pulling in and consuming everything around him. The specific literary influences that fed Wright's "hunger" do not matter, Baker claims, "because he was not in search of literary *lights*. As with the black hole, so with Wright: the light is that which can be dispensed (with). The mass remains." "The matter consumed by Wright to fuel desire," then, just happens to be "naturalistic and realistic fiction" (145–46). Then Baker "reads" the problematic passage in *Black Boy,* a reading that needs to be quoted at length:

> Reading *Black Boy* under the trope of the black hole, one might say that Wright "burns" novels to fuel *his own concentration.* He is unconcerned with novels' truth value ("It was not a matter of believing or disbelieving what I read . . ."), and their literary techniques are of no importance ("The plots and stories of the novels did not interest me . . ."). Rather, he con-

sumes them ravenously, voraciously. "I gave myself over to each novel
without reserve, without trying to criticize it; it was enough for me to see
and feel something different" . . . Wright's quest is ultimately to achieve
articulate structures of vision and feeling that constitute a correlative, supplying an equivalent to that "terribly important" *something* found absent.
What he seeks, one might say, is a *difference* that will fulfill desire. (146)

For Baker, any traces of Wright's literary sources are simply waste products
of the destructive furnace, the gravitational meat grinder (if I may be permitted my own trope), at the "Black (W)hole's" core. Thus Baker claims that
"the manifest 'unevenness' of [Wright's] prose, its pastiche, shards of theological, philosophical, and sociological discourse, sparse (sometimes mechanical) stichomythia are fragments of a 'literature' that *was*—a discursive
order reduced to zero in the interest of the black (w)hole's desire" (151).

We should probably be wary about a reading that twice, in the space of
six sentences, bases itself on what "one might say," but this is nonetheless a
bravura performance, a tour de force. The problem is that it simply doesn't
make sense, first of all in its account (or, one might say, its clear distortion) of
Wright's literal meaning; and this is particularly true of the claim that for
Wright the "literary techniques" of the books he read were "of no importance." "Plots and stories," after all, are hardly examples of "literary techniques," and Baker leaves out half of the sentence from *Black Boy* that he
quotes to support his claim, a sentence whose full text reads: "The plots and
stories in the novels did not interest me *so much as the point of view revealed*" (238).[13] This sentence, we should note, does not say that "plots and
stories" are "of no importance" but only that they are not as important as
something else. And that something else, "point of view," is an example of
"literary technique"; indeed a particular way of handling point of view, as
I've been arguing, is at once one of the main stylistic or technical markers of
literary naturalism and the central component of Wright's experiments with
naturalism in *Native Son*.

What is most troubling about Baker's reading of Wright—of Wright's
account of his literary antecedents, of his place in literary history—is not the
fact that it substitutes troping and what "one might say" for evidence and argument, nor even that it distorts Wright's literal meaning, but simply that it
seems so *unnecessary*. Why, one wonders, do Wright's achievement and his
authenticity as a "black" writer have to depend on his not working in the
same field as white naturalists, albeit in terms of his own desires and experiences? Why do these things have to depend, in effect, on his not playing
with the "big boys?" In the italicized passage that begins the chapter con-

taining his discussion of Wright, Baker insists that while *"the song's origins (as all origins) are irretrievable,"* nevertheless *"what is clear . . . is the difference between the slave's vernacular and the master's literature. . . . By writing experience in native (read: blues) as opposed to literary language, Afro-American writers have accomplished the American task of journeying from mastered existence to independent, national form"* (113–14). Does this mean that formal "independence" can never be achieved *within* a formal, generic literary tradition? Or does it mean that this prohibition applies only to *African-American* writers? If the latter is the case, the argument would seem to have implications Baker can hardly have wished. For at least since the days when Paul Laurence Dunbar and Charles Waddell Chesnutt found themselves constrained and frustrated by the *Atlantic Monthly*'s sense of its (white) American readers' tastes, it has been precisely the *"master's literature"* that has sought to consign "Negro" writing exclusively to the vernacular, to dialect.[14] And why should we worry about admitting that Richard Wright played with the "big boys?" After all, wasn't he plenty big himself?

But these observations take me beyond the specific scope of this essay. What matters here about Baker's argument is the more modest point that it distorts the relationship between the actual technical properties of *Native Son* and the formal conventions of literary naturalism, and in this it perhaps unwittingly revives some of the more unfortunate aspects of the "protest" debate. Like Baldwin, Ellison, and Howe (and Gates), Baker presents the issue in starkly either/or terms: *either* Wright's novel conforms rigidly and imitatively to the conventions of naturalism, and therefore fails as "art" (and this is the position Gates shares with all three participants in the debate); *or* the book veers completely away from naturalism, despite all appearances to the contrary, to achieve, *"independent, national form."* One at least admires Baker's attempt to shake Wright's achievement loose from the terms in which the "protest" debate and its aftermath have persistently (mis)constructed it, and doing this is clearly one of Baker's main purposes. Thus he critiques, quite brilliantly, the way in which Ellison's and especially Baldwin's accounts of *Native Son* endorse the "un-inscribed question . . . , 'What is art?'—to which "the answer proposed by bourgeois aesthetics is a response that necessarily finds Wright lacking." It is against precisely this assumption in "classical texts of Wright analysis" that Baker launches (to mix the metaphor into a kind of grotesque science fiction fantasy) his "Black (W)hole." One only wishes that Baker's project of "(W)right reassessment" had attended more carefully to Wright's actual negotiations with naturalism (142). Perhaps the gravitational pull of Irving Howe—whose role in the debate is never mentioned, interestingly, in *Blues, Ideology, and Afro-American Literature*—still requires extreme forms of resistance on the part of those who wish to engage in ideological criticism of African-American literature while sharing Ellison's dismay at Howe's argument. Still, by failing to recognize Wright's interaction with naturalist convention (a failure virtually required by his nationalist position), by going to extremes of his own, Baker runs the risk of succumbing to the very binary, neurotic distinction—between "literature" and authentic "black" utterance—that was always at the heart of the "protest" debate.

For Wright's novel *is* a negotiation with naturalism, one we could even describe, using *Gates*'s favorite trope, as a kind of "Signifyin(g)" on naturalist narrative conventions. Gates's Bloomian "metaphor for literary history" is, he explains, a "form of formal revision . . . what I am calling critical signification, or formal Signifyin(g)"; and he sees Ellison as "Signifyin(g)" on Wright "by parodying Wright's literary structures through repetition and difference." So why doesn't Gates see that this is exactly what Wright is doing to naturalism in *Native Son:* altering its "literary structures through repetition and difference"? The answer, apparently, is that he accepts, uncritically, *Ellison*'s version of Wright—of, for instance, "the heavy-handed way that Wright's naturalism was self-consciously symbolic, or of Wright's "naturalism as merely a hardened convention of 'the Negro problem'" (106–7). That Gates takes Ellison's word here isn't simply puzzling; in the context of Gates's own theory it is a serious and even foolish blunder. After all, every student of Harold Bloom should know that you can't accept the successor's anxious mis-reading of his precursor as *fact*. And if we shift to the terms of the Signifying Monkey poems, the source of Gates's own "master trope," the scope of his blunder becomes even more apparent.

Gates again and again turns to the central story in which the Monkey, through figurative language, convinces the Lion that he's been maligned by the Elephant—causing the Lion to provoke the Elephant and get stomped, after which he returns to go after the trickster Monkey. "Motivated Signifyin(g)," Gates writes, "is the sort in which the Monkey delights; it functions to redress an imbalance of power, to clear a space, rhetorically. To achieve occupancy in this desired space, the Monkey rewrites the received order by exploiting the Lion's hubris and his inability to read the figurative other than as the literal" (124). Well, if Ellison was "Signifyin(g)" on Wright through figurative patterns of "repetition and difference," and if Gates takes this parodic formal revision at face value, doesn't that identify Gates as the Lion, the one who reads the figurative literally? If so, one supposes that the Elephant, in this iteration, must be Richard Wright. Gates obviously has his reasons for misunderstanding or ignoring the implications of his own theory in this case; the same association of Wright with ideological criticism that led Baker to include Wright in his tradition would have been sufficient reason for Gates to exclude Wright from his. But the existence of a will doesn't necessarily justify the way, and Gates, too, seems to succumb to the legacy of the "protest" debate, to its need to miss or suppress what is so clearly and interestingly going on in Wright's negotiations with naturalist convention in *Native Son*.

What, then, might we learn from this case study in American literary history? Most generally, perhaps, that if literary history is going to draw its evidence from works of literature (and how could any significant literary history *not* do so, to some extent at least?) then it had better seek accuracy and care in its presentation of that evidence. "Close reading" has long been denigrated because it is supposed to entail an allegiance to the formalism of the old "New Criticism," but there is nothing inevitable in this alleged association. Nor can one imagine any other area of respectable historical or cultural inquiry in which distant reading, or the reading of isolated fragments out of context, would be considered conceptual pluses.

And the saga of critical (mis)appropriations of *Native Son* suggests another admonition: an admonition about the ways "African-American literature" has been theorized, like "Negro literature" and "Black literature" and "Afro-American literature" before it, in relation to "American literature" as a supposed whole—or, as Ellison troped it in 1941, a "broad stream." In 1989, commenting on another of Gates's books, David Lionel Smith observed that the "insistence upon viewing black texts as 'systems of signs' does not mandate the isolation of 'blackness' as a point of definition." "Quite the contrary," Smith continued,

> one can easily imagine the grouping of texts into traditional categories of genre, period, and style, without regard to 'race.' It might even be argued that the intertextual context of works cannot be fully understood so long as the works are segregated into restrictive canons based on race or gender. At the very least we might want to think more broadly in terms of *American* literature. Indeed, it might also be argued that to define literature in terms of sociological categories such as 'black' reflects a 'confusion of realms.' . . . [T]hese are points which an adequate theory of racial writing must address. It is not sufficient simply to replicate our commonplaces of social definition, thereby begging the theoretical question. (17)[15]

To say this is not, of course, to say that theory and literary history should or could be race-blind, but only that segregation, "the *isolation* of 'blackness,' " cannot help but deform our understanding of the achievements and literary histories of groups and authors so segregated. Yes, the specific terms of the "protest" debate have long since subsided. But as long as we accept an "either/or" separation of "African-American literature" from "American literature," just so long will we continue to be saddled with the rigid, binary "racial" thinking on which that debate relied.

What I am arguing specifically about *Native Son*—that in it Wright both repeats and modifies the essential narrative structure of naturalist convention—is not particularly controversial: Gates's work is only one example of a widespread interest in exploring how African-American writers have bent literary genres and conventions to their own purposes. What must be stressed, however, is that this kind of bending of genre and convention is by no means a distinctly "racial" phenomenon, something only "black" or "minority" ("vernacular") writers do to "white" ("literary") structures of power. It is rather what *all* writers do, "white" *and* "black," at least the good ones. As I have argued elsewhere, for instance, Stephen Crane and Theodore Dreiser—who just happen to be the American "naturalists" who mattered most to Richard Wright—also worked to undermine the hierarchical, class-based implications of conventional naturalist narrative.[16] Richard Wright's relation to what Ellison called the "broad stream of American literature" would thus seem to be, simply, that he was part of it, as much so as any other American writer. For as has often been observed, the idea of a "stream" (whether "broad" or "main") is not a very useful or accurate metaphor for literary history, which is probably more like a force field in which the merely conventional writers sit stationary, inert, while the most interesting—energized equally by the force of their resistance, their "originality," and by the force of the field itself—dance their own eccentric orbits. This is by no means to deny that the specific motives and contours of Wright's resistance had a great deal to do with "racial" matters, with his experience as an African American in the South, in Chicago, in New York, with his hatred of racist injustice. It is in fact my point that these matters, and particularly the way naturalist convention sought to construct his identity as "Negro writer," were crucial factors in Wright's experimental effort to write in the mode of literary naturalism without succumbing to that mode's rigid and inherently racist division of knowing "white" narrator from inarticulate "black" brute. But resistance itself is hardly a uniquely "racial" phenomenon; it is rather, as I've said, what *all* writers engage in, at least the writers who matter. We need a literary history honest and supple enough to recognize this fact—and to delight in it.

Works Cited

Baker, Houston A., Jr., *Blues, Ideology, and Afro-American Literature: A Vernacular Theory* (Chicago: University of Chicago Press, 1984).

Baldwin, James, "Alas, Poor Richard," *Nobody Knows My Name* (New York: Dell, 1961), 146–70.

———, "Autobiographical Notes," *Notes of a Native Son* (New York: Bantam, 1968; originally published in 1955), 1–6.

———, "Everybody's Protest Novel" (*Partisan Review*, 1949), reprinted in *Notes of a Native Son*, 9–17. (This essay actually first appeared in the Paris expatriate journal, *Zero*, which is where Wright first read it.)

———, "Many Thousands Gone" (*Partisan Review*, 1951), reprinted in *Notes of a Native Son*, 18–36.

Bell, Michael Davitt, *The Problem of American Realism: Studies in the Cultural History of a Literary Idea* (Chicago: University of Chicago Press, 1993).

Brodhead, Richard, " 'Why Not a Colored Man?': Chesnutt and the Transaction of Authorship," *Cultures of Letters: Scenes of Reading and Writing in Nineteenth-Century America* (Chicago: University of Chicago Press, 1993), 177–210.

Ellison, Ralph, "Recent Negro Fiction," *New Masses* 11, no. 6 (August 5, 1941), 22–26; reprinted in Gates and Appiah, *Richard Wright: Critical Perspectives*, 11–18.

———, "Remembering Richard Wright," in Ellison, *Going into the Territory* (New York: Vintage, 1986), 198–99.

———, "The Art of Fiction: An Interview" (*Paris Review*, 1955), *Shadow and Act*, 167–83.

———, *Shadow and Act* (New York: Random House, 1964).

———, "The World and the Jug," *New Leader* 46 (December 9, 1963), 22–26 and (as second half of "The Writer and Critic: An Exchange") *New Leader* 47 (February 3, 1964), 12–22; reprinted as a continuous essay, under the title "The World and the Jug," in *Shadow and Act*, 107–43.

———, and Irving Howe, "The Writer and Critic: An Exchange," *New Leader* 47 (February 3, 1964) 12–22.

Gates, Henry Louis, Jr., ed., *Black Literature and Literary Theory* (New York: Routledge, 1984).

————, *Figures in Black: Words, Signs, and the "Racial" Self* (New York: Oxford University Press, 1988).

————, *The Signifying Monkey: A Theory of African-American Literary Criticism* (New York: Oxford University Press, 1988).

————, and K. A. Appiah, eds., *Richard Wright: Critical Perspectives Past and Present* (New York: Amistad Press, 1960).

Howard, June, *Form and History in American Literary Naturalism* (Chapel Hill: University of North Carolina Press, 1985).

Howe, Irving, "Black Boys and Native Sons," *Dissent* 10 (fall 1963), 353–68; collected in *A World More Attractive* (New York: Horizon, 1963), and then, with a brief reflection on the protest debate as a whole, in *The Decline of the New* (New York: Harcourt, Brace & World, 1970, 167–89). All parenthetical page references in the text are to the version in *The Decline of the New.*

McPherson, James M., Laurence B. Holland, James M. Banner, Jr., Nancy J.Weiss, and Michael D. Bell, *Blacks in America: Bibliographical Essays* (Garden City, N.Y.: Doubleday, 1971).

Ozick, Cynthia, "Literary Blacks and Jews" (originally published in 1972), in Ozick, *Art & Ardor* (New York: Knopf, 1982), 90–112.

Reilly, John M., *Richard Wright: The Critical Reception* (New York: Burt Franklin & Co., 1978).

Smith, David Lionel, "Black Figures, Signs, Voices," *Review* 11 (1989), 1–36.

Tanner, Laura E., "Uncovering the Magical Disguises of Language: The Narrative Presence in Richard Wrights' *Native Son,*" *Texas Studies in Literature and Language* 29 (1987), 412–31; reprinted in Gates and Appiah, *Richard Wright: Critical Perspectives,* 132–48.

Watts, Jerry Gafio, *Heroism and the Black Intellectual: Ralph Ellison, Politics, and Afro-American Intellectual Life* (Chapel Hill: University of North Carolina Press, 1994).

Wright, Richard, *Black Boy (American Hunger)* (1945), in Wright, *Later Works: Black Boy (American Hunger), The Outsider* (New York: Library of America, 1991), 1–365. (This edition restores the second part of *Black Boy,* known as *American Hunger,* that was cut by Wright's publishers when *Black Boy* was originally issued in 1945.)

————, *Black Boy: A Record of Childhood and Youth* (New York: Harper & Row, 1966). (This edition, the original 1945 version of *Black Boy,* includes the conclusion Wright tacked on after the second part of the book, *American Hunger,* had been deleted by his publishers—the conclusion dropped by the Library of America edition when it restored *American Hunger.*)

————, "How 'Bigger' Was Born" (1940), in Wright, *Early Works: Lawd To-*

day!, Uncle Tom's Children, Native Son (New York: Library of America, 1991), 853–81.

————, "Introduction" to Paul Oliver, *Blues Fell This Morning: The Meaning of the Blues* (New York: Horizon Press, 1960), vii–xii.

————, *Native Son* (1940), in Wright, *Early Works: Lawd Today!, Uncle Tom's Children, Native Son* (New York: Library of America, 1991), 443–850.

————, *Uncle Tom's Children* (1938), in Wright, *Early Works: Lawd Today!, Uncle Tom's Children, Native Son* (New York: Library of America, 1991), 221–441.

Notes

Introduction

1. *Modern Language Notes* 109 (1994): 1013–15. Thrailkill, a graduate student at Johns Hopkins University, is in fact working with Walter Michaels, and her review began as a report on my realism book for Michaels's seminar on American realism (information from phone conversation with Walter Michaels, July 18, 1996).

2. *The Social Construction of American Realism* (Chicago: University of Chicago Press, 1988); *The Gold Standard and the Logic of Naturalism: American Literature at the Turn of the Century* (Berkeley: University of California Press, 1987). All parenthetical page references to *The Gold Standard* are to this edition. It should be noted that while *The Gold Standard* did not appear until 1987, the influential essays that comprise it began appearing as early as 1980.

3. *Virgin Land* (New York: Vintage Books, 1950); *The Machine in the Garden* (New York: Oxford University Press, 1964). Parenthetical page references to Smith and Marx are to these editions.

4. "Essay on American Language and Literature," *North American Review* 1 (1815): 309.

5. Chase, *The American Novel and Its Tradition* (Garden City, N.Y.: Doubleday, 1957). The idea of a pre–Civil War American "romance" tradition had earlier been suggested, albeit mainly as something to be deplored, by Lionel Trilling; see "Manners, Morals, and the Novel" (originally published in 1948), in *The Liberal Imagination: Essays on Literature and Society* (New York: Scribner's, 1976), 212. For other examples of what came to be known as the "romance hypothesis" see, for instance, Perry Miller, "The Romance and the Novel" (originally delivered as lectures in 1956), in *Nature's Nation* (Cambridge, Mass.: Harvard University Press, 1967), 241–78 and Joel Porte, *The Romance in America: Studies in Cooper, Poe, Hawthorne, Melville, and James* (Middletown, Conn.: Wesleyan University Press, 1969).

6. *Edinburgh Review* 33 (January, 1820): 79.

7. "Myth and Symbol in American Studies," *American Quarterly* 24 (1972): 435–50. Parenthetical page references to Kuklick are to this article. One token of this essay's influence is the fact that in 1974, two years after it was published, Kuklick was appointed editor of *American Quarterly,* a position he held through 1982.

8. It is an interesting mark of the period in which Kuklick himself wrote his critique that his account of the nonrepresentativeness of even popular literature does not concern itself with the way in which the myth and symbol school's version of "American culture" depends on leaving out the experiences and writings of such traditionally marginalized groups as working-class Americans, African Americans, and women.

9. "Comment" on C. Vann Woodward's "The Aging of America," *American Historical Review* 82 (1977): 597.

10. *The Crying of Lot 49* (New York: Harper & Row, 1986), 24–25, 106.

11. Thus he explains an assertion that various figures were "all equally committed to hard money" by adding that this "is not to say that they were all aware of this commitment or even that they would necessarily have recognized or acknowledged it if it had been pointed out to them" but rather that "they had involved themselves in a logic that, regardless of their own views, entailed a whole series of commitments, and it is this logic and these commitments that locate them in the discourse of naturalism" (172). And he ends his title essay by insisting that "the logic of naturalism served the interests not of any group of individuals but of the money economy itself" (178)—another master term upon whose relation to "interests" he further elaborates: "An economy . . . is, one might say, made up of people, and it acts like a person; but the person it acts like is not the people it is made up of" (179).

12. Parenthetical page references are to " 'You who never was there': Slavery and the New Historicism, Deconstruction and the Holocaust," *Narrative* 4 (1996). Michaels works out similar ideas about supposedly anti-essentialist, "cultural" ideas of racial identity in *Our America: Nativism, Modernism, and Pluralism* (Durham, N.C.: Duke University Press, 1995).

13. Also pertinent here is Michaels's comment on a tautological undercurrent in this kind of thinking. "The issue in cultural (as in racial) identity," he writes astutely, "despite the assertions of polemicists on both sides, has nothing to do with the relative priority of the group over the individual; it has to do instead with the identification of a certain set of beliefs and practices as appropriate for a person or persons in virtue of the fact that those beliefs and practices are his, hers, or theirs. What's wrong with cultural identity, in other words, is not that it privileges the group over the individual but that it (incoherently) derives what you do from what you are" (15).

14. *Errand into the Wilderness* [1956] (New York: Harper & Row, 1964), ix.

15. *The Profession of Authorship in America, 1800–1870: The Papers of William Charvat,* Matthew J. Bruccoli, ed. (Columbus: Ohio State University Press, 1968).

16. Parenthetical page references are to *Outsiders: Studies in the Sociology of Deviance* (New York: Free Press, 1963).

Chapter Two

1. "Hawthorne and His *Mosses,*" in Jay Leyda, ed., *The Portable Melville* (New York: Viking, 1952), 404–6, 418.

2. The fountainhead of this view of Hawthorne in twentieth-century criticism is D. H. Lawrence's *Studies in Classic American Literature* (Garden City, N.Y.: Doubleday, 1923). "You *must* look through the surface of American art," Lawrence writes in his discussion of *The Scarlet Letter,* "and see the inner diabolism of the symbolic

meaning." "That blue-eyed darling Nathaniel," he continues, "knew disagreeable things in his inner soul. He was careful to send them out in disguise" (93).

3. *Webster's Third New International Dictionary of the English Language Unabridged* (Springfield, Ill.: G. & C. Merriam, 1967), 1902.

4. All parenthetical volume and page references are to *The Centenary Edition of the Works of Nathaniel Hawthorne* (Columbus: Ohio State University Press, 1962ff.).

5. See, for instance, Henry James, *Hawthorne* (1879), reprinted in Edmund Wilson, ed., *The Shock of Recognition* (New York: Random House, 1943), 427–565; and William Dean Howells, *Literary Friends and Acquaintance*, ed. David F. Hiatt and Edwin H. Cady (Bloomington: Indiana University Press), esp. 47–53. See, too, Richard H. Brodhead, "Hawthorne Among the Realists: The Case of Howells," in Eric J. Sundquist, ed., *American Realism: New Essays* (Baltimore: Johns Hopkins University Press, 1982), 22–41.

6. Lionel Trilling, "Manners, Morals, and the Novel," reprinted in *The Liberal Imagination* (New York: Scribner's, 1950), 212.

7. Richard Chase, *The American Novel and Its Tradition* (Garden City, N.Y.: Doubleday, 1957), xii; F. R. Leavis, *The Great Tradition* (London: Chatto & Windus, 1948); Perry Miller, "The Romance and the Novel," in *Nature's Nation* (Cambridge, Mass.: Harvard University Press, 1967), 241–78; Northrop Frye, *Anatomy of Criticism* (Princeton, N.J.: Princeton University Press, 1957); Joel Porte, *The Romance in America* (Middletown, Conn.: Wesleyan University Press, 1969), p. ix. My own book on this subject, *The Development of American Romance: The Sacrifice of Relation* (Chicago: University of Chicago Press, 1980), is concerned less with the existence (or nonexistence) of a romance tradition in pre–Civil War America than with the question of what pre–Civil War Americans meant when they used the term "romance," and with how the meanings clustered around the term influenced the thought and fiction of so-called American romancers.

8. For objections to the romance hypothesis see, for instance, Richard Poirier, *A World Elsewhere; The Place of Style in American Literature* (New York: Oxford University Press, 1966), 8–11; David H. Hirsch, *Reality and Idea in the Early American Novel* (The Hague: Mouton, 1971), 32–48; Nicolaus Mills, *American and English Fiction in the Nineteenth Century: An Antigenre Critique and Comparison* (Bloomington: Indiana University Press, 1973); and Robert Merrill, "Another Look at the American Romance," *Modern Philology* 78 (May, 1981): 379–92.

9. Chase, *The American Novel and Its Tradition*, 18. On Chase's reversal of Hawthorne's meaning in the preface to *The Marble Faun*, see Mills, *American and English Fiction in the Nineteenth Century*, 25.

10. Trilling, *The Liberal Imagination*, 212; Chase, *The American Novel and Its Tradition*, 2; Miller, *Nature's Nation*, 247.

11. In "The Romance and the Novel," Perry Miller seems to find Melville's definition of "romance" (especially in a famous 1848 letter to John Murray, to which I refer below) more central than Hawthorne's various definitions. Still, he does quote the *Seven Gables* preface, and appears to find it in accord with what he takes Melville to be saying (*Nature's Nation*, 245.)

12. Nina Baym, *Novels, Readers, and Reviewers: Responses to Fiction in Antebellum America* (Ithaca, N.Y.: Cornell University Press, 1984), 225–35.

13. Thomas Jefferson to Nathaniel Burwell, March 14, 1818, in Paul Leicester Ford, ed., *The Works of Thomas Jefferson*, vol. 10 (New York: Putnam, 1899), 104–5. On hostility toward fiction and imagination in eighteenth- and early nineteenth-century America, see William Charvat, *The Origins of American Critical Thought, 1810–1835* (Philadelphia: University of Pennsylvania Press, 1936); my own *The Development of American Romance: The Sacrifice of Relation*, particularly 9–14; and especially Terence Martin, *The Instructed Vision: Scottish Common Sense Philosophy and the Origins of American Fiction* (Bloomington: Indiana University Press, 1961).

14. *The Letters of Herman Melville*, ed. Merrell R. Davis and William H. Gilman (New Haven, Conn.: Yale University Press, 1960), 71.

15. For an excellent account of Melville's relationship to his reading public, see William Charvat, "Melville," in Matthew J. Bruccoli, ed., *The Profession of Authorship in America, 1800–1870* (Columbus: Ohio State University Press, 1969), 204–61.

16. A belief in the fundamentally novelistic quality of *The Scarlet Letter* is shared, paradoxically enough, by both opponents and proponents of the romance hypothesis. Robert Merrill attacks the romance approach to *The Scarlet Letter* in "Another Look at the American Romance"; yet even Richard Chase, Merrill's principal target, insists that *The Scarlet Letter* "is primarily *a novel*"—with only elements of romance (*The American Novel and Its Tradition*, 68).

17. Michael J. Colacurcio, "Footsteps of Ann Hutchinson: The Context of *The Scarlet Letter*," *ELH* 39 (Sept., 1973): 459–94. For an earlier consideration of Hawthorne that also takes seriously his concern with history, see Q. D. Leavis, "Hawthorne as Poet," *Sewanee Review* 59 (Spring, Summer, 1951): 180–205, 426–58. For my own views on this matter see *The Development of American Romance*, 169–79, and *Hawthorne and the Historical Romance of New England* (Princeton, N.J.: Princeton University Press, 1971), 126–46, 173–90.

18. The notion that various characters in *The Scarlet Letter* function in one way or another as artists is widespread. It is particularly central to Joel Porte's reading of the book in *The Romance in America*, 98–114.

Chapter Three

1. *North American Review*, 35 (July, 1837), 59–73; repr., in part, in J. Donald Crowley (ed.), *Hawthorne: The Critical Heritage* (London, 1970), 55–59. For biographical information, see esp. Stewart (1948), Mellow (1980), Turner (1980). For his invaluable comments on an earlier version of this introduction, I am grateful to my colleague John Limon, whose own excellent contribution to the discussion of Hawthorne and *The House of the Seven Gables* is noted in the select bibliography. See Michael Davitt Bell (ed.), *The House of the Seven Gables* (Oxford: Oxford University Press [Oxford World Classics Edition], 1991).

2. For an excellent discussion of the invention or reinvention of Hawthorne's literary identity by Fields and others, see Richard H. Brodhead, *The School of Hawthorne* (New York, 1986), ch. 3, esp. 54–58.

3. The Centenary Edition of the Works of Nathaniel Hawthorne (Columbus, Ohio, 1962–), ix, 3–5. All future references to this edition, cited as CE, will be provided in parentheses in the text.

4. Quoted in Julian Hawthorne, *Nathaniel Hawthorne and His Wife: A Biography* (Boston, 1884), i. 383.

5. Merrell R. Davis and William H. Gilman (eds.), *The Letters of Herman Melville* (New Haven, Conn., 1960), 125.

6. Crowley (ed.), *Hawthorne: The Critical Heritage*, 195, 203, 220.

7. All parenthetical page references to *The House of the Seven Gables* are to the present edition.

8. See especially Richard Chase, *The American Novel and its Tradition* (Garden City, NY, 1957; repr. Baltimore, 1980). For my own comments on Hawthorne and "romance," see Bell (1980) and "Arts of Deception: Hawthorne, "Romance," and *The Scarlet Letter*," in Michael J. Colacurcio (ed.), *New Essays on The Scarlet Letter* (Cambridge, 1985), 29–56. [This essay appears in this book as chapter 2. Ed.]

9. Tuckerman, "Nathaniel Hawthorne," in B. Bernard Cohen (ed.), *The Recognition of Nathaniel Hawthorne: Selected Criticism since 1828* (Ann Arbor, 1969), 60; Mayo, in Crowley (ed.), *Hawthorne: The Critical Heritage*, 224.

10. William Charvat, "Introduction to *The House of the Seven Gables*" (CE, II, xx).

11. Crowley (ed.), *Hawthorne: The Critical Heritage*, 224. Similarly, the anonymous reviewer in the *Christian Examiner*—who thought the "impression" left on the reader's mind by *The House of the Seven Gables* "much pleasanter than that produced by its predecessor"—wrote that in the later book "the artistic execution [is] less perfect," and that the novel is "inferior in interest to the Scarlet Letter" (*ibid.*, 195).

12. Charvat, "Introduction" (CE, II, p. xx).

13. Hawthorne's sister Louisa was the first of many readers to see in the portrait of the judge a more specific and personal attack—on Charles Wentworth Upham (1802–75), a Salem Whig who had played a leading role in Hawthorne's dismissal from the Custom House. (See Julian Hawthorne, *Nathaniel Hawthorne and His Wife*, i. 438.)

14. *Walden*, ed. J. Lyndon Shanley (Princeton, NJ, 1971), 5.

15. In 1838, in his notebook, Hawthorne commented on a similar resolution of a feud through marriage that had occurred in his own family. (See *The American Notebooks*, CE, VIII, 74–75.)

Chapter Six

1. For a recent and mainly critical assessment of Ellison's political transformation, see Jerry Watts, *Heroism and the Black Intellectual: Ralph Ellison, Politics, and Afro-American Intellectual Life*.

2. As Baldwin himself confessed shortly after Wright's death: "I had used his work as a kind of springboard into my own. His work was a road-block in my road, the sphinx, really, whose riddles I had to answer before I could become myself" ("Alas, Poor Richard," 157).

3. For a brief bibliographical account of the "protest" debate and some of its aftermath, see McPherson et al., *Blacks in America: Bibliographical Essays*, 256–58.

4. This is also, curiously, a bit like the narrative perspective Baldwin himself adopts in these two essays, especially "Many Thousands Gone." In a typical passage here, for instance, he writes that "*we* require of *them*, when *we* accept *them*, that *they* at once

cease being Negroes and yet not fail to remember what being a Negro means—to re-member, that is, what it means to *us* (20, italics mine).

5. For the somewhat complicated bibliographical history of the Howe-Ellison ex-change, see the appropriate entries in the "Works Cited" section of this essay. While Ellison, as there noted, collected both of his responses to Howe in the *Shadow and Act* essay, Howe never reprinted his response to Ellison's first rejoinder.

6. On this last aspect of the Ellison–Howe debate, see Ozick, "Literary Blacks and Jews."

7. One might compare Ellison's account, in a 1955 *Paris Review* interview, of part of the inspiration for Ras the Exhorter (subsequently Ras the Destroyer) in *Invisible Man:* "In 1950 my wife and I . . . met some white liberals who thought the best way to be friendly was to tell us what it was like to be Negro. I got mad at hearing this from people who otherwise seemed very intelligent. I had already sketched Ras but the pas-sion of his statement came out after I went upstairs that night feeling that we needed to have this thing out once and for all and get it done with" ("The Art of Fiction," 181). The deepest irony, of course, is that this response ends up producing something very like the " 'black' anger" and "clenched militancy" Howe would be calling for eight years later.

8. For my own views on American literary naturalism in the 1890s, in the writings of Norris, Crane, and Dreiser, see *The Problem of American Realism,* 107–65.

9. Thus Charles Poore, for instance, complained in an otherwise highly favorable review in the *New York Times* (March 1, 1940) that Bigger "is able to express what he symbolizes more fluently than seems natural, considering how clearly Mr. Wright has made us see his life. . . . We can and do doubt that [the novel's 'probing inquiry into the state of the world that creates people like Bigger Thomas'] could flow so coherently through Bigger's mind." In the *New York World-Telegram* (March 2, 1940), Harry Hansen objected that "in places Bigger seems to understand more than he should." And to cite just one more example, Margaret Marshall, in *The Nation* (March 16, 1940), wrote that "Mr. Wright has not solved the admittedly difficult problem of pro-jecting in terms of an ignorant and confused, though intelligent, Negro boy the forces that motivate his actions. As a result the author often ascribes to Bigger thoughts of which he is plainly incapable." But, she adds hastily, restoring the reassuring naturalist balance, "the situation is saved because Bigger's *behavior* is *authentic* and because Mr. Wright's *analysis* of the roots of that behavior is so patently *true*" (Reilly, 45, 47, 66, italics mine).

10. The most thoroughgoing version of this approach that I know is Laura E. Tan-ner's "Uncovering the Magical Disguises of Language: The Narrative Presence in Richard Wright's *Native Son*." She writes, for instance, that "occasionally . . . Bigger the character breaks the mold into which his symbolic counterpart [constructed by the narrator] has been forced; the collision of his experience with the novel's symbolic uni-verse threatens to destabilize the narrative vision," and she sees this destabilization as deliberate on Wright's part (140). The weakness in Tanner's important and provocative argument is the absence of literary-historical context—the failure to recognize that the discrepancy between narrator and character is by no means a feature uniquely or especially pronounced in *Native Son,* and that this discrepancy is in fact significantly less pronounced in Wright's novel than in most conventional naturalist writing.

11. A year before *The Signifying Monkey*, Gates published *Figures in Black: Words, Signs, and the "Racial" Self*, which also contains a version of the "signifying monkey" argument. And in 1984 he edited a representative sampling of this "school" of criticism, *Black Literature and Literary Theory* (including earlier versions of parts of both *Blues, Ideology, and Afro-American Literature* and *The Signifying Monkey*, along with works by many others).

12. On Wright and the blues one might note, for instance, Ellison's comment toward the end of "The World and the Jug," "if you think Wright knew anything about the blues, listen to a 'blues' he composed with Paul Robeson singing, a *most* unfortunate collaboration!; and read his introduction to Paul Oliver's *Blues Fell This Morning*" (140–41)—or Baldwin's reference, in "Alas, Poor Richard," to "younger American negroes who felt that Richard did not know anything about jazz" (161).

13. Oddly enough, Baker does quote the full sentence just two pages after the passage quoted, but here, too, he is at pains to overlook its most evident meaning, glossing it rather as indicating that "the phylogenetic 'trace' of consciousness' journeyings is thus discovered as 'point of view' in realistic and naturalistic fiction. 'Point of view,' *one might say,* defined not as subjective intention but as trace of human desire, in the subjective correlative required for (W)right [*sic*] self-consciousness" (148, italics mine).

14. For an excellent discussion of this situation in Chesnutt's case, see Richard Brodhead's " 'Why Not a Colored Man?': Chesnutt and the Transaction of Authorship," in *Cultures of Letters*.

15. Smith is my colleague at Williams College, and while I hardly wish to blame him for my own argument here, I do want to acknowledge my large general debt to his clear and challenging thinking about "racial writing." I have learned more from him about this subject, and particularly about the complexities of our constructions of this subject, than from everyone else combined.

16. See *The Problem of American Realism*, 131–65.

Index

abolition, xiii, 96, 165, 168–70, 177
advertising, 112
advice manuals, 96, 101
Aiken, George L., 108–9
Alcott, Bronson, 29
Alexander, Charles, 113
Alger, Horatio, 154
allegory, 24–25, 28, 32–33, 46, 77, 130
"American Genius," 116, 130
American Revolution, 23, 69, 84–87, 92
Anderson, Sherwood, 77
Anti-Semitism, 203
antislavery. *See* abolition
Arac, Jonathan, xi
Arthur, Timothy Shay, 132–33, 134–35, 141
Astor, John Jacob, 80–81, 89
Atkinson, Samuel C., 113
Austen, Jane, 27, 68, 101, 153–54

Bailey, Gamaliel, 168
Baker, Houston, 191, 205–11
Baldwin, James, 191–93, 195–96, 201–2, 205, 207, 209, 223n. 12
Balzac, 92
Barnum, P. T., 108
Baym, Nina, 37, 136
Becker, Howard S., 10
Beecher, Henry Ward, 166, 168
Beecher, Lyman, 166–67
Benjamin, Park, 92, 113, 115–16, 123
Bentley, Richard, 79, 86–87, 90–91, 93
Bercovitch, Sacvan, xi
Best-sellers, American, 131–32, 135, 140, 143, 145, 184

bildungsroman, 178
Bird, Robert Montgomery, 106–7, 110, 119–20, 123, 128
Birney, James G., 168
blackface, 107
Blackwood, William, 99–100
"Bloody Kansas," 165
Bloom, Harold, 210
blues, 206–7, 209
Bonner, Robert, 139–40, 158, 184
book manufacturing, 69, 72
book prices, 73, 80, 82, 90, 92–93, 115–16, 118
book publishing, 69–74, 110, 115, 124, 137, 140–41
Boucicault, Dion, 109
Brackenridge, Hugh Henry, 69
Bridge, Horatio, 57–58, 61
Briggs, Charles Frederick, 117, 130–31, 138
Brodhead, Richard H., 219n. 5, 220n. 2, 223n. 14
Brontë, Charlotte, 147, 154, 178, 181; *Jane Eyre*, 147, 178
Brontë, Emily, 154
Brook Farm, 18–19, 27, 29, 42, 55
Brougham, John, 106
Brown, Charles Brockden, 69, 99, 121
Bryant, William Cullen, 67–71, 114, 116–17, 140, 184
Buckingham, Joseph T., 113
burlesque, 107
Burr, Aaron, 171
Burwell, Nathaniel, 220n. 13
Byron, Lord, 68, 70, 99, 165, 169, 173

DATE DUE

HIGHSMITH #45115